Pharmacy, Drugs and Medical Care

Fourth Edition

Pharmacy, Drugs and Medical Care

Fourth Edition

MICKEY C. SMITH, Ph. D.

Professor
Department of Health Care Administration
University of Mississippi
School of Pharmacy
University, Mississippi

DAVID A. KNAPP, Ph. D.

Professor
Department of Pharmacy Practice and
Administrative Science
The University of Maryland
School of Pharmacy
Baltimore, Maryland

WILLIAMS & WILKINS
Baltimore • Hong Kong • London • Sydney

Editor: John Butler
Associate Editor: Brian K. Smith
Copy Editor: Sandra Tamburrino-Hinz
Design: Joanne Janowiak
Illustration Planning: Lorraine Wrzosek
Production: Anne G. Seitz

Copyright © 1987
Williams & Wilkins
428 East Preston Street
Baltimore, MD 21202, U.S.A.

Accurate indications, adverse reactions, and dosage schedules for drugs are provided in this book, but it is possible that they may change. The reader is urged to review the package information data of the manufacturers of the medications mentioned.

Made in the United States of America
Third Edition, 1981

Library of Congress Cataloging-in-Publication Data

Smith, Mickey C.
    Pharmacy, drugs and medical care.

    Includes bibliographies and index.
    1. Pharmacy—Practice—United States. 2. Drug trade—United
States. 3. Medical care—United States. I. Knapp, David A.
II. Title. [DNLM: 1. Drug Industry. 2. Pharmacy Administration.
QV 736 S655pa] RS67.U6S59 1987 362.1'782   85-29524
ISBN   0-683-07762-7

                                    88 89 90 91 10 9 8 7 6 5 4

To my parents and my children,
all of whom helped to shape my work.

M.C.S.

With love to Dee A. and Wendy K.,
and to my parents.

D.A.K.

Preface to
the Fourth Edition

It seems that textbooks grow in length from edition to edition: this book grew 50 pages from the first to the third edition. The fourth edition, however, is significantly shorter, as we conscientiously attempted to present the material succinctly. Also, a survey of faculty who have used this text suggested that several chapters could be omitted since the material was covered in courses other than orientation. Thus, the chapters on social goals and ecological dimensions are no longer included, their content being treated in newly emerging social and behavioral courses. Many schools now require a health care systems course, and therefore the chapters on health manpower and the provision of health care services no longer will be found here.

We hope this shortening will make the text even more useful in a one-term introduction to pharmacy course. Of course, the book should continue to be useful as an introduction to the field for anyone desiring such information.

As always, we have attempted in the fourth edition to catch up with developments since the last edition. We have attempted, again, to anticipate some of the things that appear to lie ahead. As in the previous editions, the emphasis is on providing an orientation to pharmacy and to drugs within the context of today's dynamic medical care system. Chapter 1 provides an overview of the continuing interactions of pharmacy, drugs, and medical care. Included are discussions of the place of pharmacy in the process of care and the importance of drugs as a component of modern therapy.

Chapter 2 focuses on the primary concern of all health practitioners: the ill person. Discussion of the latest sociological studies of illness behavior is included. The pharmacist's role in patient compliance and patient counseling is stressed.

Chapter 3, on drug use, has been revised extensively to include thorough discussions of trends in drug use, what we know (and do not know) about physician prescribing, and the effect of the Food and Drug Administration's regulation on practice.

Contributor Tony Tommasello, writing from the perspective of his position of Director of the Drug Abuse Information Center for the State of Maryland, has revised and updated Chapter 4 on drug abuse.

The importance of professionalism to pharmacy practice is discussed in Chapter 5. Chapter 6 offers a look at the diverse settings in which pharmaceutical services are delivered. An appendix to this chapter includes an important codification of standards of practice for the profession of pharmacy.

Chapter 7 focuses on pharmacists themselves—what they do and how they do it. A discussion of the supply and demand for pharmacists in society also is included.

Pharmaceutical education is treated in Chapter 8, with an extensive discussion of the report of the influential American Pharmaceutical Association Task Force on Pharmacy Education. Professional experience requirements and continuing education also are included in the chapter.

Chapter 9 deals with the control of the practice of pharmacy, with special attention given to the relationship between law and ethics. Changes in Chapter 10 reflect the recent major changes in some of the national pharmacy organizations.

Finally, Chapter 11 once again looks forward and attempts to identify some of the major issues with which the profession must cope in the years to come.

Acknowledgments are due to many who have contributed to this latest revision. Especially helpful were those colleagues who have used previous editions of this book and who provided detailed suggestions in response to our survey. Of course, of utmost importance is the support of our families, who make it all worthwhile.

M.C.S.
D.A.K.

Preface to the First Edition

This book is designed to provide an introduction to pharmacy for any interested reader. Pharmacy is presented within the context of the system in which it is practiced. Thus there are discussions of many aspects of health care, including the patient and his illness, the various occupations which provide his care and the agencies which administer the system.

It is expected that the primary audience will be the pharmacy student. We would hope, however, that the book would be of value to anyone needing and seeking an appreciation of where pharmacy fits into the scheme of health things. It was impossible to discuss every aspect of pharmacy thoroughly as we would have liked to. Greater depth can be gained by consulting the references which appear at the end of each chapter. Between the time a book about health care is written and the time it is printed in today's environment, some changes may be expected to have taken place. We have tried to anticipate some of these. Short of total prescience it is impossible to predict them all. For these changes the reader is directed to the current literature.

Acknowledgements are due to many, including the following individuals, organizations and firms who have provided materials that have enriched this book. For use of their contributions we thank:

American Public Health Association

Charles Bliven	Louis Lasagna
Jack Cooper	McKesson-Robbins
Donald Dee	Peter J. Meek
Avedis Donabedian	Robert K. Merton
Arnold Goldstein	James Richards
A. J. Grimes	Christopher A. Rodowskas, Jr.
A. T. Henley	Milton I. Roemer
Richard H. Landis	Robert M. Wilson

The Editors and Publishers of:

American Journal of Nursing (American Nursing Association)
Journal of the American Pharmaceutical Association (APhA)
Medical Care (J. B. Lippincott Company)
Remington's Pharmaceutical Sciences (Mack Publishing Company)

Thanks are also due for assistance in typing the manuscript to Mrs.

Glenda Eversmeyer, Mrs. Betty McDaniel and especially Mrs. Carla Briscoe. Finally, of course, the families of the authors make it all possible, necessary and worthwhile.

M.C.S.
D.A.K

Contents

CHAPTER 5
Pharmacy as a Profession 101

CHAPTER 6
Pharmacy Settings and Types of Practice.............. 119

CHAPTER 7
Pharmacists... 161

CHAPTER 8
Pharmaceutical Education 185

CHAPTER 9
Control of the Practice of Pharmacy 209

CHAPTER 10
Pharmacy Organizations and Periodicals 237

CHAPTER 11
Toward Optimal Pharmacy Services....................... 261

List of Figures

List of Tables

CHAPTER 1

Introduction and Overview

This book deals with pharmacy, drugs, and medical care. Pharmacy is the most frequently encountered of all the health professions, responsible for dispensing over 1.5 billion prescriptions annually through community pharmacies alone. Drugs comprise by far the most commonly used form of therapy, not only in this country but in all nations of the world, and medical care is of universal interest due to the importance we all give to health.

This chapter provides a brief introduction to all three topics and explains their relationship to one another. An overview of the process of medical care is presented, along with discussions of the United States medical care system and the system of drug use. Each of these topics will be explored in greater detail later in the book.

Pharmacy and the Medical Care Process

Although pharmacists usually practice in a specific location like a community pharmacy or a hospital, their activities are interrelated with those of other medical care personnel and are affected by a variety of influences in the medical care system. That is, the policies of pharmaceutical manufacturers and wholesalers, the payment procedures of public and private insurance programs, and the attitudes and behaviors of patients all affect how pharmacy is practiced. The medical care system has evolved over the years as a response to the needs and demands placed upon it by the American people.

The interaction of persons in need of medical care with health practitioners who provide such care can be examined as a process: a series of events starting with the perception of a need for some sort of medical care service to its ultimate resolution. Examining the process of medical care in detail can provide an overview and a structure to illustrate how pharmacy fits into the overall medical care system.

Figure 1.1 illustrates the process of medical care. The process begins

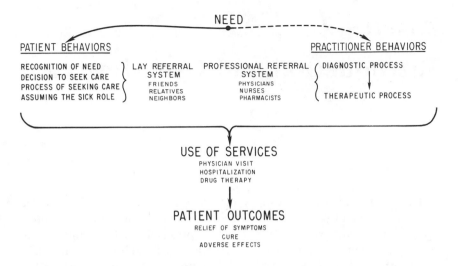

Figure 1.1. The medical care process. Revised and adapted. From: Donabedian A: Promoting quality through evaluating the process of patient care. *Med Care* 6:185, 1968.

when a person perceives a need for some kind of medical assistance. Often this is initiated by the occurrence of symptoms: pain, nausea, or headache. Sometimes the need is so obvious—a broken arm or a heart attack—that care is immediately sought. In other cases, the person must decide whether or not to seek professional care and, if so, from whom. Information is invariably sought from a variety of persons: other family members, neighbors, and friends. Most people usually have well-defined ideas about whom to ask for advice in particular situations. For example, the mother of a first-born child will turn to an acquaintance or relative with several children for advice concerning a childhood illness; a person who has recently recovered from an illness or injury may become the community expert on that condition. This "lay referral system" is often very influential in determining a person's decision to seek care. The opinions and attitudes of persons close to the individual will also affect the assumption of the sick role, that is, those privileges and responsibilities which are permitted to someone who is recognized as being sick. Privileges include permission to stay home from work or school, and receive help and sympathy, but include the responsibility to try and get well. Roughly analogous to the lay referral system is the "professional referral system," which includes physicians, nurses, pharmacists, and other health practitioners.

Note that in Figure 1.1 a solid line connects need with patient behaviors, while a dashed line links need with practitioner behaviors. In the United States health care system it is the patient who must initiate action to seek medical care. Thus, the point and timing of the initial contact with the system is up to the patient. Once in the system, the physician takes the lead in recommending steps to be taken. The complex process of diagnosis begins, assisted by consultants, laboratory workers, nurses, and others. After provisional diagnosis comes the determination and implementation of appropriate therapy, which in a majority of cases involves the use of drugs and, therefore, the pharmacist.

During the medical care process, the patient usually interacts with both the lay referral system and the professional referral system, receiving both lay and professional advice. Because of the differing perspectives of laymen and health practitioners, often patients themselves are forced to sort out a variety of opinions and advice. Ultimately, however, advice gathering and decision making result in the use of health services (e.g. a hospital stay, a prescription). The use of health services will result in some sort of outcome for the patient. Desirable outcomes include a cure for the condition, relief of symptoms, and restoration to health. In some cases the use of health services may only modify the need or indeed produce new needs, which indicates that the medical care process is at times circular. For example, a visit to a physician for treatment of an acute condition might lead to the discovery of a chronic condition such as high blood pressure which would require chronic therapy for many years. In other cases the therapy itself might result in an adverse reaction which must be countered by other forms of therapy.

The Role of Pharmacists in the Medical Care Process

Pharmacists are health practitioners and, as such, are part of the professional referral system. Because of their accessibility, pharmacists frequently are the first point of contact between a patient and the medical care system. Pharmacists may be found in over 50,000 locations throughout the United States, and their hours of practice are long, extending into the evenings and weekends, and sometimes 24 hours a day. Most pharmacies offer round-the-clock service on call in emergencies. Thus, the pharmacy is often a gateway to the medical care system, leading the patient to formal diagnosis and treatment.

Usually, however, pharmacists deal with the implementation of therapy, providing the drug products necessary for the treatment of conditions diagnosed by physicians. Because pharmacy is a profession independent of medicine, an additional control is added to the quality of drug therapy in the form of a check on physician prescribing. With the evolution of more complete patient records available in modern pharmacies, it is becoming increasingly common for pharmacists to play a more active role in the selection or refinement of drug therapy in consultation with prescribers. In addition, pharmacists provide consultation to patients on the best ways to take medication and are in a position to help patients monitor both the positive and negative effects of their therapy.

The Medical Care System

The *process* of medical care describes the interactions among patients and health practitioners in medical situations. Learning how to optimize these one-on-one interactions occupies much of the health professional's time, both in training and in practice. Often overlooked, however, is the fact that these activities are affected profoundly by many other things besides the characteristics of the specific persons involved or the technical aspects of the complaint being considered. These other things include the organization and financing of health care services, the environment of medical care, and the societal and cultural factors that pervade and influence the interaction of patients and health practitioners.

The medical care system in the United States is not one system at all (1). It includes several subsystems serving segments of the population; these subsystems may hardly be known to most middle class Americans. There is military medicine, active and pervasive, aimed at keeping the armed forces healthy and provided free to the recipients. The Veterans Administration provides primarily institutionalized care to older males. The poor frequent city hospitals, making do with a limited choice of resources, in a subsystem financed largely by Medicaid.

Even mainstream American medical care, enjoyed by most citizens and characterized by some as the best in the world, cannot be described as delivered through a distinct system. Each family in effect designs its own system, appropriate to its own needs and paid for by in large part by its own funds, either directly or through private insurance. Care is usually arranged through a family physician as needs arise. While the family has a great deal of choice in this situation, care often can be fragmented, uncoordinated, and wasteful.

Emerging alternatives for medical care delivery make a description of the system even more difficult. As the cost of care rises, insurance plans and large employers, who pay much of the cost of health insurance, are stimulating the development of different forms of providing care. These include the various forms of health maintenance organizations, preferred provider organizations, urgent care centers, and others. One major group of patients, the elderly, has about half of its expenditures for medical care paid for by the federal government under the Medicare program.

Most medical care is given in some sort of organization. Even individual physicians practice in an organized setting, supported by nurses, secretaries, billing clerks, and ancillary personnel. Formal relationships with hospitals exist, and policies pertaining to hours, back-up support, and billing arrangements affect how care is administered. Differences in organizational arrangements have a great influence on the process of care.

This influence is easily seen in organizations which are directly responsible for delivering personal health services: for example, hospitals, clinics, home health care services, nursing homes, and pharmacies. Administrative decisions can affect how efficiently health practitioners function and how satisfied they are with their work. Decisions relating to staffing patterns, hours of operation, physical layout, and the types of equipment available also will affect the quality and accessibility of care offered to patients.

Financing institutions such as Blue Cross/Blue Shield and government programs such as Medicare and Medicaid influence the provision of services by the way they structure their benefit packages and how they reimburse health practitioners. For example, insurance programs in the past offered better coverage for hospitalization than for outpatient physician visits, which often influenced physicians to hospitalize patients for procedures that could be carried out in the office. Most insurance plans have modified their policies to minimize this problem. Medicare has changed its payment policy from one of reimbursing a hospital after the fact for the costs incurred during a stay with a system of prospective payment that defines a set maximum payment based on diagnostic category. This change has had a profound influence on medical care delivery.

Many other kinds of organizations are involved in the medical care system. The educational system, including medical, dental, and pharmacy schools as well as academic health centers, provides future generations of health practitioners and is very much involved in the provisions of direct patient care services. Also important are a variety of regulatory bodies, including groups that license and regulate the practice of pharmacy and other professions, those that accredit hospitals and educational institutions, and agencies that regulate products and equipment used in medical care (e.g. the Food and Drug Administration). These organizations are concerned primarily with the providers of medical care services. There are other organizations which relate more to the recipients of service. These include, for example, labor unions that bargain for health insurance benefits for their members, employers who pay for health insurance as an employee fringe benefit, consumer cooperatives, such as the Group Health Association of Washington, D.C., which establish their own system of medical care for their members, and consumer organizations, such as the American Association of Retired Persons, which bring together members in groups to purchase medical services at a lower cost.

As the medical care system grows in complexity and cost, government at all levels has continued to have a major interest and influence. A desire to increase access to medical care by the elderly and the poor led to the establishment of Medicare and Medicaid in the mid sixties and to major efforts to increase the supply of physicians and other health personnel. As medical care costs have exploded, government attention has focused on cost management initiatives that have already led to significant changes in hospital reimbursement systems and to a plethora of strategies aimed at reducing prescription drug costs in public programs.

Uncontrollable Variables That Affect the Medical Care System

Surrounding the medical care system are several factors, beyond individuals' control, that still play a major role in the functioning of the system. Social and cultural factors, for example, have a major influence upon the medical care process. Attitudes held by patients and health professionals toward each other and toward sickness and health profoundly affect the quality of their relationship. The economic environment is important because it affects how health care resources will be allocated and paid for. With an extremely valuable commodity such as medical care services, the legal and political environment becomes especially important. Of importance are not only those laws specifically related to health care but also those which generally regulate business practices and interpersonal contacts. Contract law and malpractice insurance are but two examples.

Finally, the values that people hold regarding medical care are crucial to the way in which health care develops in any nation. For example, although there is still a great deal of disagreement as to how it should be done, there seems to be general agreement in this country that health care is a right of all people. Acceptance of this premise requires that we also accept that all persons needing medical care should have equal access to it. In addition, the medical care system must use scarce medical resources efficiently and economically, thus requiring that services provided be precisely appropriate to the client's need. As efforts are made to translate these philosophical statements into action over the years to come, the individual practices of pharmacy and medicine are bound to change. Thus, the impact of such variables, although uncontrollable, must be anticipated and planned for by all concerned.

To summarize, the medical care process may be seen as being embedded within an organizational context that is largely controllable, or at least modifiable. This context is, in turn, embedded in American society with its associated social, cultural, economic, legal, and political values. All of these things influence the intimate interactions of clients and providers seeking a solution to a specific health care problem.

The Drug Component of Medical Care

Pharmacists are primarily concerned with one aspect of the process of medical care: the use of drugs. It is an important component: 60% of physician visits result in a prescription or injection; a typical hospital patient receives six to eight different drugs during a stay; almost all nursing home patients are on multiple drug therapy.

In all of these situations pharmacists are involved, not only in providing the drug product itself but also in helping to ensure its proper use. Whereas the process of prescribing and dispensing seems quite simple, it has several unusual characteristics that need to be understood.

First, at least two sets of professional services are involved. The prescriber performs a professional function by determining the specific course of drug therapy required by a particular patient in a specified situation. The pharmacist functions professionally by ensuring that the course of therapy prescribed is appropriate and correct in every detail for the patient. Years of education and experience are involved in the proper performance of this function of drug use control. The physical supplying of the drug by the pharmacist is but a small part of the overall responsibility. The prescriber is reimbursed for diagnostic and therapeutic services. The pharmacist's charge must include not only a fee for professional services in the area of drug use control but also an amount to cover the cost of the drug product provided. Thus, there are two important components of the charge made for a prescription.

A second and unusual aspect of the prescription drug transaction is that the decision maker is different from the one paying the bill. That is, the prescriber chooses the specific drug and quantity the patient is to receive, often with the assistance of the pharmacist, and the patient pays for it. This has several ramifications. First, the prescriber is insulated from concerns about the cost of drugs. Among other things, this has led to a de-emphasis on price competition among drugs at the manufacturer's level. That is, because prescribers often do not consider price as a primary criterion in drug selection, drug manufacturers do not find it as worthwhile to compete on prices as they do on such things as company reputation and reliability, product differences, and dosage forms. The situation is becoming even more complicated now that laws in almost all states permit pharmacists to select the supplier when the product is available from multiple sources (so-called generic substitution). Price competition is much more of a factor in these situations. As high-volume, brand-name drugs lose patent protection in the years to come, competition in the drug industry undoubtedly will drastically change.

A second characteristic of the prescription transaction relates to the concentration of decision-making power in the physician (or other prescriber). Only through the act of writing a prescription can controlled drugs be sold legally in this country. Obviously, the multibillion-dollar-a-year prescription drug industry has an interest in these physicians! Because this relatively small group of individuals—about 500,000—is so powerful, the industry concentrates most of its promotional activities upon this group, allowing a much larger average expenditure per physician than it would if the promotion were aimed at a mass market of 100 million or so retail consumers. The result is that the typical physician receives a landslide of industry information and advertisements about drug products; this situation has led to much concern over ensuring that the physician can readily obtain noncommercial drug information to balance and fill out company-provided material. Thus, the importance of the pharmacist becoming more available to the physician as a source of accurate and appropriate drug information is apparent.

It should be clear by now that the prescribing and dispensing of a prescription, an act that is performed well over 1½ billion times a year and is central to both medical and pharmaceutical practice, is not so simple after all. Neither is the transaction limited to the three participants; for example, we have already mentioned the influence of the drug industry. The transaction might be better viewed as part of a larger system including the government, the industry, organized programs to pay for (and sometimes provide) drugs, the organized professional associations, and the various sources from which drugs may be obtained.

Physicians are central because their decisions are needed to provide prescription drugs. The patient, as the object of medical care, is also central and relates directly with the pharmacist at the point of dispensing. Note, however, that this is not always true. In many instances the pharmacist may not be involved at all in the dispensing process: many physicians dispense drugs routinely for profit; most dispense at least some drugs in the form of starters or samples. Planned Parenthood and similar agencies often dispense oral contraceptives without pharmacist supervision, and some of the nation's smaller hospitals are without regular pharmaceutical services. These examples are mentioned to illustrate that prescription drugs are available from many sources other than a pharmacy.

The drug industry and its contributions to medical care are difficult to overestimate; over the past decades American manufacturers have provided a majority of the significant advances in drug therapy in the world. The industry provides products and information to both physicians and pharmacists. Because of the importance of quality drug products to the health of the nation's citizens, the federal government has had a long history of interest in and regulation of the pharmaceutical industry. The Food and Drug Administration is the chief federal agency in the drug field and is broadly responsible for ensuring that all drugs marketed in the United States are safe and effective under the conditions for which they are intended.

The drug industry in America has been successful not only in producing large numbers of essential drugs but also in producing large profits for its owners. For many years the industry has been one of the most profitable industries in the United States (Fig. 1.2). As a result of these continuing high profits and the vital nature of the products involved, the brand-name drug industry has been the target of numerous congressional critics, from Senator Kefauver in the 1960s to Senators Kennedy and Nelson in the 1970s to Congressman Waxman in the mid 1980s. The most recent criticism focuses on the large increases in drug product costs since the early 1980s. At a hearing on prescription drug price increases held by his Subcommittee on Health and the Environment in July 1985, Congressman Waxman stated:

> After having risen at rates below the Consumer Price Index (CPI) for a number of years, prescription drug prices for the past several years have risen at rates far in excess of the CPI. For example, data from the Bureau of Labor Statistics show that from January 1981 to June 1985 the CPI rose 23% while prescription drug prices jumped 56%—more than double the CPI.
>
> The United States constitutes the largest and most profitable market for prescription drugs in the world. With few exceptions, prescription drugs sold in the United States cost more than in most other countries in the world, including Canada, Japan, Germany, Italy, France, and England.

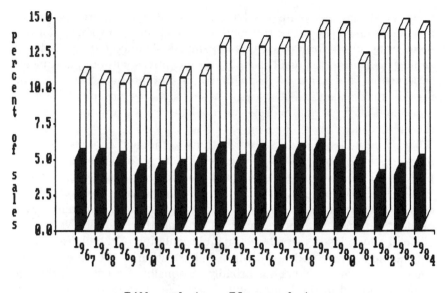

Figure 1.2. Profits per dollar of sales after taxes for all manufacturing corporations and for pharmaceutical corporations. Source: *Quarterly Financial Reports for Manufacturing, Mining, and Trade Corporations*, Federal Trade Commission (through 1981) and U.S. Department of Commerce, Bureau of the Census (since 1982).

Other criticism has concentrated upon the exceedingly high profits coupled with lack of price competition, the high concentration of producers within therapeutic categories (that is, relatively few firms produce drugs of a similar nature), and large expenditures on drug advertising directed to physicians.

The facts generally substantiate the critics' charges; the decision as to what, if anything, should be done about it is a more difficult issue. There is little question that competition in the brand-name drug industry exists mainly as product competition: that is, the discovery and marketing of improved (or competitively superior) drugs under patent protection. These products are then promoted as intensively as possible to physicians. The process is expensive—prices have been higher than they might have been under some other system and profits have been large—but many valuable products have resulted. Policy decisions in this area are not easy to make.

Third-Party Drug Programs

Increasingly important influences on the system of drug use are third-party drug programs. Until the early 1970s, virtually every prescription dispensed was paid for directly by the patient. Today, third-party programs pay about 30% of the cost of outpatient prescription drugs. The influence of these third parties (so named because they are in addition to the prescriber and patient) should not be underestimated. The individual patient paying $30 or $40 a year for drugs cannot hope to have much influence on the system as a whole. However, third parties representing thousands of drug purchasers can exert a variety of pressures upon the system because of their greater buying power. No other single issue is of greater concern to community pharmacists today.

Finally, it should be noted that the group interests of both physicians and pharmacists are looked after by their respective professional organizations. Just as the third-party payment organizations are beginning to provide representation for patients in the overall system, professional associations have long been concerned with activities and developments that affect their members.

Let us now turn our attention to the system of nonprescription drug use. Here, patients become the central figure. They are both the decision makers and the purchasers of nonprescription drugs. This means that price competition should play a larger role than with prescription drugs, and indeed it does, although product differentiation, branding, and the development of new products remain as important competitive tools. The proprietary drug industry aims its promotion at patients—consumers—and, because there are so many of them, relies upon mass advertising on television and radio and in magazines and newspapers. The more concentrated and personal promotion used with physician is far too expensive and impractical to be used with the mass market.

The government is very much involved in the regulation of nonprescription drugs; these drugs must meet the same standards of safety and efficacy as do prescription drugs. In addition, drugs to be sold directly to the public must be safe enough to be used without professional supervision (which generally means they are also less potent) and must be labeled with clear instructions as to indications and use. If a drug is not a prescription item, the law allows it to be sold in any outlet; thus, such items are found in food stores, discount houses, gas stations, and a host of other places. Pharmacies account for only about 50% of sales of this class of drugs. The result is that immense quantities of drugs are sold in the United States today without any possibility of professional monitoring or control. The pharmacists has been slow to exert his expertise in this area, even with respect to the share of nonprescription drugs sold under his nominal control.

The patient uses a variety of information sources to gain knowledge about the remedies used. The lay referral system mentioned earlier provides much information about the use of remedies by others, and this information often is used to validate or check up on the claims made for products in advertising. The physician also provides a great deal of advice on nonprescription drugs, although many patients apparently do not consult physicians primarily for advice on nonprescription drugs but save up their questions until they consult the physicians about some other matter. Then the patient will "sneak in" a question or two about self-medication, presumably at no extra charge. A number of studies have indicated that pharmacists are not consulted about nonprescription remedies as often as might be expected, given their knowledge and accessibility.

While the nonprescription drug use system is extremely important in terms of the prevalence of the use of these products, it tends to be viewed as not quite legitimate by some health professionals, particularly physicians. The drug industry is aware of this attitude and sometimes goes to great lengths to separate its prescription and nonprescription marketing activities. For example, many firms have separate divisions with different names to handle their proprietary products. Obviously, some of this differentiation is necessary because of the different marketing functions performed.

Self-medication serves important uses in this country. It provides symptomatic relief to many sufferers of minor ailments, thus relieving health professionals of the task of dealing with an immense load of less serious cases in a system that is already overloaded. But the self-medication process does require more attention from pharmacists than it gets because of the possibilities of misdiagnosis, improper drug choice, and inappropriate drug use.

Summary

This chapter has set the stage for the rest of this book. The use of drugs and the functions of the profession of pharmacy are subsequently examined not only narrowly and in depth but also in the broader context of the process of medical care and the structure of the health care system in the United States. A diagram of the medical care process shows the way in which clients and providers interact to translate health needs into specific diagnosis and treatments, often involving drugs and the pharmacist. The subsequent use of services produces outcomes which hopefully ameliorate needs but which sometimes create new ones. The practitioner-patient interaction takes place in a specific organizational setting, the characteristics of which significantly affect the process of care. The organizational setting and the clients and providers are in turn influenced by larger societal and cultural factors.

The basic transaction of providing a prescribed drug to a patient has been analyzed. It is noted that both the physician and the pharmacist provide professional services in this transaction; the patient is in the unusual position of paying for a product which another person, the physician has specified. The physician, as the central figure in the use of prescription drugs, is the focus of most of the promotional activities of the prescription drug industry.

REFERENCE

1. Torrens PR: Historical evolution and overview of health services in the United States. In Williams SJ, Torrens PR (eds): *Introduction to Health Services* ed 2. New York, John Wiley & Sons, 1984, pp 3–31.

CHAPTER 2

The Ill Person

. . . One is immediately obliged to distinguish between illness as a purely biophysical state and illness as a human, societal state. Illness as a biophysical state involves changes in bone, tissue, vital fluids, or the like in living organisms, human or not. Illness as a social state involves changes in behavior that occur only among humans and that vary with culture and other organized sources of symbolic meaning.

Eliot Freidson

Introduction

Medical care, of which pharmacy services are an integral part, is a paradoxical commodity, for while most individuals would prefer never to use it, they require and demand its ready availability. Medical (or pharmaceutical) care may be viewed primarily within the context of what it can *do* (effect a cure, relieve symptoms, return one to normal functioning) rather than for its own sake.

When an individual decides to seek care, and some may delay doing so for a variety of reasons, he brings with him a variety of expectations, some realistic and some irrational. In addition to the technical expertise which he seeks, he often expects sympathy, understanding, and consideration. Indeed, for some patients these latter characteristics are the most important of all.

Both health and sickness mean different things to different people. Their meaning is influenced by prior experience, age, education, and a variety of other personal and social factors. These same factors will also influence the patient's perceptions of his experience with pharmacy services.

It is common knowledge that all individual aspirations are not necessarily attainable in the health care system as it exists today. Some major barriers to total availability of health services are built into the current system. Others, however, are at least in part a function of the variations in individual patients and their behavior. The pharmacist, particularly the community pharmacist, is in a unique position to aid in removing barriers such as limitations in education and communication which prevent some people from finding a point of entry into the system. Indeed, the potential exists for making the pharmacist a major point of

15

entry. To do so will require a better understanding by the pharmacist of the importance of individual behavior patterns.

Definitions and Determinants of Ill Health

If one is to approach an understanding of the behavior of people seeking health care, and in so doing serve them better, there are certain distinctions that must be recognized. One of these is the conventional distinction between illness and disease.

Illness is defined, often imprecisely, by laymen as a reaction to a perceived biological alteration. It has both physical and social connotations and is highly individual, depending on state of mind and cultural beliefs, as well as physiologic and psychologic stimuli.

Disease is professionally defined, usually by physicians, and for that reason is perceived to be more precise. The definition of disease and its identification (diagnosis) in a given patient form the basis for much of the practice of medicine, including the choice of therapy. Beyond that disease has become the essential framework for the organization of the health care system and often for the organization of resources within that system.

Health professionals should recognize that the precision in the definition of disease is in fact often illusory. Physicians disagree both in diagnosis of physical and mental disorders and in the relationship between the two. It should be obvious that imprecision in the definition of disease is highly likely to lead to imprecision in therapy.

It is necessary to go a step further and point out that, by these constructions:

1. A person may have a disease and not be "ill."
2. A person may be ill and not have a disease.
3. Both disease and illness may be present.

An easy example is hypertension, a "disease" that has been precisely defined—by convention—as a combination diastolic and systolic blood pressure outside "normal" limits. This is, of course, precision by *definition*, with the fact remaining that hypertension has multiple causes, some of them not understood.

In any case, a person with the disease of hypertension may be asymptomatic and consequently not ill. Not being ill, that person may not seek care. In contrast, a person who experiences dizziness or has headaches may perceive himself as ill, seek care, and be diagnosed as disease free. These seemingly inconsequential differences may have serious consequences: failure to receive needed care in the first instance and possible waste of medical resources in the second.

A third definition that warrants brief discussion is that of *sickness*. In the context of this chapter we will refer to sickness as a condition that is socially defined, that is, a social status conferred on an individual by others. This is the approach taken by sociologists and will be important in our discussion of the sick role.

Finally, it is valuable to mention *health* or wellness. The World Health Organization's definition of health is the most widely quoted: "Health is a state of complete physical, mental, and social well-being, and not merely the absence of disease or infirmity." As this definition would conceivably exclude the existence of a dental caries or mild case of athlete's foot, it would similarly exclude virtually all of the world's population. It may be helpful, then, to think of health as an ideal state. Health, or wellness, then becomes a goal or destination, approached but never reached. Some prefer the term wellness to devote such a goal which is actively sought through positive action (good nutrition, exercise) and not merely through avoidance of contact with disease-causing agents.

With these definitions in hand, perhaps we can examine the determinants of disease, illness, and (conversely) health. Bezold (1) has argued that our state of health is determined by the interaction of four sets of interrelated variables:

1. Biology (i.e. genetic determinants)
2. Behavior (e.g. such things as smoking, drug abuse, and eating habits)
3. Pre- and postnatal environments (including physical, biological, economic, and social)
4. The health care system

Unquestionably, all of these have an influence on our individual and collective health. Inarguably, it is as difficult to assign credit for improved health status to any one of these as it is to find a single cause for most cases of hypertension.

We do know that insofar as *disease* processes are concerned, certain pathophysiologic processes are involved. These are vascular, inflammatory, neoplastic, toxic, metabolic, and degenerative. They are modified in their manifestations, however, by factors in the individual such as age, immunologic status, ingestion of medication, existence of other disease, and psychological factors. We know further that the passage of time and the accompanying social and technical changes have brought about changes in the ways we die and the diseases from which we suffer. Two sets of data will be sufficient to demonstrate this point.

Table 2.1 shows data at intervals since 1950 concerning death rates,

Table 2.1.
Age-Adjusted Death Rates for Selected Causes of Death, According to Race and Sex: United States, Selected Years 1950 to 1982 (Data Based on the National Vital Statistics System)[a]

Race, sex, and cause of death	Year								
	1950	1960	1970	1975	1979	1980	1981	1982
	Deaths per 100,000 resident population							
All causes	841.5	760.9	714.3	630.4	577.0	585.8	571.6	556.4
Diseases of heart	307.6	286.2	253.6	217.8	199.5	202.0	196.3	190.8
Cerebrovascular diseases	88.8	79.7	66.3	53.7	41.6	40.8	38.3	36.1
Malignant neoplasms	125.4	125.8	129.9	129.4	130.8	132.8	131.6	133.3
Respiratory system	12.8	19.2	28.4	32.1	35.2	36.4	37.0	37.7
Digestive system	47.7	41.1	35.2	33.2	33.1	33.0	32.2	32.1
Breast	22.2	22.3	23.1	22.6	22.3	22.7	—	—

Pneumonia and influenza	26.2	28.0	22.1	16.4	11.2	12.9	12.8	11.3
Chronic liver disease and cirrhosis	8.5	10.5	14.7	13.7	12.0	12.2	11.5	10.4
Diabetes mellitus	14.3	13.6	14.1	11.4	9.8	10.1	9.9	9.2
Accidents and adverse effects	57.5	49.9	53.7	44.2	42.9	42.3	40.2	37.1
Motor vehicle accidents	23.3	22.5	27.4	21.0	23.2	22.9	21.9	19.5
Suicide	11.0	10.6	11.8	12.5	11.7	11.4	11.3	11.5
Homicide and legal intervention	5.4	5.2	9.1	10.4	10.2	10.8	10.3	9.7
All causes—white female	963.1	917.7	893.4	804.3	738.4	745.3	730.8	709.7
All causes—while female	645.0	555.0	501.7	439.0	402.5	411.1	403.7	395.1
All causes—black male	1373.1	1246.1	1318.6	1163.0	1073.3	1112.8	—	1045.5
All causes—black female	1106.7	916.9	814.4	670.6	605.0	631.1	—	570.9

[a]From: *Health: United States, 1983.* Washington, D.C., U.S. Department of Health and Human Services, 1983, p 105.

by cause, in the United States. We see, among other things, an overall decline, dramatically so in some cases (cerebrovascular diseases and pneumonia). On the other hand, the death rate from cancer, liver disease, and homicides has increased. Further, the overall death rate differences by race and sex are striking (detail by cause is not presented).

Table 2.2 reports only on *notifiable* (i.e. communicable) diseases but shows the progress made where immunization is possible (rubeola and mumps). The data also show the disappointing record with regard to gonorrhea.

Over the years the pattern of diseases affecting the United States population has changed profoundly, generally as a result of changes in the environment, in the population's demographic composition, and in medical practice. Infectious diseases as the major cause of mortality have been replaced by chronic diseases associated with aging. At the turn of the century, infectious diseases struck the young and healthy and spread rapidly, often resulting in death. The confluence of improved sanitation, a higher standard of living, antibiotics, and vaccines reduced death and disability from infectious diseases so markedly they are now a comparatively minor cause of death.

While these disease entities have been diminishing or disappearing, new disease patterns have been emerging to take their place as the most important threat to life and health. Some of these patterns have resulted from the removal of diseases in early life (e.g. childhood infections), which has allowed time for diseases of later life (e.g. atherosclerosis) to appear. Other disease patterns, however, are comparatively new, far more prevalent than they once were, and the result of new forces in modern life and environment.

Behavior in Health and Sickness

Three types of behavior are relevant to anyone working at serving the needs of patients or potential patients. These are, with definitions:

1. Health behavior: "any activity undertaken by a person who believes himself to be healthy, for the purpose of preventing disease or detecting disease in an asymptomatic stage"
2. Illness behavior: "any activity undertaken by a person who feels ill, for the purpose of defining the state of his health and of discovering suitable remedy"
3. Sick role behavior: "activity undertaken by those who consider themselves ill for the purpose of getting well" (2).

Table 2.2.
Selected Notifiable Disease Rates, According to Disease: United States, Selected Years 1950 to 1981 (Data Based on Reporting by State Health Departments)[a]

Disease	Year							
	1950	1960	1970	1975	1978	1979	1980	1981
	Number of cases per 100,000 population							
Chicken pox	[b]	[b]	[b]	78.11	80.42	102.93	96.69	100.48
Diphtheria	3.83	0.51	0.21	0.14	0.03	0.03	0.00[c]	0.00
Hepatitis A	[b]	23.15	27.87	16.82	13.53	13.82	12.84	11.25
Hepatitis B			4.08	6.30	6.89	7.02	8.39	9.22
Measles (rubeola)	211.01	245.42	23.23	11.44	12.32	6.18	5.96	1.36
Mumps	[b]	[b]	55.55	27.99	7.81	6.55	3.86	2.20
Pertussis (whooping cough)	79.82	8.23	2.08	0.82	0.95	0.74	0.76	0.54
Poliomyelitis, total	22.02	1.77	0.02	0.00	0.01	0.02	0.00	0.00
Paralytic	[b]	1.40	0.02	0.00	0.00	0.01	0.00	0.00
Rubella (german measles)	[b]	[b]	27.75	7.81	8.38	5.36	1.72	0.91
Salmonellosis, excluding typhoid fever	[b]	3.85	10.84	10.61	13.49	15.06	14.88	17.44
Shigellosis	15.45	6.94	6.79	7.78	8.95	9.15	8.41	8.66
Tuberculosis[d]	80.50	30.83	18.22	15.95	13.08	12.57	12.25	11.94

Table 2.2. — continued
Selected Notifiable Disease Rates, According to Disease: United States, Selected Years 1950 to 1981 (Data Based on Reporting by State Health Departments)[a]

Disease	Year							
	1950	1960	1970	1975	1978	1979	1980	1981
	Number of cases per 100,000 population							
Venereal diseases[e]								
Syphilis[f]	146.02	68.78	45.46	38.00	30.00	30.68	30.38	31.98
Primary and secondary	16.73	9.06	10.94	12.09	10.00	11.38	12.01	13.73
Early latent	39.71	10.11	8.11	12.57	9.07	9.40	8.96	9.24
Late and late latent	76.22	45.91	25.05	12.81	10.64	9.70	9.26	8.86
Congenital	8.97	2.48	0.97	0.43	0.20	0.20	0.12	0.13
Gonorrhea	192.45	145.33	298.52	472.91	468.30	459.44	443.27	435.24
Chancroid	3.34	0.94	0.70	0.33	0.24	0.38	0.35	0.37
Granuloma, inguinal	1.19	0.17	0.06	0.03	0.03	0.03	0.02	0.03
Lymphogranuloma, venereal	0.95	0.47	0.30	0.17	0.13	0.11	0.09	0.12

[a]From: *Health: United States, 1983.* Washington, D.C., U.S. Department of Health and Human Services, 1983, p 125.
[b]Not reported nationally.
[c]Rates greater than 0 but less than 0.005 are shown as 0.00. The total resident population was used to calculate all rates except venereal diseases, for which the civilian resident population was used.
[d]Data subsequent to 1974 are not comparable to prior years because of changes in reporting criteria that became effective in 1975.
[e]Newly reported civilian cases.
[f]Includes stage of syphilis not stated.

The pharmacist has been most involved in the second of these, to a lesser degree in the third, and only minimally in the first. We will look at them in reverse order.

The Sick Role

Understanding of the "sick role" or behavior expected of a person defined as sick is made easier by placing it in historical perspective. Treatment, both medical and social, of the sick person has changed with the level of civilization. At the most primitive level the member who was ill was left to fend for himself or die, with no obligation placed on his neighbors to come to his aid. As civilization advanced, illness was frequently ascribed to evil spirits, and methods of assistance were limited to incantations and sometimes magic potions. The Old Testament, while changing the frame of reference somewhat, still placed illness in a religious context and is rife with references to illness as punishment for sin, either the patient's own or those of his family.

The New Testament brought about a sharp change in attitudes even to the point of allocating "grace" to those who associated with or aided the sick. By the eighteenth and nineteenth centuries secular authorities had become influential in health care and, as it became obvious that health care contributed to the common good, "contributions to the care of the sick grew larger and larger, finding in the course of time, social security as its most striking expression" (3).

In spite of this progress, vestiges of the old attitudes remain. We still have difficulty adopting a wholesome attitude, for example, toward mental illness, and a subconscious uncomfortable reaction to crippled persons is still widespread. All of this background is necessary to an understanding of the behavior pattern which society expects of those who are officially "sick." Sociologist Talcott Parsons has characterized the sick role as consisting of two rights and two duties (4).

> *Rights*: Freedom from blame for illness
> Exemption from normal roles and tasks

The rights are bestowed conditionally, however, and are appropriate only if the patient fulfills his duties.

> *Duties*: To do everything possible to recover
> To seek technically competent help

Obviously, there are deviations from this model but, when such deviance occurs, society's approval is usually withheld.

The sick role gives the individual a reasonable excuse for making claims on others for care and also provides a reason for failure. People

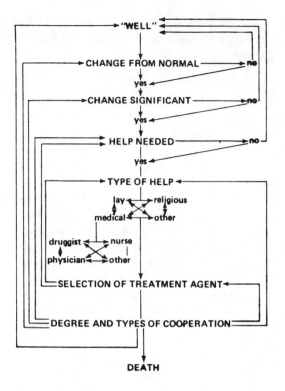

Figure 2.1.   Decision steps in the sickness career. Source: Twaddle and Hessler (5).

with symptoms (i.e. who are "ill") can, with confirmation, adopt this special social role. A person can enter the sick role if a doctor confirms that the person is ill or if the family or friends of the individual are willing to accept the status "sick." Thus, illness (individually defined) becomes sickness (socially defined), especially if a physician confirms the existence of disease.

Illness Behavior

Understanding of the behavior of people when they are ill has been enhanced by viewing this behavior as a "sickness career" (5). Figure 2.1 graphically portrays this process.

The sickness career begins with a state of wellness. As already noted, being well or healthy will mean different things to different people. There have been a variety of studies of this phenomenon, and the general criteria by which people view themselves as well include:

1. A feeling of well being
2. An absence of symptoms
3. An ability to perform normal personal and work functions

Although these will not be uniform from person to person, their meaning for any given individual will form a baseline of health against which to judge changes.

When a change from a state of wellness is perceived, there will again be varying reactions. Most people, even those who feel well, are able to identify the presence at any time of some symptoms. Often they will view these as normal, although they may trigger a desire for further information.

Ultimately a decision must be made about the significance of symptoms. Twaddle and Hessler (5, pp 125–127) report that a variety of factors go into determining if a change in health status is significant. These factors are:

1. Interference with normal activities and functions (e.g. bowel habits, work ability, leisure activity)
2. Clarity of symptoms (e.g. sharp pains or symptoms visible to family or friends are likely to be judged important)
3. Tolerance threshold (some people can tolerate more pain, either because of personal characteristics, cultural factors, or the nature of their work)
4. Familiarity with symptoms (common symptoms that one has had previously and recovered from are likely to be viewed as less serious than those which have not been previously experienced).
5. Assumptions about cause (e.g. in the case of chest pain it may be viewed as anything from a heart attack to indigestion).
6. Assumptions about prognoses (if long-term incapacity or possible death is associated with the symptom, it is likely to be viewed as more serious).
7. Interpersonal influence (refers to effects of the lay referral system discussed in Chapter 1).
8. Other life crisis (in some cases a symptom that might have been viewed as normal assumes greater proportions in the face of family or work crisis).

Once a symptom is viewed as significant a decision must be made whether help is needed and, if so, what kind of help is needed. The enormity of sales of nonprescription drugs attests to the fact that self-treatment is often the first method of treatment chosen. If, consistent with the sick role, the individual chooses to seek professional help, it is likely that the lay referral system as well as prior experience will again come into play, both in the initial decision to seek help and in the choice of type of help chosen.

Irving Zola identified five triggers affecting the timing of a patient's decision to seek medical care. They are as follows (6):

1. An interpersonal crisis occurs that serves to call attention to the symptoms, causing the patient to dwell on them.
2. Social interference occurs as the symptoms begin to threaten a valued social activity, such as work.
3. The individual receives sanctioning for seeking care, that is, others encourage the patient to seek care.
4. The patient perceives the symptoms as threatening in nature.
5. The symptoms are seen as similar to previous symptoms, or to those with which the person is familiar because relatives or friends have had them.

Once help is sought, for purposes of this discussion usually from a physician, the drug use process (described in Chapter 3) begins. Within this process a wide range of patient behaviors remains, including the degree to which that patient will comply with professional recommendations. Research has shown that the degree of patient compliance varies greatly and is influenced, again, by a variety of personal, psychological, social, cultural, and economic factors.

According to Christensen's comprehensive review of drug taking compliance studies (7), negative influences on compliance include:

1. Length of treatment
2. Desire to continue in the sick role
3. Complexity of the medication regimen
4. Incidence and severity of side effects especially if unexpected
5. Extremes of age
6. Living alone
7. Personality disorders
8. Prophylactic use of drug
9. Asymptomatic status
10. No immediate negative consequences of noncompliance
11. Lack of explanation by physician

It should be apparent that the potential role of the pharmacist in compliance is extraordinary. This will be explored further in Chapter 3.

Some idea of the degree to which variation exists in patient reaction to symptoms can be gained from a review of the data in Table 2.3, which shows response of a sample of rural patients to a selection of symptoms.

The final step in the sickness career is comprised of a range of

Table 2.3.
Proportion of Frequently Reported Symptoms without Medical Treatment[a]

Symptom	Percentage without medical treatment	Total
Repeated sinus attacks	40.3	467
Repeated back trouble	31.7	202
Chronic nervous trouble	21.5	186
Hemorrhoids	61.9	134
Overweight	55.3	159
Ear problem	25.9	189
Vision problems	51.3	154
High blood pressure	15.7	376
Heart trouble	11.4	123
Arthritis or rheumatism	42.0	371
Hay fever	50.8	120
Allergy	27.4	168
Bad sore throat	34.6	130
Bad shortness of breath	33.3	108
Irregualr heart beat	21.4	112
Serious stomach pain	54.3	116
Painful or swollen joints	46.5	101
Insomnia	61.5	143
Swelling ankles	47.1	136

[a]Either self-treated or untreated.

outcomes ranging from death to a chronically ill status to a return to wellness.

Health Behavior

Hardest of all health-related behavior to predict is that of the "healthy" individual. Included in such behavior are decisions to obtain preventive or detection tests as well as activities, such as dental hygiene and good nutrition, designed to maintain a state of wellness. The individual has no clearcut symptoms to prompt such action, yet the time, effort, and money spent on this type of activity are potentially the most productive of those spent on any health care activity.

One of the most widely accepted explanations of people's health behavior is the "Health Belief Model" shown in Figure 2.2. Briefly, the model proposes that an individual is psychologically ready to take action relative to a given condition, for example, cancer prevention. The

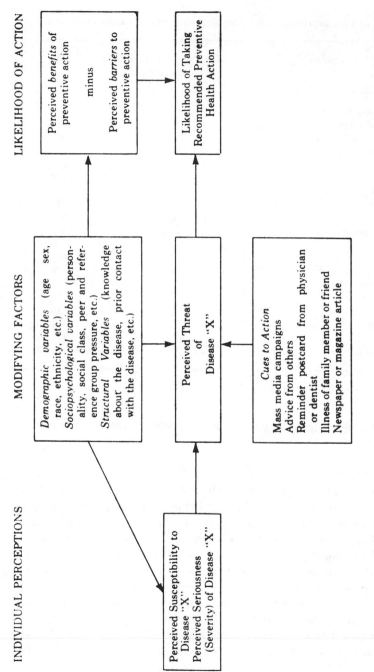

Figure 2.2 The Health Belief Model as a predictor of preventive health behavior (after Becher et al.). From Rosenstock IM: Historical origins of the health belief model. *Health Education Monographs* 2:334, 1974.

degree of such readiness is influenced by the extent to which that individual feels susceptible to the condition and views the condition as one with serious personal consequences.

The individual must also believe that a proposed action (e.g. a Pap smear) is both feasible and appropriate to use, that it would reduce susceptibility to the condition or to the seriousness of the condition, and that taking the action presents no serious psychological or other barriers.

Finally, some sort of cue or stimulus is needed to trigger an action response.

The pharmacists may conceivably perform useful functions in any of these steps: in the first by health education efforts, in the second by providing the convenience factor, and in the third by providing cues. In any case the pharmacist is likely to be involved because drugs are involved in almost any episode involving health problems.

In a study conducted in Columbus, Ohio, of nearly 3000 illness and injury incidents, researchers found that drug therapy in general and self-medication in particular played a central role in treatment.

> Over 90% of all incidents involved the use of drugs, and over 70% involved the use of drugs without a doctor contact. Treatment occurred rapidly; in almost ⅓ of the cases it was begun within 4 hours of the onset of the symptoms. The most frequently reported strategy was the use of non-prescribed drugs within the first 4 hours (8).

The importance of self-medication is perhaps explained by the difficulty in establishing contact with a physician. "The number of doctor attempts was greater than the number of doctor contacts. An average of 7 hours was required just to make a doctor contact after the person had initiated an attempt" (9).

The Pharmacist and Patient Behavior

It should be apparent from the foregoing discussion that variations in human behavior may be important determinants in whether and how an individual seeks and receives medical care. Talbot has concluded that:

> ... if the health care professions are to continue to make major gains, it must be recognized that most human diseases and disabilities are due to a multiplicity of factors. Of these, some are responsible for creating conditions which predispose the occurrence of disease in some form, while others serve as the specific immediate mechanism through which the condition is made manifest.
>
> The sources of human wellness and disability are social,

behavioral, and biophysical in nature. It follows that medicine in the aggregate must develop the ability to identify and to deal with all of them (10).

This "aggregate" includes the pharmacist. The stages in health, illness, and sick role behavior offer opportunities and obligations for pharmacy. Some of these are a traditional part of pharmacy practice; others have not been fully delineated. This in no way lessens their potential importance. A few examples may help to illustrate how the pharmacist may best serve the patient.

A review of Figure 2.1 will show several points at which pharmacists may serve their clients.

During the symptom experience stage, the potential patient is quite likely to enter the pharmacist's domain, either to obtain a product for relief of one or more symptoms or to receive assistance in interpreting the symptoms, or both. The pharmacist has both the responsibility to offer only such products as provide safe and effect symptomatic treatment and the responsibility to be knowledgeable enough to interpret symptoms sufficiently well so that the patient is neither unduly delayed in obtaining the services of a physician nor acts as a drain on our overburdened health care system without need.

Since the patient assuming the sick role is expected to try to get better, he may choose self-medication as a means to that end. He should receive guidance in his choice if this is appropriate, or he should be told, when necessary, that such action is inappropriate. The pharmacist may, in fact, be the first one approached in the medical care contact stage because he is readily available. Depending upon the nature of such contact, he may assist in finding access to the system, he may aid in locating the proper medical services, and, most importantly, he may provide the pharmaceutical services and products which the physician ultimately prescribes.

Considerable study has been done in Wales on the perception of the patient concerning prescriptions written for him by the doctor. Many patients actually believed that prescriptions were not always what they wanted but that the doctor used the prescription as a way of getting them out of the office. The researchers in Wales believed that in the majority of cases the patients were acquiescent in the presence of the doctor, but once they left his office they reviewed what had happened and used their drugs and their doctor's advice in light of that review. The Welsh researchers believed that the patient sometimes lost his perspective in the doctor's office but upon reentering the "real" world tended to manipulate therapy to his/her own choosing. As the researchers pointed out, "if a patient leaves the surgery with a prescription and does not return, it is easy for the doctor to assume that the patient has taken the medication as indicated, that the medication has worked, and that the patient has been cured" (11). One possible result is an unrealistically positive assessment of drug efficacy by prescribers.

The problem of patient compliance with physician recommendations, particularly with regard to prescription drugs, is one which is critical to a successful outcome and which is particularly amenable to pharmacist intervention. As Figure 2.3 shows, "hypo-compliance" is as much a medical problem in hypertension as the hypertension itself.

Where drug therapy is involved, the outcome of the physician-patient encounter typically involves a prescription. The physician, through the medium of the prescription, requests the pharmacist to dispense to the patient a specified number of units of a specific drug in a specific dosage form at a specific dose. He further requests the pharmacist to provide written instructions, through the medium of the prescription label, directing the patient to consume the drug according to the prescribed schedule. The patient is then expected to consume the medication as directed; he is expected to comply with his prescribed drug therapy regimen.

From this it can be seen that patient compliance with a prescription drug regimen is a two-stage process. First, the patient must take the prescription to the pharmacist (often the physician completes this act by telephoning the prescription to the pharmacist) and have it dispensed. At the second stage the patient must use the drug at the rate and for the duration prescribed. Although it occurs in only about 3% of the cases, the patient may choose not to have his prescription dispensed. If he chooses not to comply with this prerequisite first stage of the process, he cannot be compliant with the second stage.

The most frequently reported reason for noncompliance is forgetfulness. Patients simply forget to take some doses of the medication. Another reason frequently reported is the perception by the patient that he feels better and no longer needs the medication, so he prematurely discontinues taking the drug. Side effects are also reported by patients to be responsible for their discontinuing the medication.

Patient interviews often also reveal that the patient does not correctly understand the directions on the prescription label. We found that patients instructed to take antibiotics "one capsule four times daily" more often understood that they should take the intended four capsules each day than did patients instructed to take "one capsule every six hours." Patients in the latter case did not know that they should take the medication around the clock, which was implied but

There are two sides to every story...

Hypertensive

Hypo-compliance

*Hypo-compliance is the failure or inability of hypertensive patients to follow prescribed therapy.

The need for antihypertensive therapy [1,2]

In the well-known VA studies of 1967-70, patients with mild to moderately severe hypertension treated with antihypertensive therapy experienced significant beneficial results.

1 Effects of treatment on morbidity in hypertension. II Results in patients with diastolic blood pressure averaging 90 through 114 mm Hg. Veterans Administration Cooperative Study Group on Antihypertensive Agents. J A M A 213 1143, 1970.

2 Effects of treatment on morbidity in hypertension. Results in patients with diastolic blood pressures averaging 115 through 129 mm Hg. Veterans Administration Cooperative Study Group on Antihypertensive Agents. J A M A 202 1028, 1967

Profile of the hypo-compliant hypertensive:
Her first antihypertensive R_x was for a 2-months' supply. Now, 5 months later, she's back for another 2-months' supply...

Will she be back?

What you should know about hypo-compliance

• **Hypo-compliance** leads to undermedication, risk of serious complications, increased morbidity and mortality.

• **Hypo-compliance** —As an important part of the professional health team, you can help the hypertensive patients you serve by making them aware of the importance of *fully* complying with their physicians' advice and taking their medication as prescribed.

• **Hypo-compliance** —This important message on hypertensive hypo-compliance is now being communicated to all physicians in your area by USV representatives.

Figure 2.3. Courtesy of USV Pharmaceutical Corporation, Tuckahoe, NY.

not explicitly stated on the label. Many other instances of incomplete or confusing instructions could be cited by any pharmacy practitioner. This is a problem area that effective patient counseling can remedy easily.

Cooperation with medical agencies includes undergoing treatment procedures for the illness and following the prescribed medical regimen. If, for example, a diagnosis of infection is determined by the physician, he may prescribe a course of antibiotic therapy. The patient obtains his prescription and complies with the directions on the label. After a period of time, but before the completion of the full course of therapy, the patient's symptoms may sufficiently subside or disappear and he may perceive continuation of the antibiotic regimen as incongruous with his responsibility to relinquish the sick role. He may perceive that taking the medication is part of being sick, not part of being well, and that he is acting inappropriately with respect to resuming his normal roles. Yet, if he prematurely terminates the full course of antibiotic therapy, his decision may result in the development of a subsequently more serious infection, since only the least viable microorganisms may have been affected by the short course of therapy and the most resistant organisms remain to multiply and "reinfect" the host.

The patient's decision to either continue or to terminate therapy is predicated on his perception of the consequences of each decision. His perception of the consequences is based in part upon the information he has relative to those consequences. Thus, the pharmacist may help ensure patient compliance to a drug therapy regimen by providing information to persuade the patient that his most rational decision is to continue the full course of therapy. Indeed, it is the pharmacist's responsibility to his patient to counsel him effectively as to the proper use of his medications.

It should also be noted that the term compliance brings with it at least two dangers. The first is the view that the doctor always knows best. This may bring with it blind adherence to directions even in the face of untoward and undesirable effects. The second is the failure to make the patient a part of the treatment process, thereby eliminating a valuable participant. Zola (11) has argued that the patient must be involved, must demand: "A demystification of expertise, a right to know everything about one's body, and a sharing of power in any decision affecting one's life." He prefers a change from "medication compliance" to "therapeutic alliance."

Freidson has noted that:

> ... the laymen who do enter the [medical] consulting room are not a representative sample of the total population. Entrance into the

consulting room follows an organized social process that is highly selective. The grounds for selection are not the profession's conceptions of illness, and the organization of the process is in important ways independent of the organization of the profession (12).

There is every reason to believe that the laymen who enter the pharmacy at the community level are a much more representative sample of this population. The potential exists for the pharmacist, through his ready availability and a studied application of triage techniques, to assist in making the consulting room population both more representative of the population as a whole and more representative of medically rather than socially defined needs. Note should be taken that even the pharmacist may not come into direct contact with the patient, particularly the very young, very old, or very ill patient; this fact is yet another intervening, complicating variable in the process.

The pharmacist should also be alert to the possibility of "overmedication," even under medical supervision. "The doctor's contribution to overmedication is to be seen in the context of his recurrent need to balance the time available for practice against the time demanded for medical care" (13).

Muller estimates, based on statistics on medical practice provided by the American Medical Association, that office-based physicians see in their office more than 90 patients per week. For general practitioners this figure is nearly 130. She estimates that this gives the physician about 17 minutes to spend with each of his patients, assuming some time in the hospital.

> The act of prescribing in this situation conforms to the requirements of the successful termination strategies in psychological theory.... The prescription is a signal for the approaching end of the encounter, it both summarizes and carries forward the relationship, it is an expression of concern, and it deals with the interests of both parties perceived as equitable.
>
> By keeping the length of appointments within bounds, the doctor does not have to extend his work day to satisfy requests for appointments and to maintain his income: nor does he have to cut down his income by seeing fewer patients. He can turn his patients over to aides for instructions, physical therapy, or other ministrations, but he would have to be compensated for the cost incurred by doing so (13).

It is particularly important for the community pharmacist to recognize his very special place in the health care delivery system for those in lower socioeconomic classes.

Strauss has recognized that lower income families often use the pharmacist as a first or sometimes the only step in treatment (14).

The pharmacist can assist in breaking the vicious poverty-illness-poverty cycle that characterizes the experience of lower income patients. There are several suggested methods of intervention, and the alert and concerned pharmacist can assist in each. They are:

1. Speeding up the initial visit for medical care
2. Improving patient experience in medical facilities
3. Improving communications about necessary regimens
4. Increasing in other ways the likelihood of patient compliance with necessary regimens
5. Increasing the likelihood of needed follow-up

Although lower income patients experience greater problems in these areas, the concepts apply to all patients.

The pharmacist has great potential as well for assisting the public in productive and beneficial *health* behavior. One of the principal methods of doing so is by providing the cues to action. This may be accomplished through verbal reminders or through displays. Particularly promising opportunities exist for influencing young adults to acquire and maintain good health habits, particularly in relation to drugs. There is still a major deficiency in curricula and personnel for this purpose which pharmacists could help to fill.

Summary

In this chapter a discussion was presented of the differences in the ways in which a person may behave when he is ill and when he is not ill. The importance of the perception of the individual of his relative illness or wellness was expressed, and application of these behavior patterns in pharmacy practice is made. It should be apparent from the material presented in this chapter that the stages of illness behavior provide a multitude of opportunities for pharmacist activity, many of which have not been adequately exploited to date. The knowledgeable pharmacist who is willing to study the patient as an individual will find it possible to fulfill his professional role to the fullest extent.

REFERENCES

1. Bezold C (ed): *Pharmaceuticals in the Year 2000.* Washington, D.C., 1983, p 30.
2. Rosenstock IM: Why people use health services. In Mainland D (ed): *Health Services Research.* New York . Milbank Memorial Fund, 1967, pp 94–127.
3. Roemer MI (ed): *[Henry E.] Sigerist on the Sociology of Medicine.* New York, MD Publications, Inc., 1960, pp 9–22.

4. Parsons T: Definitions of health and illness in the light of American values and social structure. In Jaco EG (ed): *Patients, Physicians and Illness*. New York, The Free Press of Glencoe, 1959, pp 165–187.

5. Twaddle AC, Hessler RM: *A Sociology of Health*. St. Louis, C.V. Mosby, 1977, p 124.

6. Zola IK: Illness behavior in the working class. In Shostak A, Gomberg W (eds): *Studies of the American Worker*. Englewood Cliffs, NJ, Prentice-Hall, 1964, p 160.

7. Christensen DB: Drug-taking compliance: A review and synthesis. *Health Serv Res* 13:171–187, 1978.

8. Knapp DE, Oeltjen PD, Knapp DA: Anatomy of an illness. *Med Marketing and Media* 9:20–22, 1974.

9. Talbot NB: The need for behavioral and social science in medicine. In Knowles JH (ed): *Views of Medical Education and Medical Care*. Cambridge, MA, Harvard University Press, 1968, p 48.

10. Anon.: Doctors "overestimate" the number of patients who want medicine. *Pharm J* 209:369, 1972.

11. Zola IK: The social and psychological implications of compliance. Proceedings of the Interprofessional Conference on Compliance with Medical Regimens by the Hypertensive Patient. University of Mississippi, 1975, p 35.

12. Freidson E: *Profession of Medicine*. New York, Dodd, Mead & Company, 1970, p 279.

13. Muller C: The overmedicated society: Forces in the marketplace for medical care. *Science* 176:488–492, 1972.

14. Strauss AL: Medical organization, medical care and lower income groups, *Soc Sci Med* 3:143–177, 1969.

CHAPTER 3

Drug Use

Drugs play an enormous role in modern medicine and in society at large. About 60% of all physician office visits result in at least one drug being prescribed (1). In 1983 community pharmacists dispensed 1.5 billion prescriptions—seven for every man, woman, and child in the United States. At an average price of nearly $8.50 per new prescription, the annual expenditure totaled about $16.7 billion (2), and these figures do not include prescriptions purchased through mail-order plans, hospital outpatient pharmacies, or the 2000 prescription departments in supermarkets, department stores, and discount houses.

Drugs available over the counter (OTC) without prescription also play an important role in self-treatment. A typical family medicine cabinet may contain 15 to 20 different nonprescription products. Sales of these products totaled $4.3 billion in 1983 (3).

Drug use by institutionalized patients is even more pervasive. Although precise data are not available. an average hospital patient receives six to eight different medications during a typical stay. In long-term-care facilities, where patients usually are elderly, 90% receive three or more drugs all the time, and 15% receive ten or more (4).

Trends in Drug Use

Obviously, not all drugs are the same and summary figures can only give a vague notion of the role drugs play in therapy. Table 3.1 presents the therapeutic categories which accounted for the largest number of total prescriptions in 1983. More than half of all prescriptions were written for products in one of these categories. The types of drugs range from the curative, such as many of the anti-infectives, to palliatives, such as the pain relievers and cough and cold preparations, to substances which replace or modify natural substances in the body, such as the hormones.

Table 3.2 lists the 50 most frequently prescribed drugs in 1979 and

Table 3.1.
Prescriptions for Leading Therapeutic Categories (1983)[a]

Category	% of all prescriptions
Cardiovasculars	14.6
Antibiotics/anti-infectives	12.6
Psychotherapeutics	8.0
Analgesics	7.0
Cough/cold	5.4
Antiarthritics	4.7
Total: top six categories	52.4

[a] From: Annual prescription survey. *Drug Topics* 128(6): 29, 1984.

Table 3.2.
Fifty Most Frequently Prescribed Drug Products 1979 and 1983 (New and Renewal Prescriptions)[a]

Drug and manufacturer	1979 rank	1983 rank
Valium (Roche)	1	4
Inderal (Ayerst)	2	2
Ampicillin (unspecified)	3	**[b]
Tylenol/Codeine (McNeil)	4	3
Lasix Oral (Hoechst-Roussel)	5	7
Dyazide (SK&F)	6	1
Tetracycline syst. (unspecified)	7	**
Lanoxin (B-W)	8	5
Dimetapp (Robins)	9	16
Dalmane (Roche)	10	17
Actifed (B-W)	11	**
Aldomet (MSD)	12	12
Darvocet-N 100 (Lilly)	13	10
Penicillin VK (unspecified)	14	**
Keflex (Dista)	15	11
HydroDiuril (MSD)	16	39
Erythromycin syst. (unspecified)	17	**
Clinoril (MSD)	18	41
Motrin (Upjohn)	19	9
V-Cillin K (Lilly)	20	**
Indocin (MSD)	21	28
Tagamet (SK&F)	22	6
Empirin Comp./Codeine (B-W)	23	32
Donnatal (Robins)	24	37

Table 3.2.—*continued*
Fifty Most Frequently Prescribed Drug Products 1979 and 1983 (New and Renewal Prescriptions)[a]

Drug and manufacturer	1979 rank	1983 rank
Premarin Oral (Ayerst)	25	13
E.E.S. (Abbott)	26	14
Hygroton (USV)	27	33
Librium (Roche)	28	79
Benadryl Caps./Tabs. (P-D)	29	35
Prednisone oral (unspecified)	30	**
Slow-K (Ciba)	31	19
Dilantin Sodium (P-D)	32	24
Isordil (Ives)	33	31
Elavil (MSD)	34	**
Amoxicillin (unspecified)	35	**
Fiorinal (Sandoz)	36	50
Synthroid (Flint)	37	18
Phenobarbital (unspecified)	38	**
Aldoril (MSD)	39	36
Lomotil (Searle)	40	**
Hydrochlorothiazide (unspecified)	41	**
Mycolog (Squibb)	42	**
Ilosone (Dista)	43	**
Tranxene (Abbott)	44	26
Ovral (Wyeth)	45	**
Diabinese (Prizer)	46	22
Antivert (Roerig)	47	**
Vibramycin (Pfizer)	48	**
Ortho-Novum 1/50-21 (Ortho)	49	44
Percodan (Endo)	50	**

[a] From: *Pharmacy Times*, April 1980, p 34, and April 1984, p 28 (from National Prescription Audit, IMS America).

[b] Not in top 50, in most cases because of changes in reporting procedures.

their ranks in 1983. Rank changes both up and down can be noted resulting from changing patterns of therapy and from the introduction of new, popular medications. Only eight of the drug products (Valium, Premarin, Dimetapp, Dilantin, Indocin, Benadryl, Donnatal, Hydro-Diuril) have been in the top 50 since 1966.

Notice that a list of the most frequently prescribed drug *chemicals* (i.e. ingredients) would be different. A 1982 study by the Food and Drug Administration (FDA), using the same data source as that used in Table 3.2, found the ten most frequently prescribed drug chemicals to be (in order): hydrochlorothiazide, codeine, combination oral contraceptives,

Table 3.3.
Expenditures for Nonprescription Drugs (1983)—In thousands[a]

Category	Total expenditures	Expenditures in pharmacies	% expenditures in pharmacies
Cough/cold	$1,522,690	$856,726	56
Analgesics	1,634,932	849,953	52
Vitamins	1,304,689	803,911	62
Antacids	779,955	390,124	50
Laxatives	389,595	268,813	69
Diet aids	555,238	224,785	40
Contraceptives	322,452	186,071	58

[a] From: Annual drugstore sales survey. *Drug Topics*, 128(22):1984.

erythromycin, propanolol, triamterene, potassium, diazepam, amoxicillin, and digoxin (5).

The top 50 products accounted for about 35% of all prescriptions in 1980; the top 100, 49%; and the top 200, 62% (6). Thus, despite the thousands of drug products available, relatively few are prescribed in large numbers. Of course, a less frequently prescribed drug is not unimportant to a patient who needs it, so a major function of pharmacy is to be able to obtain any drug product quickly as required.

The FDA study cited above reported a 28% increase in prescription drug use in the 11 years between 1971 and 1982. Most of this increase came from larger prescription sizes (5).

Table 3.3 shows the extent of use of nonprescription drugs as measured by consumer expenditures or sales. Americans spent well over a billion dollars in 1983 on cough/cold medicines alone, and 44% of those dollars were spent in nonpharmacy outlets. Overall, more than 40% of nonprescription drug expenditures were made in nonpharmacy outlets.

Drug Use Process Models

Before examining the more obvious uses of drugs as medication, it may be useful to remember that drugs have many uses in our society. Svarstad (7) has identified 11 different classes of human motives in which drugs serve some function (see Table 3.4). A review of these should show the pervasive influence of drugs in our society. It is helpful to point out that almost all of these functions are served, at one time or another, by drugs obtained through legitimate medical channels. Not included in the Svarstad list is one additional function—sexual—as the main use of oral contraceptives is to permit sexual activity with reduced risk of pregnancy.

Table 3.4.
Human Motives and the Functions of Drugs[a]

Motive	Function
Prevent, treat, and cure disease; relieve pain and discomfort	Therapeutic function
Relieve feelings of personal failure, grief, stress, fear, loneliness, sadness or inferiority	Psychological support function
Relax and enjoy the company of others; experience pleasurable sights, sounds, tastes, smells, and feelings; satisfy curiosity or desire for new and unusual experiences	Recreational function
Relieve fatigue and improve academic, athletic, or work performance	Instrumental function
Manage or control the behavior of demanding patients, disruptive children, political dissidents, and other persons	Social control function
Beautify the skin, hair, or body image	Cosmetic function
Gain social status, approval, or prestige	Status-conferring function
Express feelings, values, preferences, interest, or concern	Expressive-symbolic function
Seek religious meaning, salvation, or transcendent experiences	Religious function
Gain knowledge and understanding of human behavior	Research function
Allay hunger or control the desire for food	Appetitive function

[a] From: B. L. Svarstad: The sociology of drugs. In Wertheimer AI, Smith MC (eds): *Pharmacy Practice*. Baltimore, University Park Press, 1981, p 261.

In order to organize what is known about drug use in a *medical* context, a framework for analysis has been developed which views drug use as a process occurring over time and consisting of several identifiable stages or steps. These include:

1. Perception of a need for a drug
2. Selection of a specific drug product
3. Choice of a regimen

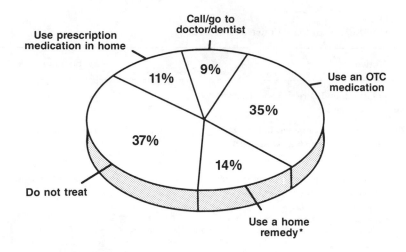

(Total adds to 106% because more than one action was taken in some cases.)

*Home remedies include salt-water gargles for sore throat and baking soda paste for bee stings—not medicines.

Figure 3.1. How people take care of everyday health problems. Source: Harry Heller Research Corporation: *Health Care Practices and Perceptions: A Consumer Survey of Self-Medication*. Harry Heller Research Corporation, 1984.

4. Obtaining the drug product
5. Administration/consumption of the drug product
6. Feedback

Each of these stages involves decisions which must be made by one or more persons, including health professionals, such as physicians, nurses, and pharmacists, or lay people, such as patients or relatives of patients. The correctness and appropriateness of each of these decisions influence the success of the entire drug use process. Thus, the business of drug giving and drug taking is hardly a simple process. Understanding its complexities is of vital importance to the health professional. Reference to Figure 3.1 will also put drug use into a broader context.

Perception of Need for a Drug

The first stage in the drug use process involves deciding whether a drug of some kind would be appropriate in a specific situation. The situation could involve a physician treating a patient, a mother helping a sick child, or a person medicating himself. In some situations the decision may not be prompted by an acute problem. For example, a need for immunization may stem from enrollment requirements at school, the desire to visit a foreign country where vaccination is required, or a general orientation to preventive care. In any case, at this stage the concept "drug" has not yet been refined to the need for a specific product.

Apparently, it does not take much to reach this stage. The threshold for perception of need for a drug is very low. Drugs are one of the most common forms of therapy. In a longitudinal study conducted in 1968 (8), investigators followed the health behavior of 278 households over a 30-week period. Panelists kept detailed diary records of their activities related to all incidents of illness or injury occurring in the household. They also recorded details of all drug procurements. Of 3381 incidents of illness or injury reported, over 90% involved the use of drug therapy. It was also found from a further analysis of 2814 cases with complete time information that this need for a drug occurs soon after the onset of symptoms. In over 60% of these cases, one or more drug products was used within the first 4 hours and before any contact with a physician was made. Although the study respondents took medication frequently and quickly, an analysis of the types of illnesses reported shows that over 60% were common ailments for which symptomatic relief through the use of drugs is well established.

The nonprescription (OTC) drug use process in one which, in spite of its importance, is still imperfectly understood. The most recent and most extensive study was that conducted in 1983 on behalf of the Proprietary Association (9). According to that national survey of more than 2000 people, about one in three health problems is treated with an OTC medication (see Fig. 3.1).

According to the survey, Americans experience an average of 4.5 health problems per person per 2-week period. The survey noted, however, that neither OTC nor prescription drugs were used to treat slightly more than half of the problems reported: "Of the 9,148 problems reported by the sample, 51% were either not treated or treated with a home remedy." Some 37% of those problems were not treated and 14% were treated with home remedies, such as salt or baking soda mouthwashes for gum problems and hot water soaks for ingrown toenails (see Table 3.5).

OTC drugs were most commonly used for problems that the survey said "would be considered either annoying or which would make daily functioning difficult if the symptoms were not alleviated." OTC drugs were most frequently used for lip problems, athlete's foot, chronic

Table 3.5.
Problems with Highest Incidence of Treatment by Home Remedy[a]

Ten problems with highest incidence of home remedy	Adult problems treated by home remedy (%)	Hypothesized actions
Ingrown toenail	40	Soak in hot water
Gum problems	36	Mouthwash such as salt water, baking soda
Sore throat not associated with cold	30	Hot liquid
Burns other than sunburn	28	Cold water/butter
Overindulgence of alcohol	25	Home brew
Acne/pimples	25	Soap and water
Minor cuts and scratches	24	Adhesive bandage
Overweight	22	Diet
Bunions/corns/calluses	22	Soak in hot water
Pain associated with injury	21	Hot or cold compresses/heating pad

[a] From: Harry Heller Research Corporation: *Health Care Practices and Perceptions.* Washington, D.C., Harry Heller Research Corporation, 1984.

dandruff, and common cold (see Table 3.6). The problems most likely to be treated with prescription medicine already on hand were asthma, ulcers, skin infections, hay fever/related allergies, arthritis/rheumatism, and migraine headaches.

The survey found that 43% of people who use OTC drugs take the product for only 1 day. "Those problems for which OTC medications are primarily used for one day tend to be acute and short term, such as asthma and overindulgence of alcohol," the report said. For example, 81% of consumers who took an OTC for overindulgence of alcohol used the product only 1 day, as did 73% of those using OTC products for asthma and 60% of those who took an OTC for headache relief.

Among the problems most likely to be untreated are age or "liver" spots, bruises, baldness, sleeping problems, underweight, minor fatigue, overindulgence of food, minor anxiety, diarrhea, and cough not associated with a cold (see Table 3.7). The report noted that these problems "tend to be non-serious over the short term, although some could be serious if they persisted over a long period of time."

Table 3.6.
Problems with Highest Incidence of Treatment by Nonprescription Medication[a]

Ten problems with highest* incidence of treatment with an OTC medication	Adult problems treated with an OTC medication (%)
Lip problems	71
Headache	69
Athlete's foot	64
Chronic dandruff	61
Common cold	61
Painful dry skin	58
Migraine headache	56
Menstrual problems	54
Premenstrual problems	54
Sinus problems	53

[a] From: Harry Heller Research Corporation: *Health Care Practices and Perceptions.* Washington, D.C., 1984.

Table 3.7.
Problems Most Frequently Untreated[a]

Ten most frequently untreated problems	Adult problems not treated during interview period (%)
Age spots/"liver spots"	87
Bruises	75
Baldness	75
Underweight	69
Sleeping problems	68
Minor fatigue	62
Overindulgence of food	57
Diarrhea	56
Minor anxiety	51
Cough not associated with a cold	50

[a]From: Harry Heller Research Corporation: *Health Care Practices and Perceptions.* Harry Heller Research Corporation, Washington, D.C., 1984.

A Canadian study (10), this time conducted by mail, found results consistent in a general way with those just cited. Canadian consumers believed that the availability of a drug on the market was an implicit governmental guarantee that it was safe. The Canadian researchers hypothesized a self-medication model (see Fig. 3.2) that is helpful in

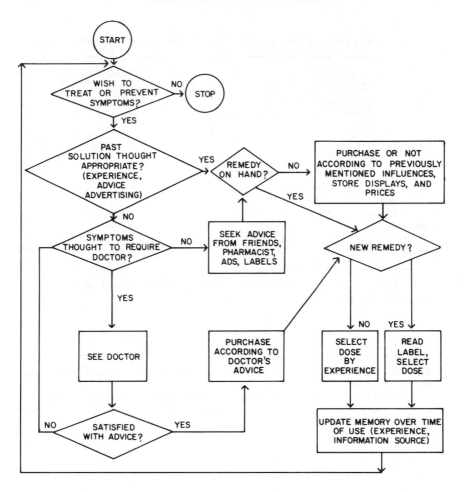

Figure 3.2.   Self-medication model. From: Hustad TP, Courtney AE, Heeler RM: An emerging model for purchase and consumption of non-prescription drugs. *J Consumer Affairs* 13(1):81–85, 1979.

understanding the behavior of OTC users *and* may serve as a framework for future research.

As far as the use of prescription drugs is concerned, the physician finds them useful for a wide variety of therapeutic purposes. Important to the understanding of the drug use process is the fact that drugs may serve needs other than those strictly related to pharmacologic activity. For example, it is well known that there is a placebo effect associated with the use of drugs. Thus, many patients may receive beneficial effects from drug therapy even though it may be difficult to prove a pharmacologic effect. For this reason, when manufacturers submit data in support of a new drug product, the FDA requires proof that the drug's activity is not caused by the placebo effect. It should also be noted that the effect of suggestibility does not always work in a positive fashion. A mere discussion of side effects with some patients is enough to initiate their occurrence.

Besides pharmacological and placebo uses of drugs, physicians may use drug therapy for other reasons. These may be patient centered or physician centered. Some examples of patient-centered uses include stimulating patient expectations for improvement or recovery, meeting patient expectations for action from the physicians, and boosting patient morale in intractable cases. Thus drugs may be used for psychological reasons as part of a more comprehensive therapeutic plan.

Physician-centered uses include gaining time to diagnose more precisely the condition while maintaining control of or contact with the patient. Such action also helps to legitimize the doctor-patient relationship. For example, the physician may prescribe an innocuous compound in order to satisfy the patient that something is being done while the physician proceeds to process lab tests. By manipulating the quantity of the prescription, the prescriber can to some extent control the return of the patient for a renewal prescription. Sometimes drugs may serve as a substitute for other forms of treatment perceived by the prescriber as being unavailable. For example, a physician may prescribe psychotropic drugs for a patient for whom psychiatric care may be out of the question for economic reasons. Finally, reaching for the prescription pad is a convenient and efficient method of ending a patient visit.

Some of these "latent" functions of the prescription are summarized in Table 3.8. Latent functions are consequences which are neither intended nor always recognized (11). This is in contrast to the "manifest" (intended and recognized) functions of prescriptions which are:

1. Method of therapy
2. Legal document
3. Record source
4. Means of communication

Further discussion is beyond the scope of this text but is available in the reference cited.

It must be stressed that nonpharmacological uses of drugs are not necessarily bad. Prescribing is linked to the condition of the patient in one way or another, and if placebo uses are being exploited deliberately, subtherapeutic doses usually are prescribed. A very important

Table 3.8.
Latent Functions of the Prescription[a]

Visible sign of the physician's power to heal (drug)
Symbol of the power of modern technology (drug)
Sign that the patient is "really" ill (drug)
Legitimizes the long-term illness without cure
Concrete expression that physician has fulfilled his contract
Reasonable excuse for human contact with physician
Satisfactorily terminates the visit
Fits the concept of modern man that he can control his own destiny
Expression of physician's control
Indication of physician's concern
Medium of communication between physician and patient
Source of satisfaction to the physician
Identifies the clinical situation as legitimately medical
Legitimizes sick role status (see Chapter 2)
Symbol of patient stability
Symbol of patient control
Excuse for failure
Means of patient goal attainment
Evidence of physician as an activist
Evidence of pharmacist activity
Research source on utilization and treatment
Political tool
Medium of exchange
Sampling medium
Method of clinical trial
Method of differentiating legal drug status

---

[a]From: Smith MC: The prescription: Everything you wanted to know but didn't think to ask. *Am Pharm* NS18(6):31–33, 1978.

aspect of therapy seems to be the skillful use of nonpharmacological applications of drugs. On the other hand, the decision between patient satisfaction and rational drug therapy sometimes constitutes a serious ethical dilemma for the physician, as does the possibility of using refill restrictions and "secret" formulae to ensure repeat patient visits. It has also been argued that the use of placebos is dishonest (or at least paternalistic) and tends to undermine patient trust in the physician.

Selection of a Specific Drug Product

Once a decision has been made to use a drug of some kind, a specific drug product must be selected from among the many hundreds available. This process involves decisions concerning the appropriate therapeutic category, active ingredients, and manufacturer. In the case of prescription drugs, about 85% of all new drug orders specify a brand name and thus a manufacturer. Considerable attention has been paid to the selection of drug products by physicians. Studies of prescribing patterns focus initially on the drug products selected. A number of studies using criteria specifying the pharmacological appropriateness of the prescribed drug for the diagnosed condition have detected an uncomfortably high frequency of what has been termed "irrational prescribing."

Irrational prescribing by physicians is linked to a variety of causes, including inadequate physician training in pharmacology, difficulty in obtaining necessary drug information, over-reliance on drug advertising, and the large number and variety of marketed drugs.

One of the possible reasons for overprescribing is the physician's bias toward illness. Scheff (12), in fact, refers to a "medical decision rule" in which it is better to find (diagnose) a disease that does not, in fact, exist (a type I error) than not to find a disease that is present (a type II error). There is considerable evidence to support such a bias which, if it does exist, would lead logically toward increased prescribing.

This is only one of the many factors involved in the complex process through which a physician proceeds in choice of drug therapy. The "simplified" model shown in Figure 3.3 is representative of a number of efforts to portray the process graphically.

A major culprit in charges that physicians prescribe imperfectly has frequently been prescription drug advertising. Real evidence of the influence of such advertising is sparse (13), but advertisements such as that shown in Figure 3.4 add to the image of the prescriber as a sort of thoughtless decision maker.

In recent years the pharmacist had begun to play an increasingly important role in "drug product selection." That phrase is a second-generation term, following the term "substitution" for the practice in which a pharmacist selects the source of a drug product for which a physician has written a prescription—either by the generic name of the drug itself or by a brand name. (Only in the latter case, and only if the pharmacist selects a product *different* from that which was prescribed, does *substitution* occur.)

Drug product selection has been and continues to be, although to a decreasing extent, a thorny intraprofessional economic, legal, ethical, and interprofessional issue. In regard to the last of these it is notable that the two major professional organizations reached an important agreement on definition of terms in 1983, which, it was hoped, would lead to further understanding. These helpful definitions are reproduced as Table 3.9.

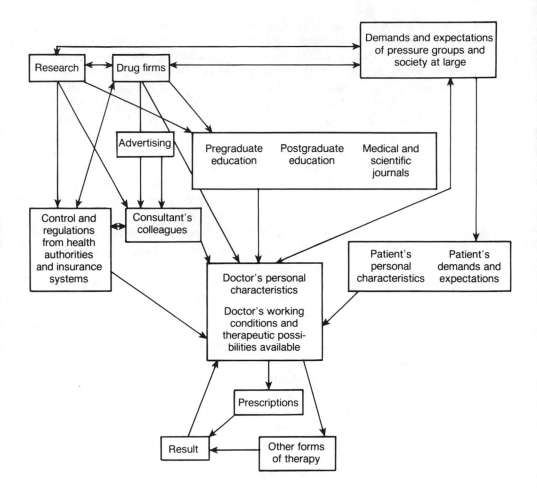

Figure 3.3. A simplified model of the factors that affect drug prescription. Note: Diagnosis considered constant. From: Hemminki C: The role of prescriptions in therapy. *Med Care* XIII(2):151, 1979.

From the pharmacist's point of view, the authority for drug product selection brought with it increased responsibility. The kinds of decisions necessary are shown in Figure 3.5. Since nearly two-thirds of all prescriptions are written for drugs available from at least two sources, the decision-making scope for the pharmacist is tremendous.

Consumers selecting self-medication drugs for symptomatic relief are hampered by a lack of technical knowledge. Therefore, advertisements, the lay referral network, and past personal experience must be relied

For a solid year we've been guaranteeing success with Macrodantin in acute U.T.I....

*Symptom-free, or we pay for your next choice...
because there's still nothing more effective.*

This year we're renewing that guarantee.
That should tell you something.

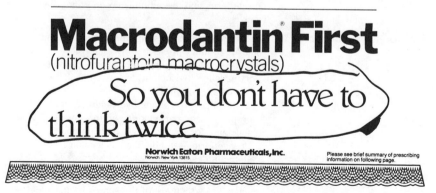

Macrodantin® First
(nitrofurantoin macrocrystals)

So you don't have to think twice.

Norwich Eaton Pharmaceuticals, Inc.
Norwich, New York 13815

Please see brief summary of prescribing information on following page.

Figure 3.4. Prescription drug advertisement.

Table 3.9.
Terms Defined by American Pharmaceutical Association
and American Medical Association[a]

Term	Definition
Drug product selection	The act of selecting the source of supply of a drug product in a specified dosage form.
Chemical equivalents	Those multiple-source drug products which contain essentially identical amounts of the identical active ingredients in identical dosage forms, and which meet existing physical–chemical standards in the official compendium, the USP–NF.
Biological equivalents	Those chemical equivalents which, when administered in the same amounts, will provide the same biologic or physiological availability, as measured by blood levels, urine levels, etc.
Therapeutic equivalent	Those chemical equivalents which, when administered in the same amounts, will provide the same therapeutic effect as measured by the control of a symptom or disease.
Generic substitution	The act of dispensing a different brand or an unbranded drug product for the drug product prescribed (i.e. chemically, the exact same drug entity in the same dosage form, but distributed by different companies). Examples: 1. Rufen brand of ibuprofen for Motrin brand of ibuprofen. 2. Unbranded generic ampicillin for Polycillin.
Pharmaceutical alternates	Drug products that contain the same therapeutic moiety and strength but differ in the salt, ester, or dosage form, and are administered by the same route.
Pharmaceutical substitution	The act of dispensing a pharmaceutical alternate for the drug product prescribed. Examples: 1. Salt — codeine sulfate for codeine phosphate or tetracycline hydrochloride for tetracycline phosphate complex. 2. Ester — propoxyphene hydrochloride for propoxyphene napsylate or erythromycin ethyl succinate for erythromycin estolate. 3. Dosage form — ampicillin suspension for ampicillin capsules.
Therapeutic alternates	Drug products containing different therapeutic moieties but which are of the same pharmacological and/or therapeutic class that can be expected to have

Table 3.9.—*continued*
Terms Defined by American Pharmaceutical Association
and American Medical Association[a]

Term	Definition
	similar therapeutic effects when administered to patients in therapeutically equivalent doses.
Therapeutic substitution	The act of dispensing a therapeutic alternate for the drug product prescribed. Examples: 1. Chlorothiazide (Diuril) for hydrochlorothiazide (HydroDiuril). 2. Chlorpheniramine maleate (Chlor-Trimeton) for brompheniramine maleate (Dimetane). 3. Prednisone for prednisolone.

[a]From: *Am Pharm*, NS24, (2):64, February 1984.

upon. Much decision making is made by trial and error; if a remedy fails to treat symptoms rapidly, the layman usually seeks medical advice.

The pharmacist is an important factor in the OTC product decision. As Table 3.10 shows, pharmacists frequently are asked to recommend brands of OTC products.

Pharmacists are in a strategic position to influence drug selection decisions of both prescribers and patients, and generally are taking a more active role in this step of the drug use process.

Selection of Regimen

This is an important and sometimes overlooked aspect of the drug use process. The effect of a drug product can be influenced significantly by varying the route of administration, dosage form, dosage regimen, and length of therapy. Obviously, the dosage must be varied to meet the individual needs of patients. A 100-pound woman requires a different regimen than does a 270-pound man. Unfortunately, evidence of under-dosing and overdosing has been reported, and it seems that little effort is made to adapt dosage regimens to patient differences such as weight, age, and sex.

There are some psychological overtones to the selection of regimen as well, particularly in the area of route of administration. For example, some patients strongly believe that a drug will not work well unless it is injected, whereas others associate a bitter-tasting liquid with effectiveness.

DRUG PRODUCT SELECTION FLOW CHART

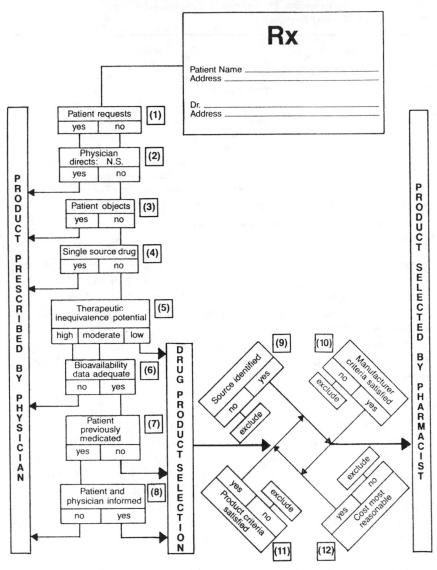

Figure 3.5. Drug product selection flow chart. From: Wanke LA: Lesson # 679–401–82–15. *Drug Store News*, November 1, 1982.

Table 3.10.
**Percentages of Nonprescription Drug Sales in Which the Pharmacist Was
Requested to Recommend a Product[a]**

Product class	Percentage			
	1981	1982	1983	1984
Acne preparations	34.6	34.5	37.5	37.8
Added-strength analgesic	N/A	33.5	39.0	37.5
Arthritis pain product	N/A	32.1	39.8	37.4
Antacid	32.0	33.2	37.7	35.4
Cough remedy	54.1	49.0	53.3	53.9
Diarrhea preparation	49.3	46.5	50.8	52.7
Diet aid	N/A	35.4	38.9	37.4
Hemorrhoid preparation	37.0	34.1	34.8	36.7
Laxative	38.1	34.8	43.5	37.8
Pregnancy testing kit	44.2	38.8	44.3	38.9
Sleeping aid	38.3	32.5	42.1	39.7

[a]From: *American Druggist,* 190 (3):24, 1984.

Obtaining the Drug Product

As obvious as it may seem, it must be noted that a drug must be
physically obtained before it may be consumed by the patient. In most
ambulatory care settings, this requires that the patient leave the physician's office and go elsewhere to obtain the drug. This presents serious
problems in maintaining continuity of care because the prescriber often
has no way of determining how accurately or even whether the prescription is dispensed and consumed. Very limited information exists
about whether or not patients actually obtain prescribed medication. In
the outpatient setting, apparently a very high percentage—in excess of
90%—have their prescriptions dispensed (14). Improved methods of
pharmacist-physician communication are necessary to provide continuous care and monitoring for patients.

We are continuing to learn about the factors involved in the acquisition of a prescription drug. An example of the complexity of this
process is shown in Figure 3.6. The diagram indicates, in simplified
form, the results of statistical analysis of data obtained from 300
persons aged 65 and over. It shows that certain predisposing variables,
largely demographic, combined with certain enabling factors and
coupled with the patient's perceived morbidity, are likely to lead to use
of a prescription drug.

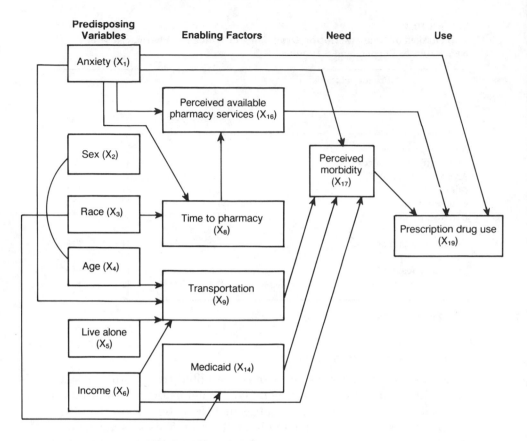

Figure 3.6. Path diagram relating predisposing, enabling, and need for care factors to prescribed medicine use. From: Smith MC, Sharpe TR: *Barriers to and Determinants of Drug Use Among the Elderly.* Final Report to the Andrus Foundation. University, University of Mississippi, 1983.

Self-medication products may be obtained from a wide variety of outlets, most of which feature the products on self-service shelves. This wide and easy availability leads to stockpiling in home medicine cabinets. Households inventoried in the 1968 study mentioned earlier (8) averaged over 17 nonprescription drug products on hand. Such stockpiling may lead to drug-related problems such as accidental poisoning.

Administration/Consumption of Drugs

Patients may either consume drug products themselves or have the medication administered to them. Hospital inpatients typically rely on nurses to administer medication. The technical functions of supplying and administering the drugs must be carried out accurately or else the effectiveness of the drug therapy may be compromised, no matter how appropriate it may have been in all respects up to this stage. Devising and implementing an error-free drug administration system is not easy. In large hospitals hundreds of drug orders and thousands of doses must be processed and dispatched to the correct location within the institution in time for the scheduled administration. Similar logistic problems are faced by thousands of nursing homes and extended care facilities.

Much attention is paid to the problem of patient compliance with medication on an ambulatory basis. Because in this situation it is extremely difficult to monitor patient behavior, it is hard to obtain a clear picture of the effect of the pattern of consumption of the drug. Assuming that the choice of drug and regimen is appropriate, obviously the degree of patient compliance is an important factor in the outcome of therapy. Many compliance studies agree that patients often vary the dosage, frequency, and duration of medication, sometimes interfering significantly with the intended therapeutic response. An example is the frequent discontinuance of antibiotic therapy within 2 or 3 days because the symptoms disappear. This permits the regrowth of the offending organism and a recurrence of the infection. The role of the pharmacist in improving patient compliance is discussed in Chapter 2.

We add at this point that compliance can be understood quite well in the context of the Health Belief Model (see Fig. 2.2). Indeed, Becker and Maiman have adopted it to this purpose. Their version is shown in Fig. 3.7.

Recognition of the importance of compliance in drug development is shown in Fig. 3.8. (It is interesting to note the advertising style. Apparently neither the doctor [see Fig. 3.4] *nor* the patient has to "think twice.")

Effects of Drug Therapy

Feedback serves as a powerful reinforcer of behavior in all areas, and drug use is no exception. Prior personal experience with a particular drug, either by a prescriber or a patient, is often a major determinant in future use. Unfortunately, the effects of drug therapy are extremely difficult to measure and interpret correctly. Thus, feedback often may be judged incorrectly, leading to improper drug use decisions. Laymen are not trained drug evaluators and, with the exception of those physicians who are also clinical pharmacologists, neither are most prescribers.

Some of the factors that can confound the evaluation of a drug's true effects include the following:

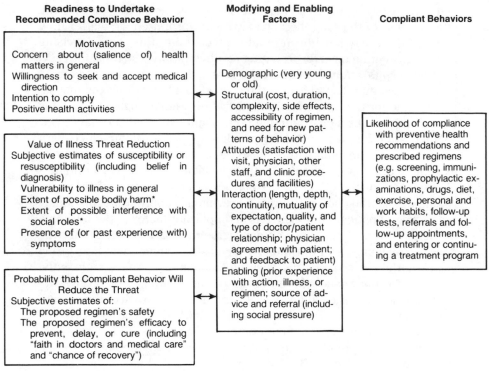

Readiness to Undertake
Recommended Compliance Behavior

Modifying and Enabling
Factors

Compliant Behaviors

Motivations
Concern about (salience of) health matters in general
Willingness to seek and accept medical direction
Intention to comply
Positive health activities

Value of Illness Threat Reduction
Subjective estimates of susceptibility or resusceptibility (including belief in diagnosis)
Vulnerability to illness in general
Extent of possible bodily harm*
Extent of possible interference with social roles*
Presence of (or past experience with) symptoms

Probability that Compliant Behavior Will Reduce the Threat
Subjective estimates of:
The proposed regimen's safety
The proposed regimen's efficacy to prevent, delay, or cure (including "faith in doctors and medical care" and "chance of recovery")

Demographic (very young or old)
Structural (cost, duration, complexity, side effects, accessibility of regimen, and need for new patterns of behavior)
Attitudes (satisfaction with visit, physician, other staff, and clinic procedures and facilities)
Interaction (length, depth, continuity, mutuality of expectation, quality, and type of doctor/patient relationship; physician agreement with patient; and feedback to patient)
Enabling (prior experience with action, illness, or regimen; source of advice and referral (including social pressure)

Likelihood of compliance with preventive health recommendations and prescribed regimens (e.g. screening, immunizations, prophylactic examinations, drugs, diet, exercise, personal and work habits, follow-up tests, referrals and follow-up appointments, and entering or continuing a treatment program

* At motivating, but not inhibiting, levels.

Figure 3.7. Hypothesized model for predicting and explaining compliance behavior. From: Becker MH, Maiman L: Strategies for enhancing patient compliance. *J Community Health* 6:113–135, 1980.

1. **The difficulty of separating coincidental effects from cause-effect relationships**. Many illnesses are self-limiting, but drugs used coincidentally for treatment may be believed to provide a cure even if they are ineffective pharmacologically. Perhaps this is a factor in the frequent prescribing of antibiotics for the common cold; usually the cold goes away in a week and, if a prescriber gets into the habit of using antibiotics, he eventually may convince himself that the reason the cold goes away is because an antibiotic was used.

2. **The failure to separate pharmacological effects from placebo effects**. Both are important components of drug therapy, and certainly placebo uses are appropriate and effective in many cases. It is important, however, that the physician and the pharmacist clearly understand the distinction between pharma-

Patients on Surmontil don't have to think twice.

All most of them need is one 100 mg capsule two hours before bedtime after initial dose titration.

No forgotten doses.

No escalation of side effects.

In fact, specifying Surmontil 100 mg, h.s., is a positive therapeutic step that may further reduce an already low incidence of side effects.

And help assure compliance.

SURMONTIL® 100 mg*
(trimipramine maleate)
JUST ONE CAPSULE h.s.

Because depressed patients don't need any more trouble.

*Also available in 25 mg & 50 mg capsules

© IVES LABORATORIES 1983

Figure 3.8. Surmontil advertisement.

cological and placebo effects so that proper drug use decisions may be made.

3. **The lack of patient feedback**. A lack of patient contact after treatment may be interpreted by the prescriber as being a result of the success of the drug therapy used. Obviously, this might not be the case. The patient might have gone to see another physician, decided to bear up under the problem until it went away by itself, or even have died. Unfortunately, such reasoning is itself reinforced by advertising such as that for a prescription sedative which states, "when your patient doesn't call the next day, you'll know she slept."

4. **The failure to recognize side effects or relate them to the use of a particular drug product**. This sometimes occurs because it is difficult to monitor patients, especially in an ambulatory situation. Thus, feedback which might have modified a prescriber's future use of drugs is not easily obtained.

In summary, the drug use process is complex and involves many stages and many separate decisions. In order to ensure optimal drug use, attention must be paid to making the proper decisions at each stage. We will now discuss some of the major problems associated with drug use and the efforts made to control them.

Problems Associated with Drug Use

Louis Lasagna, a physician who frequently comments on the way drugs are developed, manufactured, and used, has described the impact of modern drugs on medical practice:

> The pharmaceutical revolution, while yielding significant benefits, has also generated its share of problems. The production of potent new drugs has given the physician the power not only to modify disease processes for the benefit of his patients but also to produce new and serious side effects, as individual drugs cause unwanted toxicity or interact with other drugs or with foods to do pharmacologic mischief (15).

Drugs have been described as a two-edged sword combining the potential benefit of therapy with the risk of therapeutic misadventure. A figure of 10% frequently is cited as the incidence in which an unwanted reaction to a drug may occur. In a study of adverse drug reactions in the hospital setting, Visconti described an adverse reaction as:

> ... any response in a patient to a drug properly administered in the accepted dose range, that was unintended and undesired by the prescribing physician, necessitating a reduction in drug dosage, discontinuation of the drug, administration of an antidotal drug, hospitalization or prolonged hospital stay (16).

Although medicinal chemists invest considerable effort in modifying the structure of drugs to maximize benefits and minimize risk, they will likely never succeed in developing products that are completely risk free. The ultimate responsibility for determining and evaluating the benefit-to-risk ratio for a particular patient is the prescribing physician. Society accorded this responsibility to physicians with the establishment of the legal category of prescription drugs in the early 1950s. In order for society to receive the largest net benefit from prescription drugs, physicians must take care to use them appropriately.

Drug products themselves are inanimate objects—powerful tools with great potential to do good or to cause harm. How they are used is of ultimate importance. Harmful adverse results cannot legitimately be blamed on drugs if they are prescribed inappropriately, anymore than computers can legitimately be blamed for errors caused by inappropriate programming.

And yet drugs are blamed for much in our society. We are accused of being a "drug-taking society," one in which there is a "pill for every ill." If a drug is implicated as the cause of a serious side effect or is not effective for every advertised indication, a typical solution is to take it off the market, when in fact it might be an essential drug when used appropriately in certain patients. Attempts to control adverse drug effects are likely to be less successful overall when aimed at the drug than when aimed at the conditions under which the drug is used.

On his first day at the FDA in 1979, Commissioner Jere Goyan told a national television audience that the number of prescriptions for ambulatory patients could be cut in half " . . . and still meet the real needs of people for medications, and make the American people overall healthier" (17). This statement reflects the widely held belief that physicians, for whatever reason, are placing too much reliance on drugs and are prescribing excessively. Certain therapeutic classifications frequently are cited in this regard, including antibiotics, sedative/hypnotics, and tranquilizers.

Overprescribing may have numerous negative effects. The most obvious is the unnecessary exposure of the patient to the risk of adverse effects without the change of benefits. Overprescribing can add substantially to the cost of medical care. In addition, in some cases, although the risk to an individual patient may be small, the danger to society in general may be high. For example:

> Antibiotics differ from other drugs in that they are not only exert a therapeutic effect but also alter the ecology of the microflora of the body and the environment. Thus, antibiotic usage conjures up an image of fallout akin to that from a leaking nuclear reactor. There is legitimate concern about the development of antibiotic resistance

and its transmission by plasmids as a result of excessive use of antibiotics by physicians, veterinarians and manufacturers of animal feed (18).

On the other hand, there are some areas in which *underprescribing* is a significant concern. For example, most authorities believe that the prevalence of high blood pressure in this country should warrant the use of more antihypertensive medication. And even antibiotics, thought to be overprescribed as a category, may be prescribed for too short a period of time in the treatment of certain infections.

In summary, because drugs are so diverse and medical needs so varied, attempts to categorize prescribing problems as overprescribing or underprescribing are not very helpful. It is more helpful to recognize that *inappropriate* prescribing of one sort or another frequently occurs and that serious attention needs to be given to methods which lead to a more appropriate prescribing.

Inappropriate Prescribing

In 1969 President Johnson's Task Force on Prescription Drugs reported on a systematic review of several general types of inappropriate prescribing:

> The use of drugs with demonstrated efficacy.
> The use of drugs with an inherent hazard not justified by the seriousness of the illness.
> The use of drugs in excessive amounts, or for excessive periods of time, or inadequate amounts for inadequate periods.
> The use of a costly duplicative or "me-too" product when an equally effective but less expensive drug is available.
> The use of a costly combination product when equally effective but less expensive drugs are available individually.
> The simultaneous use of two or more drugs without appropriate consideration of their possible interaction.
> Multiple prescribing, by one or several physicians for the same patient, of drugs which may be unnecessary, cumulative, interacting, or needlessly expensive (19).

There have been many studies which have concluded that prescribing practices are less than ideal. One of the most convincing was that conducted by Rucker (20). He tested the hypothesis that the most frequently prescribed drugs are clinically superior to competitive products. Using ten independent measures of therapeutic acceptability, Rucker found that less than half of the drug entities satisfied the criterion of clinical superiority. Indeed, he concluded that at least 25% probably should be excluded altogether as drugs of choice.

Improving Drug Use

This discussion of the problems related to drugs and their use illustrates the importance of and need for attention to the improvement of drug use. Certainly no one is in favor of or intends inappropriate prescribing, and health professionals, drug manufacturers, and consumers share the common goal of seeking maximum benefit from therapeutic agents. This section discusses approaches taken to improve drug use by regulatory agencies, third-party programs, health professionals, and consumers.

Regulation: The Food and Drug Administration

Although the regulation of medical practice is in the hands of the states, federal regulation related to drugs has a great effect on prescribing. Specifically, actions of the FDA involving the labeling and advertising of drugs have a major influence on prescribing, although the technical mandate of the agency is limited to the regulation of the drug product.

Because of the importance of the FDA and its responsibilities as outlined in the Food, Drug and Cosmetic (FDC) Act, it is useful to trace its legislative history. The precursor to today's FDC Act was passed in the early 1900s. It was the era of the muckrakers, and one of them, a socialist writer named Upton Sinclair, was appalled by the degrading working conditions of laborers in the Chicago meat-packing industry. He wrote a novel entitled *The Jungle*, which vividly described the situation. The public indeed was aroused but, contrary to Sinclair's intent, they were much more concerned over the filthy and unsanitary conditions under which their meat was being packed than they were with employment conditions. Their arousal proved a major stimulus to the passage of the Pure Food and Drug Act in 1906. This legislation required that drug products (as well as food) be *pure*, and it prohibited adulteration and misbranding.

By the early 1930s deficiencies in the legislation were becoming apparent, and a 5-year battle to strengthen drug legislation was begun in Congress. It took a tragedy, however, to precipitate action on a stronger law. A drug manufacturer looking for a suitable vehicle for the new wonder drug, sulfanilamide, dissolved the active ingredient in diethylene glycol, which was a good solvent and produced a pleasant tasting and elegant elixir. Unfortunately, the solvent was not tested for safety, and turned out to be a deadly poison. One hundred and seven deaths resulted, including those of many children. An additional death was added later when the chemist who formulated the elixir committed suicide. Soon thereafter, the FDC Act of 1938 was passed. This law established the FDA and required premarketing clearance of drug products, with the requirement that they be proved not only pure but *safe* for use as labeled.

In 1951, the Durham-Humphrey Amendment was passed. This amendment established two classes of drugs, prescription and nonprescription.

Later in the 1950s, attention was again focused on the drug industry by the Senate hearings of Estes Kefauver. Although the hearings went on for a number of years and considered a wide range of drug-related topics, the major emphasis was on the economics of the industry and the cost of drugs. Then, in the early 1960s the thalidomide tragedy occurred. Its effects were felt mainly in Europe, but some United States citizens were involved even though the drug was kept from the United States market by the FDA. The publicity accompanying the birth of hundreds of malformed infants was enough to stimulate Congress to act again. In 1962 the Kefauver-Harris Amendments to the FDC Act were passed. These amendments require manufacturers to prove that their drugs are not only pure and safe but also *effective* for use as indicated on the label. The amendments also gave the FDA authority to regulate prescription drug promotion and strengthened in other ways the control of the agency over drug manufacturing and marketing.

To summarize, the functions of the FDA today fall into several major categories:

1. Premarketing clearance of all new drugs for purity, safety, and effectiveness
2. Regulation of all labeling and advertising of prescription drugs; the agency cooperates with the Federal Trade Commission on regulation of nonprescription drugs
3. Regulation of drug manufacturing practices, including establishing good manufacturing practices, monitoring their application, and initiating recalls if necessary
4. Establishing and implementing bioequivalence regulations
5. Engaging in postmarketing surveillance to detect unanticipated adverse and therapeutic effects of drugs

After the passage of the 1962 amendments there remained the problem of what to do about the 3000 already approved prescription drugs being marketed for about 16,000 claimed indications which had never been reviewed for effectiveness. Because of limited resources, the FDA could not handle the massive review required to bring these drugs into compliance with the law. Therefore, they contracted with the National Academy of Sciences/National Research Council (NAS/NRC) to conduct the Drug Efficacy Studies (DES). Some 30 expert panels composed of emminent scientists and physicians in appropriate fields were established to review the evidence for each claim being made for the 3000 marketed drugs. Each claim for each drug was placed into one of six categories: effective, effective with reservations, probably effective, possibly effective, lacking substantial evidence of effectiveness, or ineffective as a fixed combination. The reviews were essentially completed by 1969.

> Of the 16,573 drug claims evaluated by the NAS/NRC, 3,493 or 21.1% were found to be lacking in substantial evidence of effectiveness, or were found ineffective as a fixed combination. Another 7,145 or 43.2% were found 'possibly effective' and 2,112 or 12.7% 'probably effective.' Only 3,823 claims—23% of the total—were found flatly 'effective' (21).

During the implementation phase of the review, manufacturers were given the opportunity to substantiate claims which were found wanting, or else they were required to change label indications or in some cases to completely withdraw products from the market.

By 1970, although the FDA had acted upon thousands of drugs, several hundred with one or more less-than-effective indications remained on the market. Many of these were fixed-ratio combination products of an effective ingredient with one or more less-than-effective ingredients. In most cases no safety issue was involved, the products were large money makers for the manufacturers, and the FDA chose not to devote the resources necessary to force the products off the market. In 1970 the American Public Health Association and the National Council of Senior Citizens sued the FDA to force compliance. The judge set a timetable for the FDA to complete action on the products; this timetable expired in 1976. After renewed litigation, the FDA agreed in September 1980 to:

1. Add more staff to expedite the project
2. Give priority to the biggest selling drugs
3. Notify all doctors of the names of all drugs which lack evidence of effectiveness . . . (22)

In late 1984 the American Public Health Association reported that the "effectiveness of drugs on the market [would be] assured at long last"(23). The association reported that of the drugs reviewed by the FDA, 1092 had been found to be not effective for any indication and the remaining 2259 were found to be effective for some indication. The majority of *these*, however, were found to be ineffective for some indication and required labeling changes.

Despite its central role in drug regulation, the FDA is significantly limited in what it can do to directly affect prescribing. Once a drug has been marketed, the agency has little control over how it is used by physicians. Usually, complete information about drug effects is simply not available at the time of marketing, and the FDA could not formulate strict usage guidelines if it wanted to. As a result, FDA action after a drug has been marketed is limited to issuing information bulletins or to withdrawing the drug from the market entirely. Often the publicity accorded to questions about a drug in the news media is the most effective way of influencing prescribing.

The OTC Review

In February 1972 the FDA launched the most massive effort ever undertaken to evaluate all nonprescription medicines sold in the United States. The purpose of this study, called the Over-The-Counter (OTC) Drug Review, was to apply modern standards of science to these medicines and to ensure that they were safe, effective, and properly labeled for consumer use without professional supervision. The FDA began the review with 17 panels of outside scientific and medical advisors.

When the FDA convened its first OTC advisory panel to study antacid and antiflatulent (anti-gas) ingredients, the agency thought all results would be in and published within 5 years. The antacid/antiflatulent panel results encouraged that optimism. The panel met seven times, and the final agency rules (monographs) for antacids and antiflatulents were published in the Federal Register on June 4, 1974—a little over 2 years after the panel's first meeting.

But subsequent panels found many more ingredients, in more categories, than they expected. In addition, many combinations of ingredients as well as single entities had to be studied, and panel reports had to be harmonized with previous review publications. While growth of the Review represented a big jump in the reviewers' workload, it justified the review's focus on ingredients rather than on products. The FDA estimated that there were some 300,000 OTC medicine products sold in the United States as the Review began, making a product-by-product review impossible.

During 500 meetings over 9.5 years, the panels examined 722 ingredients, submitted their recommendations, and disbanded.

After October 17, 1981, the Review became entirely an internal staff process at the FDA, with certain mandated periods for public comment. The Department of Health and Human Services (FDA's parent department) will publish final orders for all 72 product categories, thus completing the Review.

One surprising consequence of FDA scrutiny of OTC and prescription drugs has been a series of decisions to change the status of dozens of them from legend to OTC. This shift has had some economic consequences which are yet to be fully evaluated. Only half of the practicing pharmacists surveyed in 1984 indicated that they felt such shifts were good for pharmacy, although the President of the American Pharmaceutical Association (APhA), Maurice Bectel, spoke in favor of the idea (24).

What *did* occur as a result of this activiy was a revival of APhA interest in the concept of a class of drugs not requiring a prescription available only in pharmacies. In this instance APhA proposed a transitional period of pharmacist-only distribution between prescription and nonprescription states.

Organizational Influences: Third-Party Payment Programs

Third-party programs, such as private health insurers, Medicaid programs, and health maintenance organizations, have a financial interest in the quality and cost of the drugs provided for their beneficiaries. They also have the size and the organizational ability to affect drug use significantly. As drug costs grow, so does the interest in establishing organizational controls over drug use. Examples of approaches being used include establishing formularies, setting drug cost limits, and developing auditing or drug utilization review procedures.

Formularies. A formulary is simply a list of drug products to be paid for by a program. If functioning properly, the choice of drugs included will be based first upon therapeutic considerations and second upon economic ones. The establishment of the content of the formulary should be firmly in the control of health professionals, including ample representation by pharmacists.

Cost Limitations. Programs such as the Maximum Allowable Cost (MAC) program of Medicaid have been established to limit drug product reimbursement to a predetermined level. As applied to multiple-source drugs, it encourages the dispensing of more economical products. Because MAC deals only with multiple-source drugs and not with drug selection otherwise, it has little influence on the appropriateness of prescribing.

Audit and Utilization Review Procedures. These procedures seek to develop profiles of prescribing for individual physicians in an attempt to detect patterns which are either outside normal ranges or of predetermined screening criteria for appropriate drug use. Because it is well established that much prescribing is now inappropriate, comparing individual prescribing patterns to average prescribing is not likely to be fruitful. On the other hand, use of predetermined screening criteria can be successful if the criteria are conscientiously constructed by well-qualified pharmacists and physicians. The process must include the necessary follow through to correct problems detected from the review.

Through the use of these and other approaches, third-party programs are in an excellent position to improve drug use. Unfortunately, implementation of these procedures has often been sloppy and inadequate, and ineffective implementation means not only that the procedure will fail in the specific program, but also that unwarranted doubt will be cast on the efficacy of the approach itself.

The Role of Health Professionals

It would be expected that the health professionals who deal with drugs would exert a certain amount of control of their own. This is indeed the case. Two major methods of professional drug control are used with a good deal of success. The first is the pharmacy and therapeutics committee, which is now an effective means toward rational drug therapy in a substantial proportion of the hospitals of this country. The pharmacy and therapeutics committee usually is composed of physicians, nurses, and one or more pharmacists (usually serving as secretary) whose tasks include the establishment of drug use policy for the entire hospital. This includes in most cases maintaining a formulary of drugs from which physicians practicing in that hospital must select for their patients. The pharmacy and therapeutics committee concept has been tried outside the institutional setting in a few communities with success, and there is every indication that the expansion of this application will continue.

The second method increasingly used by health professionals in all settings is drug prescribing review. Discussed previously in the context of third-party programs, drug prescribing review is also applicable in hospitals, health maintenance organizations, nursing homes, and even community pharmacies, regardless of the source of payment. The procedure is conceptually very simple: determine criteria for appropriate prescribing and compare incoming prescriptions to the criteria. Because of the complexity of individual cases, criteria cannot possibly cover all possibilities, but they do not have to in order to be useful. Even relatively simple screening criteria based only upon the information on a prescription can detect large numbers of apparently faulty prescriptions (25). Failing the simple screening criteria does not prove the prescription is wrong, of course, but should be sufficient to prompt a call to the prescriber.

The practicing pharmacist is in an ideal position to conduct an implicit form of drug prescribing review every time a prescription is dispensed. Pharmacists are becoming ever more aware of their important role in ensuring appropriate prescribing and are increasingly using their superior drug knowledge to complement the physician's expertise in diagnosis.

Consumer Influences

There is a variety of ways by which the individual and collective consumer may control drug use and distribution. Organizations such as Consumers' Union have devoted considerable effort to identifying for their members methods of reducing drug costs. Consumer involvement has been encouraged by the publication of a variety of consumer-oriented books and articles aimed at increasing the consumer's awareness of the pharmacy system.

Organizations representing the interests of the elderly such as the National Retired Teachers Association and the Gray Panthers have become increasingly active in the drug area, stimulated by the fact that persons over 65 use four times the amount of drugs than do younger persons. With the impetus created by planning for the 1980 decennial White House Conference on Aging, many pharmacy associations and schools of pharmacy are developing special educational programs for the elderly on the use of drugs.

In recent years the Health Research Group, an arm of Public Citizen (the Ralph Nader organization), has become increasingly active in the drug field. The group pays special attention to the activities of the FDA and has been vigorous in its attempts to ensure that the agency carries out its mandate in the best interest of the consumer. Despite the organization's small size and voluntary nature, it has been extremely successful in its efforts to prod the FDA into action. In addition, it has published a number of pamphlets and books related to drugs and drug use.

A major thrust of many consumer organizations is to "activate" patients and make them feel more responsible for understanding all aspects of their prescribed therapy. This was also one of the stated purposes of the FDA program of patients package inserts (PPIs). As proposed, PPIs would be distributed to the consumer with the purchase of certain prescription drugs. The PPI would be a simplified version of the physician package insert, and would explain the benefits and risks of the medication, provide necessary warnings, and advise how to take the drug. Although a step in the right direction toward the goal of better informed consumers of medication, the PPI program was logistically and politically difficult to implement.

It is clear that patient information regarding prescription drugs is a continuing and legitimate topic of discussion. In 1984 CBS conducted a major study of consumers' knowledge and awareness of prescription drug topics(26). Apparently aimed at "testing the water" concerning the possibility of prescription drug advertising to consumers (see Chapter 11), the study nevertheless yielded some valuable information. Among the findings were the following:

1. People are informed only marginally about prescription drugs in this country.
2. There are six different types of information or knowledge that people have about prescription drugs:
   - Safety and efficacy
   - Proper home use
   - General health information
   - Misuse and dependency
   - Liability
   - Cost and value
3. Households in the study report the most familiarity with issues relating to proper home use of prescription drugs, and the least familiarity with safety and efficacy of prescription drugs and with the liabilities of manufacturers and advertisers.
4. People report needing more information on all issues related to prescription drugs. In particular, they want more information about safety and efficacy and proper home use of prescription drugs(see Table 3.11).
5. Consumer needs for information about prescription drugs far outstrip current levels of knowledge about prescription drug topics.
6. The widest discrepancy between what is now known and what people would like to know about prescription drugs is found in the areas containing their limitations, content and ingredients, comparisons, liability, and alternatives.
7. There is a high level of concern in this country about prescription drug issues. At least two-thirds of all prescription-using households say that they are highly concerned about prescription drug costs, drug dependency, people taking unneeded drugs, and drugs being prescribed too readily.
8. Traditional sources like the physician and pharmacist are considered the most useful sources of information about prescription drugs. Nontraditional sources like friends, family, and mass media are seen as less useful.

Summary

The most frequently used form of therapy in medical practice is the drug. Data were provided in this chapter on the extent of drug use in the

Table 3.11.
Reported Need for Information About Prescription Drug Issues[a]

		Importance[c]		
	Mean Level[b]	High	Moderate	Low
Safety and Efficacy				
Side effects	4.47	87	8	5
Interaction with food	4.35	85	10	5
Doctors' evaluation of effectiveness	4.35	83	11	5
Safe for treatment	4.28	80	14	5
Safety record	4.26	81	12	6
Effectiveness	4.22	79	14	6
Information on prescription drugs	3.96	67	24	8
Limitations	3.95	68	22	9
Contents and ingredients	3.95	67	21	11
Effectiveness comparisons among drugs	3.92	67	22	10
Proper Home Use				
Dosage	4.44	86	7	6
When to take	4.29	82	10	7
Storage	4.20	79	14	7
Protect children	4.20	76	10	12
General Health Information				
Symptoms	4.17	77	16	7
Specific symptoms	4.09	74	18	8
Alternatives to prescription drugs	3.90	66	21	12
Public health issues	3.83	63	26	10
Alternative methods of taking prescription drugs	3.65	56	24	17
Misuse and Dependency				
Physical and psychological dependence	4.01	70	19	10
Dependence	4.01	70	19	10
Misuse	3.85	65	21	13
Liability				
Manufacturers' liability	3.81	62	22	14
Advertisers' liability	3.65	56	24	18
Cost and Value				
Effectiveness of generic prescription drugs	3.96	70	18	11
Brand vs. generic prescription costs	3.81	63	23	13
Prescription vs. OTC costs	3.65	64	23	13

[a]From: Bectel MJ: The Rx-OTC switch: Good for pharmacy. *Am Pharm* NS21(4):84, 1984.

[b]Very important, 5; quite important, 4; somewhat important, 3; not very important, 2; not at all important, 1.

[c]For convenience, values for very important and quite important, and not at all important, have been combined into high and low importance, respectively.

country, along with some information on the most frequently prescribed therapeutic categories and specific products. Nonprescription
drugs also were discussed. Drug use is more complicated than the mere
prescribing and dispensing of drugs. The drug use process consists of
several identifiable stages, including the perception of a need for drugs,
the selection of a specific drug product, the choice of a regimen,
obtaining the product, administration/consumption of the drug, and
feedback. Understanding the complexities of each stage is very important to the pharmacist. We have seen in this chapter that drugs are
associated with a variety of problems, some medical, some social, and
some economic. Efforts to overcome these problems and to control
drugs and drug use were described. Major attention was paid to legal
controls and the legislative history and development of federal drug law
and the FDA. Other influences on prescribing such as third-party
programs, health professionals (including pharmacists), and consumers
are also important.

REFERENCES

1. *National Ambulatory Medical Care Survey, 1981 Summary*. Washington, D.C., U.S.
   Department of Health and Human Services, 1983.
2. Annual prescription survey. *Drug Topics* 128(6):29, 1984.
3. Annual drugstore sales survey. *Drug Topics* 128(22): 1984.
4. Office of Long Term Care: *Physicians' Drug Prescribing Patterns in Skilled Nursing
   Facilities*. Washington, D.C., U.S. Department of Health, Education, and Welfare, June
   1976, p 13.
5. *Drug Utilization in the U.S.—1982*. Washington, D.C., Food and Drug Administration, 1983, p 11.
6. The top 200 drugs. *Pharm Times* 50(4):28–29, 1984.
7. Svarstad BL: "The sociology of drugs." In Wertheimer AI, Smith MC (eds): *Pharmacy
   Practice*. Baltimore, University Park Press, 1981, p 261.
8. Knapp DA, Knapp DE: Decision making and self-medication: Preliminary findings. *Am
   J Hosp Pharm* 29(12):1004–1012, 1972.
9. Harry Heller Research Corporation: *Health Care Practices and Perceptions*. Washington, D.C., Harry Heller Research Corporation, 1984.
10. Hustad TP, Courtney AE, Heeler RM: An emerging model for purchase and consump-
    tion of non-prescription drugs. *J Consumer Affairs* 13(1):81–85, 1979.
11. Smith MC: The prescription: Everything you wanted to know but didn't think to ask.
    Am Pharm NS18(6):31–33, 1978.
12. Scheff TJ: *Being Mentally Ill*. Chicago, Aldine Publishing, 1966, pp 105–127.
13. Smith MC: An analysis of the impact of print advertising on prescribing. In Morgan J,
    Kagan D (eds): *Society and Medication: Conflicting Signals for Prescribers and
    Patients*. Lexington, MA, Lexington Books, 1983.
14. Hammel RW, Williams PO: Do patients receive prescribed medication? *J Am Pharm
    Assoc* NS4:331–337, 1964.
15. Lasagna L: The pharmaceutical revolution: Its impact on science and society. *Science*
    166:1227, 1969.

16. Visconti JA: An epidemiologic and economic study of adverse drug reactions in patients on the medical service of a university teaching hospital. Unpublished Ph. D. dissertation, University of Mississippi, 1969.
17. *F-D-C Reports.* November 26, 1979, p 7.
18. Kunin CM: Antibiotic accountability. *Engl J Med* 301(7):380, 1979.
19. Task Force on Prescription Drugs: *Final Report.* Washington, D.C., Department of Health, Education, and Welfare, 1969, p 21.
20. Rucker TD: The top-selling drug products: How good are they? *Am J Hosp Pharm* 37:833–839, 1980.
21. Bryan PA: DESI who? *FDA Consumer*, October 1972, p 14.
22. Wolfe SM, Coley CM: *Pills that don't work.* Washington, D.C., Health Research Group, 1980, p 198.
23. Anon.: FDA nears end of 22-year clean-up of ineffective prescription drugs. *Nation's Health.* 14:8, 1984.
24. Bectel MJ: The Rx-OTC switch: Good for pharmacy. *Am Pharm* NS21(4):84, 1984.
25. Knapp DA, Brandon BM, West S Leavitt DE: Drug use review: A manual system. *J Am Pharm Assoc* NS13(8):417–420, 433, 1973.
26. CBS Television Network: *The CBS Consumer Model: A Study of Attitudes, Concerns, and Information Needs for Prescription Drugs and Related Illnesses.* New York, 1984.

CHAPTER 4

Drug Abuse

Anthony C. Tommasello, M.S.

Director, Drug Abuse Information Center, State of Maryland, School of Pharmacy, University of Maryland

The Medicated Society

America is a highly developed technologic society, and it seems as if it will continue to grow, given an adequate fuel supply and a work force of individuals motivated towards the continued technological growth of their country (1). Such an environment exists on the premise that through technological advances the ills of society can be brought under control. This can be carried down to the level of the individual participant in such a system. One need only spend several minutes reading, watching, or listening to any public medium and he will readily begin to appreciate the advantage of the technological society.

America has produced machines that can wash a table full of dishes and dry them in an hour. Americans who emit "offensive body odor" have a host of perfumes, deodorants, and antiperspirants with which to spray themselves. If a person has trouble sleeping at night, an inexpensive OTC medication will "help make you drowsy so you can fall asleep easily." The message essentially is that if a problem or discomfort exists, a solution can be provided.

The American public has been seduced by advertising campaigns into purchasing merchandise, drugs included, which they may not have bought in the absence of these advertising efforts. John Kenneth Galbraith argues that the role of advertising in the past has been to inform the public when products which they have demanded are available; today it seems that the purpose of advertising is to stimulate and create public demands for products which are most profitable for the manufacturer to sell (2) and to promote product loyalty (3). A study of the impact of television beer advertising indicates that product selection is affected rather than total consumption. Even a cursory survey of early afternoon and late evening television advertisements reveals the extent to which drug use is promoted to the public.

"A pill for every ill" is a statement which often sums up the patient's expectations upon entering the health care system, and why not? Television advertisements extol the pharmacological age and, if their products prove unsuccessful, the person has the option of entering the health care system where a physician exists who can surely supply the needed medication. And so through the years Americans have come to realize that indeed even the daily tensions brought about by living in a world with a pace too rapid for many to keep up with can be eliminated through the use of drugs.

If America is a medicated society it is not alone, for in other countries the use of psychoactive drugs is on a par with this country's. Past studies indicate that 15% of all persons in the United States employ the use of minor tranquilizers or sedatives to help them through the day (4). In Belgium and France this figure is 17%, Sweden and Denmark have percentages equal to the United States, West Germany and Great Britain demonstrated a 14% figure, while the Netherlands, Italy, and Spain show the lowest percentage figures of 13, 11, and 10%, respectively.

The question which holds relevance for this chapter is whether or not this level of drug use promotes drug misuse and abuse or indeed whether this level of drug use in and of itself is drug misuse. To answer this question we must first examine some of the factors which contribute to how society defines these terms.

What Is Drug Abuse?

One should realize that drug abuse is a broad term, and it would be well to examine the ambiguity with which it is surrounded. Glasscote et al. (5) state that "drug abuse" is the least specific of the terms used in the field, and, paradoxically, for that reason it may be most useful. Its applicability ranges all the way from a single experimental use of marihuana to "addiction to heroin." R. G. Smart points out that "there are good reasons for the continuing vagueness and confusion." For example, "lack of clarity helps to maintain, among competing parties in a dispute, the idea that one side has won" (6).

In 1972 the President's Advisory Commission on Narcotics and Drug Abuse defined drug abuse as the use of a drug under one of the following circumstances:

1. In amounts sufficient to create a hazard to one's own health or to the safety of the community
2. When one obtains drugs through illicit channels
3. When one takes drugs on one's own initiative rather than on the basis of professional advice (7)

Smart (6) is quick to point out that this definition may be too broad as it would include all use of cigarettes (what physician would advise smoking?), a great deal of the use of alcohol (50% of fatal automobile accidents involve a drunken driver), and all use of OTC medicine unless directed by a physician. Also included in this definition would be all use of marihuana regardless of the amount or frequency of use.

From the confusion surrounding this issue has emerged the idea of arriving at a workable definition which has usefulness for a specific purpose. If a person uses heroin once, is that drug abuse? Could daily use of marihuana be considered drug abuse? How about daily use of cigarettes or alcohol? The reader will decide for himself based upon his values, as well as his knowledge, opinions, and attitudes about various types of drug use. However, if we are to discuss drug abuse in this chapter, we must reach a decision concerning the meaning of the term; we must have a workable definition. So without further argument the following definition is offered for the purposes of this chapter and as a focal point for independent exploration and classroom discussion concerning this controversial issue.

> Drug abuse is the deliberate, excessive, nontherapeutic use of a drug, measured by either dose or frequency or route of administration, which proves detrimental to the individual, either physically or psychologically.

Drug Use, Drug Misuse, and Drug Abuse

In this section four types of drug use situation will be described and differentiated, with the objective identifying the sector from which the majority of drug abuse originates. These four types are (a) therapeutic drug use, (b) religious drug use, (c) cultural drug use, and (d) social drug use.

Therapeutic drug use involves a direct and reliable drug effect relationship. Indeed, the value of a therapeutic agent is the extent to which drug effects are reproducible in a variety of individuals. The safety and effectiveness of prescription drugs are established through years of preclinical studies and controlled, blinded clinical trials. For instance, if an antihypertensive agent sometimes lowered blood pressure but sometimes raised blood pressure, it would never become accepted as a valuable (adjunct to) therapy. In the therapeutic drug use situation, the patient's response to the drug has little to do with the environment in which the drug is taken (the setting) or the person's state of mind or level of mood (the set) at the time the drug is consumed. Therapeutic effect has been established through controlled trials. While the patient's desire to improve may enhance the effectiveness of drug therapy, it is not a requirement for effective drug therapy. Thus, in a hypertensive crisis blood pressure is reduced even in unconscious patients.

Another important aspect of therapeutic drug use is that directions for use accompany the drug. Prescription drugs are dispensed with explicit instructions typed on the label, and OTC drugs have directions typed on the container. If one uses the drug in a way that violates the instructions for use, he must accept the consequences of misuse. There are implicit rules associated with religious and cultural drug use. In the social drug use category, no rules exist except by group consensus. In some groups status is achieved by the most outrageous drug using/abusing behavior, while in others drug abstinence is the norm.

In the religious context the drug is often used symbolically and drug effects are not sought. On the other hand, there are religious sects such as the Native American Church of the United States which employs drugs to induce trance states (8). The drug use in this situation is restricted to the shaman or high priest during most ceremonies but at times a communal experience is centered around the psychoactive effects produced by peyote. It is considered sacrilegious to debase the sacred symbol by employing it for its drug effect, and the use of peyote outside of the sacred ceremony is taboo.

Cultural drug use can be viewed as a normal part of a daily routine. The drugs used frequently are from the stimulant category, although marihuana use in Jamaica seems to be culturally embedded. For instance, the coffee break is a routine part of the American business day, and cigarettes are consumed by many individuals without the slightest notion that they are ingesting a potent psychoactive compound. In the hills of the Andes, crushed coca leaves are chewed early in the morning before the workers take to the fields. In all instances of cultural drug use the drugs are consumed in a natural form. That is, no effort is made to isolate the active substance and consume it in its pure form.

Social drug use can be described as the use of drugs to enhance social interactions, usually in a party atmosphere. Although Americans by and large have ambivalent attitudes about social drug use, there are some guidelines within which drug use in social situations is acceptable. First, the dose of the drug is usually kept low, thereby allowing set and setting to play an important part in producing the effect that one gets following the drug ingestion. Second, because the use of drugs in the social setting is for the purpose of increasing social interactions, drug users must stay in control to the extent that they are accountable for their actions.

In the social drug use situation the contribution of set and setting are extremely important. One might even suppose that set and setting are more important factors in determining responses to low doses of psychoactive drugs in social situations. As an example, consider the young man who smokes a small amount of marihuana in the company of his best friends while listening to his new stereo component system. Now imagine that right in the middle of his favorite song, with the volume adjusted accordingly, the speakers suddenly go dead. In an instant the setting has changed: where before there was music, now there is silence. Equally important, imagine the change in mood which occurs when he realizes that he just spent a year's savings on a stereo system that does not work. In this situation, direct drug effects are relatively unimportant.

Entrepreneurs in the recreational drug use industry have capitalized on the contribution of set and setting influences on drug effect. Elaborate smoking devices, expensive cocaine paraphernalia, and drug-oriented accessories such as jewelry and belt buckles add to the allure of drug use and allow one to make a personal statement about his identity in a drug using subculture.

The growth of the paraphernalia industry has not gone unnoticed. The open sale and promotion of these goods, especially to minors, has caused communities to organize and bring pressure on "head shops" to close or restructure their merchandising policies. As of November 1, 1979, Georgia, Indiana, and North Dakota had passed statewide anti-paraphernalia laws, and similar ordinances have been adopted in 77 local jurisdictions of 13 other states (9). Generally, the laws which are based on a "Model Paraphernalia Industry Regulatory Act" restrict sales of any tobacco products or smoking devices to minors. Laws which attempt to prohibit the sale of all paraphernalia without regard to age have not been adopted or have been overthrown on the grounds that they are vague and unconstitutional. The promotion of drug-related materials still occurs but is now largely concentrated in special interest periodicals such as *High Times* (10).

The very fact that such widesweeping laws are unconstitutional or unenforceable indicates that our drug-using society finds it impossible to prohibit selected drug use while allowing and promoting other drug use. Thus, social drug use has gained more than a foothold in our culture. Regardless of the health questions involved and the legal status of certain drugs, a large segment of our population will continue to use drugs socially and recreationally which they find bring them pleasure and enjoyment.

In most cases drug abuse, however it is defined, results from social drug use that gets out of control. Man has been using drugs socially at least since the discovery of the fermentation process; drug abuse has been with man for the same amount of time. It seems that when large numbers of people use drugs socially, an unfortunate side effect is that some portion of users will suffer from abuse of the drug. That is, the drug use will adversely affect some major life function area such as family, physical health, work, or psychological stability (11).

It is elementary to distinguish between the four types of drug use situations described above, but where does social drug use end and drug abuse begin? A group of adults gathered together drinking alcoholic beverages and discussing the politics of the United States is called a cocktail party. This is social drug use. When adolescents gather together, smoke marihuana, and talk about the ills of society, they are called drug abusers. Only two things differ: the age of the users and the drug used.

There are variables which are identifiable and can be used to distinguish social drug use from drug abuse. They are: (a) the dose of the drug, (b) the frequency of drug administration, (c) the route of drug administration, and (d) the conditions under which the drugs are consumed. These variables will now be examined in more detail.

(a) *The dose of the drug.* There are two drugs that are well accepted in America: alcohol and tobacco. A third, marihuana, is emerging but is still considered illicit. But even if the discussion is limited to alcohol and tobacco, one can readily see that uses and abuses exist. John Seldon, whose life spanned the years 1584 to 1654, said "'Tis not the drinking that is to be blamed but the excess." Indeed, it is the excessive use of alcohol which causes the medical problems evident in the millions of alcoholics (12) in the United States. An often quoted figure is that 10% of American drinkers are Alcoholic and that 50% of the alcohol sold in the United States is consumed by 10% of the population. Similarly, the medical profession recognizes that the risk of lung cancer increases as the consumption of cigarettes increases. Generally, it is pharmacologically accepted that as the dose of any drug is increased the risks associated with its use also increase.

(b) *The frequency of drug administration.* As the interval between episodes of drug use decreases, risks increase. Someone who smokes a pack of cigarettes a week runs less risk of adverse effects than someone who smokes a pack a day. If one begins to consider other psychoactive drugs, especially depressant drugs such as alcohol, one will realize that the frequency of administration can be increased to the point of constant intoxication.

(c) *The route of administration.* Many so-called "drugs of abuse" are therapeutic agents meant for oral administration; however, for purposes of the drug abuser they are injected. The insoluble material in the tablet travels through the bloodstream until it reaches a vessel which is too small in diameter to allow the particle to pass. Repeated injection causes the buildup of these solid particles until damaging effects are noticeable (13). Another consideration is that the toxicity of a drug varies with the route of administration, and on an equal dose basis, intravenous use is generally the most toxic.

(d) *Conditions under which the drugs are consumed.* Several behavioral criteria have been suggested which characterize the person with a "drinking problem" (14). Three hold relevance here: (a) anyone who must drink in order to function or to cope with life has a drinking problem, (b) anyone who goes to work intoxicated has a drinking problem, and (c) anyone who is intoxicated and drives a car has a drinking problem. These criteria could easily be extended to drug use other than alcohol.

In an attempt to detect Alcoholism, several questionnaires have been developed. The CAGE test asks four simple questions focused on Cuttingdown, Annoyance by criticism, Guilty feeling, and Eye openers in regard to drinking alcohol (15). Other screening tests are longer and ask more detailed questions about the consequences of one's alcohol use (16). The point is that as one considers the four aspects of drug use listed above, it is the impact on one's life that determines use, abuse, or addiction.

The Drugs

Not all drugs manufactured are liable for abuse because, unless a drug affects the central nervous system, it will produce no changes in perception or mood. Here again we run into a problem of semantics over the question of what constitutes a drug. Eric Josephson writes that one pharmacologist feels that:

> Any substance that by its chemical nature alters a structure or function in the living organism is a drug.... Pharmacological effects are exerted by foods, vitamins, hormones, microbial metabolites, plants, snake venoms, stings, products of decay, air pollutants, pesticides, minerals, synthetic chemicals, virtually all foreign materials (few are completely inert), and many minerals normally in the body (17).

Josephson comments, "to this list may be added water."

Any attempts to work with this definition would be cumbersome, but it provides some idea of the number of substances which can produce changes in the mind or body.

Drug abusers and social drug users limit their drug use to three classes of drugs: those that depress or those that stimulate the central nervous system and those that produce changes in normal perception so that the world is viewed in a novel way. Table 4.1 lists those drugs which fall into these three major categories of drugs of abuse. The list is by no means definitive, and street chemists who manufacture illicit drugs are finding ways to create new drugs by making minor chemical alterations to existing compounds. These "designer drugs" attempt to improve on the euphoria-producing effects of their forerunners and to circumvent the illegal status of specific chemical formulae. Unfortunately, small changes in the molecular design of a drug can alter the pharmacology and toxicology of a drug in unknown ways. Street drug manufacturers are more concerned about making money than about producing safe drugs.

An examination of the table will reveal that drugs of abuse include not only prescription and OTC medicines but also a host of street drugs which have no medicinal value but are potent psychoactive agents. Also included are a group of substances usually not thought of as drugs but which nevertheless have psychoactive properties.

The category of depressant drugs is by far the most extensive. Most are prescription medications such as morphine, the barbiturates, and the minor tranquilizers, although alcohol is by far the most extensively used and abused depressant drug. The major tranquilizers, those used in the treatment of major psychiatric disorders, tend not to be abused although abuse of amitriptyline hydrochloride (Elavil), a drug used in the treatment of depression, has been reported (18). Some, such as diphenhydramine, are found in OTC sleep medications (19), whereas others such as heroin have no therapeutic place in the American health care system except in experimental studies. The nondrug intoxicants in this category include volatile solvents such as toluene and benzene. Although the mechanisms of action differ, all the drugs listed in this category have one thing in common. By depressing the activity of the central nervous system, they produce in the user a brief euphoria, a temporary relief from the psychologic discomfort of human inhibitions, and a resultant escape from the pressure of life in the real world.

Drugs in the stimulant category have the opposite effect in the user. The central nervous system is excited, and fatigue can temporarily be fought off. The abuser who injects amphetamine intravenously (mainlines) receives for his efforts a strong rush sometimes described as a total body orgasm, followed by a period of activity which when it terminates leaves the individual drained of both physical and psychic energy (20). Smaller doses taken by mouth are used by students and truck drivers as a method of maintaining mental alertness. When the drug is used in this manner, the extreme effects noted in the mainliners are not seen and serious consequences rarely result. Although amphet-

Table 4.1.
Classification of Drugs

Locally acting agents
Antibiotics
Vitamins
Cardiovascular agents

Therapeutic Drugs

Antineoplastics
Antitoxins
Muscle relaxants
Diuretics
Hormones

Drugs affecting the central nervous system

Anticonvulsants   Drugs of abuse   Analgesics   Antipyretics

Depressants   Stimulants   Psychedelics

		Major	Minor
Alcohol	Methamphetamine	Lysergic acid	Marihuana
Narcotics (opioids)	Amphetamine	diethylamide	Hashish
Natural (morphine, codeine)	Nonamphetamine[a]	(LSD)	
Semisynthetic (heroin)	(phenmetrazine)	Mescaline	
Synthetic (methadone,	Caffeine	Psilocybin	
meperidine)	Cocaine	Dimethoxymethylamphetamine	
Barbiturates	Strychnine	[DOM (STP)]	
Short acting (thiopental)	Nicotine	Dimethyltryptamine (DMT)	
Long acting (phenobarbital)	Propellants (freon)	Paramethoxyamphetamine	
Intermediate acting		(PMA)	
(secobarbital,		Δ^9Tetrahydrocannabinol	
pentobarbital, amobarbital)		(Δ^9THC)	
Nonbarbiturates[b] (methaqua-		Hashish (oil)	
lone, glutethimide)			
Volatile solvents (toluene,			
gasoline)			
Tranquilizers			
Major (phenothiazines)			
Minor (diazepam, chlor-			
diazepoxide)			
Anesthetics			
Ether			
Nitrous oxide			
Phencyclidine (PCP)			

[a]Many drugs used as anorexants are also stimulants although they are chemically different from amphetamines.

[b]Many drugs used as hypnotics are unrelated chemically to the barbiturates although they produce similar effects.

amine is available by prescription, its use has been restricted severely, and now it reaches the streets primarily through a chain of illicit drug distribution originating from a point of synthesis in some clandestine laboratory.

The potent stimulants are legally prescription drugs and are subject to scheduling laws to be discussed later. The mild stimulants caffeine, phenylpropanolamine, and ephedrine are utilized as ingredients in most OTC stimulants and weight loss products. The potential toxicities of these substances should be noted (21).

Finally, we arrive at the list of psychedelic drug substances, which is subdivided into major and minor psychedelics for one important reason. Although the psychedelic experience is reported to be fundamentally the same, marihuana in dried leaf form is hardly potent enough to produce the full-blown break with reality produced by potent psychedelics such as LSD. In *The Doors of Perception* Aldous Huxley describes his experiment with mescaline as being an experience in colors, geometric figures, and revealing insights into various works of art (22). Others have had frightening encounters with psychedelic drugs when they failed to move freely through the psychedelic experience and became trapped in a terrifying mental episode. Unfortunately, these "bad trips" are sometimes made even worse by emergency room treatment, and the person may suffer psychological damage until the feelings experienced during the trip are worked through (23).

Because the psychedelic drugs are not considered medically useful, they are not produced by ethical drug manufacturers except in small quantities for research purposes. Some natural products, such as psilocybin and mescaline, may be found on the street in the natural form as encapsulated crushed organic material, but these dosage forms tend to be scarce. Because of the limited supply of the natural products and the street demand for psychedelic drugs, it has become profitable to manufacture these substances illicitly for street sale. Because the FDA is not in the business of validating street drugs for purity and identity, the purchaser is unprotected from the unscrupulous activity of the illicit drug underworld.

In discussions of psychoactive drugs, the rebound effects are often overlooked. This pharmacological reaction is in the opposite direction of the original drug effect and occurs when the sought after effect wears off. Depressant drugs produce rebound effects such as anxiety, nervousness, and irritability. Stimulant drug rebound effects include lethargy, fatigue, and craving for more drug. The rebound effects of psychedelic drugs could be described as boredom, lassitude, and a reduction in motivational energy.

These rebound effects eventually subside and the user's psyche returns to its baseline level. However, in some instances drug users react to the rebound experience by taking more of the drug in an attempt to reverse the rebound discomfort. While this does relieve the rebound distress to some degree, this effect also will wear off and the subsequent rebound will be more severe than before.

This is an extremely brief description of the actions of these three categories of drugs, and it is in no way intended to be a review of the pharmacology of these substances. The reader is encouraged to pursue the topics presented here until his curiosity is satisfied, for the behavioral pharmacology of drugs of abuse is an interesting topic and worthy of study.

Drug Schedules

The topic of drug schedules was previously mentioned as part of the government's efforts to curb the abuse of certain drug substances. The federal government, through the Drug Enforcement Administration (DEA) and the FDA, is responsible for ensuring that abusable drugs are confined to their role in therapy and not diverted for sale on the illicit market. Toward this end psychoactive drugs are placed into one of the five categories of the drug schedule chart (Table 4.2).

The schedules are set up on the basis of the importance of the drug in medical practice, its potential for abuse, and its ability to produce either psychological or physiological dependence. Heroin, for example, is placed in Schedule I since (a) it has no therapeutic use in medicine, (b) it has an extremely high potential for abuse, and (c) it easily causes strong physical and psychological dependence. Other substances are scheduled accordingly.

Depending on the schedule in which a drug is placed, it will be subjected to certain manufacturing and dispensing limitations. Schedule I drugs may not be prescribed for any purpose, and manufacturing is limited to government-certified drug houses. Schedule II drugs may be manufactured in limited quantity and dispensed only by a written prescription which cannot be refilled. The restrictions become less stringent as one moves from Schedule I to Schedule V. Prescription drugs not on the schedule are not subject to these limitations.

Sources of Drugs

In the medical model presented earlier, a person seeks therapeutic advice and treatment from a physician in either private practice or in a hospital setting. Logically, then, the physician becomes the target of those who wish to acquire drugs for other than therapeutic purposes.

Table 4.2.
Schedules of Drug Classification According to the Comprehensive Drug Abuse Prevention and Control Act of 1970

Schedule	Criteria for admittance	Examples
I	a. High potential for abuse b. No accepted medical use in the United States c. A lack of accepted safety for use uder medical supervision	LSD Heroin Marihuana Mescaline
II	a. High potential for abuse a. High potential for abuse b. Currently accepted medical use in the United States, currently accepted with severe restrictions c. Abuse may lead to severe psychological or physical dependence	All narcotics All amphetamines All barbiturates except phenobarbital Phencylidine (PCP)
III	a. Potential for abuse less than substances in Schedules I and II b. Well-documented and approved medical use c. Abuse may lead to moderate or low physical dependence or high psychological dependece	Talwin Doriden Compounds containing limited quantities of narcotic drugs Benzodiazepines
IV	a. Low potential for abuse relative to substances in Schedule III b. Accepted medical use in treatment c. Abuse may lead to limited physical or psychological dependence	Meprobamate Phenobarbital Chloral hydrate
V	a. Low potential for abuse relative to substances in Schedule IV b. Accepted medical use c. Limited physical or psychological dependence liability	Cough syrups containing codeine Preparations containing narcotics in quantities less than Schedule III

The physician in private practice listens to the complaints of the drug abuser, which, unknown to him, are fabricated with the intention of acquiring psychoactive drugs. In many cases the physician responds according to his medical training and the Hippocratic Oath and prescribes drugs to alleviate the symptoms presented. In doing so the physician becomes the source of drugs for this abuser until discovering the fraudulent nature of the complaints. This may never occur, because the pseudopatient may move on to another physician long before he is discovered, in order to leave open the possibility for a return visit. In this manner the drug abuser obtains a continuous supply of psychoactive agents by utilizing the services of many different physicians.

The next step in the medical model is to have the physician's prescription dispensed. Often it is a genuine prescription even though it was obtained through dishonest means. The pharmacist may be totally unaware of the patient's intent and therefore have no reason to become suspicious. The prescription is dispensed, *no laws have been broken* by the health practitioners, and a con artist has obtained his goal.

Recent changes in federal drug scheduling laws have played a large role in discouraging this type of activity. However, psychoactive drugs not on the schedule continue to be dispensed in quantities which exceed the estimated need.

In several instances criminal procedures have been used to obtain psychoactive drugs from the health care system. Intricate rings of criminal activity evolve. In one case in a large Northeastern city, the following events took place. Bogus prescription pads were printed in the basement of a downtown row home. Prescriptions were written for 100 Dilaudid tablets, a synthetic narcotic, with instructions to take as needed for severe pain. A physician's phone number was included along with his narcotics prescribing number allocated by the DEA. The prescriptions were accurate in every detail. If a pharmacist called the physician, and many did, an authoritative voice answered verifying the authenticity of the prescription, along with the information that it was written for the bearer's grandmother who was terminally ill with cancer.

After receiving several of the same prescriptions, one pharmacist decided to look up the physician's phone number in the telephone book. He became suspicious when he found none listed and notified the authorities. Investigation revealed that the ring consisted of several men. One wrote the prescription and played the role of the physician, while the others had the prescriptions dispensed in various pharmacies in the city. The "physician's" phone number turned out to be that of a public telephone booth, and the "physician" was a narcotics addict with a great deal of street knowledge about narcotic drugs and prescribing practices. Each day that the ring operated, ten prescriptions were dispensed for 100 tablets each, a street value conservatively estimated at $5000. No one knows how long the ring operated undetected.

Other methods of fraudulently obtaining prescription drugs include altering valid prescriptions and writing phony prescriptions on stolen blanks.

Recently, pharmacy thefts have increased dramatically. Increased effectiveness of law enforcement efforts to intercept drugs being smuggled into the country and the increased demand for psychoactive drugs for nontherapeutic use may be the cause. These forces make the street price of pharmaceutical grade drugs attractive enough for people to risk arrest and prosecution for theft of scheduled substances. Unfortunately, the rise in pharmacy crime has brought with it an increase in assaults against pharmacists. The response has been the passage of the Controlled Substances Registrant Protection Act of 1984. This law makes drug theft a federal crime which could result in FBI action and federal prosecution. The law is too new for comment on its impact, but already there is controversy surrounding its enforcement. Federal agents prefer not to become involved in the investigation of cases unless more than $5000 in drugs have been stolen, there has been a death, or the possibility existed that a death could have occurred in the theft. Pharmacists argue that any impact the law may have had on pharmacy crime will be minimized by these interpretations (24).

Of course, not all drugs of abuse are obtained by the methods mentioned above. Friends, family, and neighbors play a large role in supplying drugs to the user, abuser or experimenter. In view of the fact that an estimated 29% of the women and 13% of the men in the United States are receiving psychotherapeutic drugs regularly (4), it is no wonder that the family medicine cabinet is an excellent initial source of drugs for the adolescent experimenter. In passing from the experimental to the occasional user stage, the drug abuser will look to sources of drugs that carry less danger of exposure. Friends, if chosen properly, can be an excellent source of drugs.

Eventually, one begins to realize that friends get their supply from somewhere. In fact the chain of illicit drug distribution is not too unlike the legitimate distribution of prescription drugs discussed elsewhere in this book. The one tremendous difference is that since the federal government has put severe manufacturing restrictions on all legal sources of selected psychoactive drugs, a vast underground system of clandestine laboratories has developed to supply drugs to the illicit market.

Is the final product of these underground laboratories put through quality control procedures for purity and accuracy of dose content? Statistics from street drug analysis laboratories nationwide suggest that the rate of misrepresentation in street drug sales has remained fairly constant at about 50%. Many drugs analyzed have been found to be impure or completely different substances from that of their purported identity (25, 26). In some cases the impurities have been shown to possess severe toxicity. A product sold in California as "synthetic heroin" was found to contain MPTP (1-Methyl-4 phenyl-1,2,5,6 tetrahydropyridine).

MPTP has been shown to cause development of permanent Parkinson's disease symptoms in at least 150 persons who used this street product (27). One thing is clear: there is no consumer protection agency for people who purchase drugs on the street. The drug abuser must put his faith in the reliability of his connection, who in most cases bought the drug from a larger supplier. Even when the products bear licit company trademarks, it must be remembered that capsules can be opened and diluted with any powder, and tablet designs can be copied.

Somewhere in the chain of illicit drug distribution there exists a person known as the pusher. Supposedly he is the man who gets the experimenter to take the first step, and then just sits back and waits for business to roll in. Doubtless there are some members of a peer group who are more coercive than others, just as there are those who feel an insecure need to follow blindly. But in the final analysis it is the individual user who actively seeks out the person who can supply his drug.

One can see there is a variety of methods by which it is possible to obtain drugs for nontherapeutic purposes. If a person's will to obtain a drug is strong enough, he will find a way to obtain it regardless of the methods or risks involved.

The Drug Abuser

There is no single statement that characterizes the drug abuser. While it was once thought that drug abuse was a black inner city problem, now it is realized that this is hardly the case. The problem is not black or white, Chicano or Indian, black inner city, or white middle class. Drug abusers can be found in any sampling of the population. Of the heroin user, Charles Winick writes:

> Let us assume that we were to get a chronic heroin user to talk about the subject of careers of heroin users. What kind of user should make the presentation? A masochist, counterphobic personality, or an oral passive type? Someone with an emotional conflict? A Chicago cool cat, an Oakland mellow dude? A person with endocrine dysfunction? Someone who is medicating himself? A proponent of the hang-loose ethic? A head or a freak? A double retreatist or someone else suffering from anomie? One who lacks impulse control? An extremely intelligent person, making an astute adaptation to the realities of ghetto life? A victim of the knowledge of how to relive withdrawal distress? Or a risk discounter (28)?

There just is no stereotype.

Drug use can be classified according to certain motivational characteristics. For instance, Dohner presented 13 motives for "non-medical,

Table 4.3.
Functions of Drugs[a]

Function	Example
Esthetics	Use of marihuana by jazz musicians
Aphrodisiac	Mostly folklore
Ego disruption	LSD, other hallucinogens
Ideological	Use of peyote by antiwhite Indians
Political	Use of opium by Japanese in attempt to demoralize Chinese in 1930s
Psychological support	Tranquilizers
Religion	Marihuana in Jamaica, peyote in Native American Church
Research	Behavioral studies
Social control	Peyote "confessions"
Therapeutic	Any medical application
War and other conflicts	Biological warfare

[a]From: Barber B: *Drugs and Society.* New York, Russell Sage Foundation, 1967.

mood-altering agent use" and suggested that the motives were applicable to adults as well as adolescents (29). Dohner's list is: *1*, curiosity, *2*, imitation, *3*, peer pressure, *4*, pursuit of well being, *5*, instant achievement, *6*, relaxation, *7*, recreation, *8*, psychological support, *9*, rebellion, *10*, insight and identity, *11*, esthetics, *12*, mystical-religion, and *13*, aphrodisiac. Another list of drug functions, with examples, is given in Table 4.3.

Some people are experimental users and never get beyond that stage, while others use drugs occasionally. Some drug abusers rarely mix drugs and use their drug of choice whenever possible. Others are polydrug abusers who do not seem to discriminate among drugs and who use stimulants as readily as depressants or hallucinogens and often in combination.

The Road to Addiction

Our understanding of addiction has its roots in studies done from the late 1940s through the middle 1950s. During this period, the majority of people with addiction problems were dependent on alcohol or narcotic drugs. Studies carried out at the Addictions Research Center in Lexington, Kentucky, drew on populations of alcoholic and narcotic addict patients admitted to the national treatment center located in that town. When deprived of their drug, these individuals experienced an abstinence syndrome typified by objective signs of distress. These included weight loss, cardiovascular changes, gastrointestinal distress, and in some cases of alcohol dependence, psychosis and seizure. Thus, addiction was described by the World Health Organization (WHO) as follows in 1957:

1. An overpowering desire or need (compulsion) to continue taking the drug and to obtain it by any means
2. A tendency to increase the dose
3. A psychic (psychological) and generally a physical dependence on the effects of the drug
4. A detrimental effect on the individual and on society (30)

Since then the definition of addiction has been refined to take into account a number of changes in the epidemiology of drug abuse. The most notable of these is the proliferation of substances available for abuse. Drugs such as marihuana and amphetamine do not lead to withdrawal distress typical of narcotics or alcohol in that physical dependence is absent in spite of extremely compulsive patterns of abuse and clearly intense psychological dependence. Thus, physical dependence is no longer considered a requirement in the diagnosis of drug addiction.

Dr. Jerome Jaffe proposes that addiction be viewed as "a behavioral pattern of compulsive drug use, characterized by overwhelming involvement with the use of a drug, the securing of its supply, and a high tendency to relapse after withdrawal." He adds that "it is possible to be physically dependent on drugs without being addicted and to be addicted without being physically dependent" (31). This viewpoint is becoming generally accepted, and compulsive use of such agents as caffeine, nicotine, and marihuana is considered addiction (32).

The question is, how does one come to be addicted? It is obvious that one must first use the drug and find it rewarding in some way. Either the drug effects per se are pleasurable or the use of the drug fills a psychological need such as acceptance into a peer group or rebellion against parental values. If the drug use fills a physical or psychological need, there is a tendency for the individual to continuously repeat the drug experience. After a time the initial fondness for the drug may develop into psychological dependence so it is administered with increasing frequency. Why some people develop psychological dependence and some do not is an unanswered question.

Depending on the amount and frequency of drug abuse, some degree of tolerance will develop, meaning that the user must take more of the drug to achieve the same "high." The next step in the addictive cycle is crucial and depends upon the pharmacological properties of the drug. Once tolerance has developed, termination of drug use may or may not produce the series of physical discomforts known as the withdrawal syndrome. This syndrome is related to the drug's effect, and the pharmacological properties of the drug will determine the withdrawal signs and symptoms experienced. Most central nervous system depressants have been shown to cause objective signs of withdrawal and are thus said to produce physical dependence. The person physically dependent needs to use the drug continually simply to prevent the occurence of the withdrawal syndrome. This effect is discovered somewhere in the addictive cycle when the user recognizes that obscure feelings of malaise dissipate when the drug is consumed. At this final stage the triad of addiction—tolerance, psychological dependence, and physical dependence—is complete, and the person is said to be addicted according to WHO standards (see upper cycle in Fig. 4.1 on the genesis of addiction).

In an alternative scenario the individual follows the same pattern of introduction to the drug, continued use, and psychological dependence. However the drug being used happens not to produce physical dependence. When this person stops using the drug, an abstinence syndrome is experienced but without the physical distress associated with physical dependence. Even though there is no objective withdrawal pattern, the abrupt termination of drug use creates a psychological void in the person's life, which ultimately leads to relapse in most cases unless there is some therapeutic intervention. This course of events is conceptualized by the lower cycle in Figure 4.1 and is properly diagnosed as addiction under the Jaffe definition.

Treatment for the Drug Addict

The decision to enter treatment results from a complex interplay of an individual's perception of the rewards of drug use in the face of the experience of negative consequences of drug-using behavior. The rewards may be considered as the degree to which drug use satisfies Dohner's 13 motives presented above. The negative consequences of drug abuse tend to occur in four major life function areas. These are; interpersonal relations; productivity; self-concept; and health. As the rewards of drug use diminish and the negative consequences of drug abuse increase, the balance favors a decision to terminate drug use.

Eventually one may seek professional intervention if self-directed attempts to quit have been unsuccessful.

Basically, there are two types of treatment available to the drug addict: (a) maintenance on a drug which will prevent withdrawal

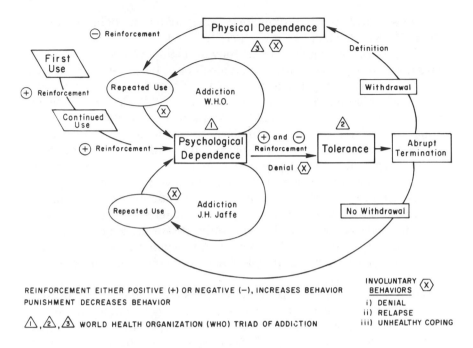

Figure 4.1. The genesis of addiction.

discomfort and (b) detoxification from the addictive substance, with supportive therapy to keep the patient drug free.

Many people assume that maintenance therapy is a new treatment method; however, in the early 1900s programs were in operation to supply narcotic addicts with continuous supplies of morphine. The programs were only minimally successful and, with the exception of one clinic in Shreveport, Louisiana (33), were ended shortly after they began. The concept of maintenance therapy for narcotic addicts was ended with the Harrison Act, which made it illegal for physicians to prescribe narcotics for the purpose of maintaining a person's addiction. Then in 1965 the *Journal of the American Medical Association* published a paper by Drs. Vincent Dole and Marie Nyswander (34), reporting on their success in treating narcotics addicts with daily doses of methadone, a synthetic narcotic developed by the Germans during World War II (35). Soon afterward, methadone maintenance clinics began springing up all over the country. At the present time methadone maintenance is an accepted method of treating narcotic addicts, and the clinical use of methadone is controlled by FDA regulations (36).

Statistics indicate that approximately 75,000 addicts are being treated in about 575 maintenance programs (37).

The converse of maintenance therapy is abstinence therapy. Alcoholics Anonymous (AA) operates on an abstinence basis using recovering alcoholics as role models and establishing a broad support system for continued sobriety. The AA is responsible for the recovery of many alcoholics from various walks of life. Al Anon has helped many spouses of alcoholics, and Alateen has similarly helped many sons and daughters of alcoholics understand alcoholism and how they are affected by it.

Other types of drug dependencies also are treated on an abstinence basis. After a short period of detoxification involving a gradual reduction in the dose of the addictive drug, the patient is enrolled into a counseling program designed to help him re-enter society by improving job skills and developing social skills often absent in the drug abuser. A new self-help group called Narcotics Anonymous (NA) is basically identical to AA but attracts people whose primary drug dependency is different from alcohol.

Before leaving the issue of treatment, it should be pointed out that, especially in the maintenance modality of treatment, counseling is the intregal part of the therapeutic regimen. Even the FDA regulations on methadone demand at least weekly contact between the patient and the counselor. Also, methadone cannot in any way be considered a panacea for drug dependence. It is merely a tool in the overall rehabilitative process of which the ultimate goal is to produce a well-balanced, functional individual.

The Role of the Pharmacist

Pharmacists have a functional role in the treatment of drug dependence. First, they can work in a methadone maintenance clinic having responsibility over the preparation and dispensing of medication to patients. The position demands precise accuracy in record keeping and dispensing, as well as a working relationship with the program personnel and with the patients. In most cases they will be considered the most knowledgeable individuals on the treatment staff regarding the pharmacology of drug therapy. They frequently will be asked to consult with the physician in arriving at the patient's maintenance dose, as well as calculating any dose changes required during treatment.

Second, pharmacists in drug treatment programs can function in a counseling capacity, especially when dealing with polydrug abusers who frequently mix drugs, greatly increasing the potential for toxic responses. To many patients and counselors, pharmacology has a vague meaning, and the professional guidance that pharmacists provide will help clarify drug actions and side effects. They can set up inhouse training programs for counselors to increase drug knowledge and understanding among staff regarding patient complaints about drug therapy.

Third, pharmacists can play a major role at the state and federal levels of addiction treatment. Both the state and the federal governments have responsibility for ensuring quality patient care for the drug abuser. Pharmacists can check program records to ensure compliance with regulations, they can suggest methods for record keeping which might improve the ease and accuracy of reporting, and they may be able to suggest changes that will facilitate medical care while maintaining compliance with government regulations.

In terms of drug abuse prevention, pharmacists have important contributions to make. First, by maintaining proper patient records, community pharmacists can keep a check on patients who shop among physicians to acquire multiple prescriptions for psychoactive drugs. They should keep a close watch on the number and frequency of renewal requests, being aware that psychoactive substances frequently produce tolerance.

A second important function of community pharmacists is interaction with physicians. When pharmacists become aware of dangerous situations resulting from multiple physician treatment or overprescribing by one physician, it is their duty to become involved in the interest of the patient. In many instances an alternate course of drug therapy can be recommended that has a reduced drug abuse liability.

It is not known to what extent forged prescriptions add to the availability of drugs for illicit sale. However, pharmacists should always be aware of prescription fraud and be cognizant of the role they play in encouraging or discouraging this type of drug "connection." Apparently, there is no crime in possessing a forged prescription; however, it is illegal to receive legend drugs under false pretenses. Therefore, there are two approaches pharmacists can take when presented with a potentially forged prescription: first, verify the fraudulent nature of the prescription by contacting the prescriber, and dispense the prescription after notifying the local authorities. The person receiving the prescription can be arrested for receiving legend drugs under false pretenses. A second course of action is to inform the prescription bearer that the medication will be dispensed after contacting the physician. If the prescription is fraudulent the person usually will leave the pharmacy very quickly (38).

It is important to recognize that both courses of action result in the fraudulent prescription being left in the hands of the pharmacist. Any course of action which returns a suspected forgery to the bearer should be avoided. Before leaving this subject, realize that even if the prescription is valid, the interest indicated by making contact with the prescriber will remind the physician that pharmacists are important members of the health care team. In most cases physicians are relieved to know that some aspects of the responsibility for monitoring a patient's health care are shared with another competent professional.

Pharmacists can act in the role of a teacher and become involved in drug abuse education. All patients are potential students awaiting instruction in drug-related matters. Often this role is never realized. All too often patients never get to talk with pharmacists. Patients should be instructed in the proper use of all drugs, especially psychoactive substances. They should be cautioned about possible drug interactions with alcohol when appropriate. In many cases when anorexic medications are prescribed, the patient may not be aware of the stimulant side effects. They should be warned that sedative hypnotic drugs are potent medications which should be stored securely so that they are inaccessible to children.

Pharmacists can become active in the community. Local elementary and high schools can benefit from a well thought out and carefully planned presentation on drugs (33). Adult groups such as the PTA and Lions Club often welcome an open discussion about drugs.

One thing should be kept in mind when acting the role of educator. The drug abuse epidemic of the 1960s gave birth to a great many self-proclaimed drug-experts. These well meaning people often provided misinformation, half-truths and twisted facts in their attempts to provide drug abuse information. As a result, drug education took a giant step backward, and the credibility of those who spoke about drug abuse suffered serious and ongoing damage. In view of the controversy which surrounds the drug use scene, this may have been a blessing in disguise, for now audiences are reluctant to believe someone who "has all the answers." However, factual presentations of two sides of a controversial issue (marihuana research, for instance) are well received by adolescents as well as adults.

Pharmacists can become active in community drug education efforts. The 1980s have seen the introduction of a variety of community-based drug abuse prevention approaches. A strategy that has been successful in organizing community action is a school-based movement. Teams of teachers, students, community organizers, business owners, police, drug counselors, clergy, and parents are formed. They undergo special training in drug abuse and addictions and become instrumental in promoting prevention activities in their locale. Pharmacists can participate either as team members or as resource individuals when prevention efforts are organized. These and other community organizations can benefit from a well-thought-out and carefully planned presentation on drugs (39).

A cautionary note is in order. It is often the case that people expect drug abuse lectures to have a prevention thrust. This unfortunately leads to presentations of the casualties of drug abuse or worst case scenarios of drug use. Adults seem to have a penchant for believing that the complex adolescent behavior of drug involvement can be altered significantly by authoritative antidrug messages. They often see drug information lectures as prevention exercises. A more realistic approach is to recognize that in our highly drug-oriented society a basic understanding of pharmacology is a critical educational necessity (40). While pharmacists should address the effects of alcohol, marihuana, and other drugs in these presentations, it should be done in such a way that basic pharmacological principles such as dose response relationships, pharmacokinetic principles, and side effect vs. adverse effect analysis are emphasized. Thus, participants come to understand the effects of these drugs from a broader perspective than a simple listing of problems associated with abuse.

An increasingly important area of pharmacist involvement is within our own profession. Chemical dependence on alcohol or other drugs has been shown to be a problem among health professionals (41). Most notably, physicians have established self-help organizations to offer confidential intervention to their colleagues. Other health professions have begun similar efforts.

In the State of Maryland the Pharmacist Rehabilitation Committee operates as a treatment broker, referring pharmacists to appropriate confidential care. In addition, the Committee establishes a middle ground between pharmacists' problems in practice and the State Board of Pharmacy, which has the authority to suspend or revoke a license to practice. A contractual agreement spells out the conditions upon which the Committee will play an advocacy role for the pharmacist should the State Board bring action against his or her license. The contract calls for ongoing therapy and abstinence from psychoactive drugs. The Committee receives referrals from pharmacy employers and the State Board, and in some cases pharmacists self-refer after learning that the Committee offers an escape from what has developed into an unsolvable dilemma. Similar programs exist in other states. The State Pharmaceutical Association is the usual point of first contact.

The existence of these committees in the various health professions indicates the need for all pharmacists to be knowledgeable about chemical dependence. We owe our profession the interest in keeping it healthy and the desire to show compassion to our colleagues. Pharmacists should educate themselves to recognize the signs and symptoms of chemical dependence and should become familiar with the operation of their association's pharmacy rehabilitation group. They can urge their association to develop continuing education programs on this topic and become instrumental in establishing a rehabilitation committee if none exists.

Summary

In *The Natural Mind,* Andrew Weil postulates that getting high is an innate drive in man (42). Children can be seen whirling themselves around until they collapse from dizziness, and hyperventilation is a natural method of altering perceptions. In our medicated society sooner or later just about everyone will ingest some psychoactive substance. It is hardly any wonder that of this vast number of people some will find the "high" so pleasurable that they will be willing to devote their life to it, never realizing that drugs are but one means of achieving such a sensation.

There are many unanswered questions in the drug abuse field. Are treatment methods any better now than they were in the days of the Shreveport Clinic? Is there any hope of curing drug addiction through pharmacological means? What causes a person to use drugs to his own self-evident detriment? Can society comfortably hold some drugs to be socially acceptable while labeling any other drug use "drug abuse?" What should be the basis for society's choice of acceptable intoxicants? The list of questions could go on and on.

The field is wide open, and pharmacists have a role to play.

REFERENCES

1. Toffler A: *Future Shock.* New York, Random House, Inc., 1970.
2. Coombs RH, Fry LJ, Lewis PG (eds): Mass media inducements: Enticements to begin. In *Socialization in Drug Abuse.* Cambridge, MA, Schenkman Publishing Co., Inc., 1976.
3. Deleted in press.
4. Balter M, Perry HJ, Mellinger GD, Cisin IH, Manheimer DI: National patterns of psychotherapeutic drug use. *Arch Gen Psychiatry* 28:769–783, 1973.
5. Glasscote RM, Sussex JN, Jaffe JH, Ball J, Brill L: *Treatment of Drug Abuse: Programs, Problems, Prospects.* Washington, D.C., Joint Information Service of the American Psychiatric Association for Mental Health, 1972.
6. Smart RG: Addiction, dependency, abuse or use. In Josephson E, Carroll EE (eds): *Drug Use: Epidemiological and Sociological Approaches.* Washington, D.C., Hemisphere Publishing Corporation, 1974.

7. Rappolt RT, Singh JM, Multer LH, Lal H: *Drug Addiction, Clinical and Sociological Approaches*. Washington, D.C., Hemisphere Publishing Corporation, 1974.

8. Diaz JL: Ethnopharmacology of sacred psychoactive plants used by the Indians of Mexico. *Annu Rev Pharmacol Toxicol* 17:647–675, 1977.

9. Wynne RD,   : Community and legal responses to drug paraphernalia. DHEW Publication No. (ADM) 80963, 1980.

10. *The New York Times*, July 29, 1980.

11. Weller RA, Halikas JA: Objective criteria for diagnosis of marihuana abuse. *J Nerv Ment Dis* 168:98–103, 1980.

12. *Fifth Special Report to the U.S. Congress on Alcohol and Health*. DHHS Publication No. (ADM) 84-1291. Rockville, MD, National Institute on Alcoholic Abuse and Alcoholism, 1984.

13. Soin JS, McKusick A, Wagner HN, Jr.: Regional lung-function abnormalities in narcotic addicts. *JAMA* 224:13, 1973.

14. Problem drinking and alcoholism. In *Alcohol and Alcoholism Problems, Programs and Progress*. DHEW Publication (HSM) 72-9127. Rockville, MD, National Institute on Alcohol Abuse and Alcoholism, 1972.

15. Ewing JA: Detecting alcoholism: The CAGE questionnaire. *JAMA* 252 (14):1905–1907, 1984.

16. Morse RM, Hurt RD: Screening for alcoholism. *JAMA* 242 (24):2688–2690, 1979.

17. Josephson E: Introduction. In Josephson E, Carroll EE (eds): *Drug Use: Epidemiological and Sociological Approaches*. Washington, D.C., Hemisphere Publishing Corporation, 1974.

18. Cohen MJ, Hanbury R, Stimmel B: Abuse of amitriptyline. *JAMA* 240:1372–1373, 1978.

19. *Physician's Desk Reference for Nonprescription Drugs*, ed 5. Oradell, NJ, Medical Economics Company, Inc.,

20. *STASH Capsules*. Madison, WI, The Student Association for the Study of Hallucinogens, vol 1, no. 1, 1974.

21. Pentel P: Toxicity of the over-the-counter stimulants. *JAMA* 252(14):1898–1903, 1984.

22. Huxley A: *The Doors of Perception*. New York, Harper & Row Publishers, Inc., 1970.

23. McCabe OL: Psychedelic drug crisis: Toxicity and Therapeutics. *J Psychedelic Drugs* 9:107–121, 1977.

24. Siegelman S: Editor's report. *Am Drug* September 1984, November 1984, January 1985, February 1985, April 1985.

25. Street drug rip-off. In *The Maryland Anonymous Drug Analysis Service Statistics*, 1973–1974.

26. The 1977 drug analysis results. *Pharm-Chem Newsletter* 7:2, 1978.

27. Memo to state drug abuse agencies from CDC, 1984.

28. Winick C: Some aspects of careers of chronic heroin users. In Josephson E, Carroll EE (eds): *Drug Use: Epidemiological and Sociological Approaches*. Washington, D.C., Hemisphere Publishing Corporation, 1974.

29. Dohner VA: Motives for drug use: Adult and adolescent, *Psychosomatics* 13:317–324, 1972.

30. World Health Organization, Expert Committee on Mental Health: *Addiction Producing Drugs*, 7th report of the WHO Expert Committee, WHO Technical Report Series. Geneva, 1957.

31. Jaffe JH: Drug addiction and drug abuse. In Goodman LS, Gilman A: *The Pharmacological Basis of Therapeutics*, ed 5. New York, The Macmillan Company, 1975.

32. Newman RG: The need to redefine 'addiction.' *New Engl J Med* 308(18):1096–1098, 1983.

33. Waldorf D, Orlick M, Reinarman C: *Morphine Maintenance: The Shreveport Clinic 1919–1923*. Washington, D.C., The Drug Abuse Council, Inc., 1974.

34. Dole VP, Nyswander M: A medical treatment for diacetylmorphine (heroin) addiction. *JAMA* 193:80–84, 1965.

35. Goodman LS, Gilman A: *The Pharmacological Basis of Therapeutics*, ed 5. New York, The Macmillan Company, 1975.

36. *Federal Register* 45(184):62694–62718, 1980.

37. National Institute on Drug Abuse: *National Drug Abuse Treatment Survey*, 1978.

38. *Pharm Alert* 9:2, 1978.

39. Smith MC, Mikeal RL, Taylor JNM: Kids, drugs and druggists. *J Am Pharm Assoc* NS10:454–457, 1970.

40. Tommasello T: Maryland's Student Committee on Drug Abuse (SCODAE). *J Am Pharm Assoc* NS20(12):26, 1980.

41. Bissell L, Haberman PW: *Alcoholism in the Professions*. New York, Oxford University Press, 1984.

42. Weil A: *The Natural Mind: A New Way of Looking at Drugs and the Higher Consciousness*. Boston, The Houghton Mifflin Company, 1972.

CHAPTER 5

Pharmacy as a Profession

Let us take a view of the relative position of the dispenser and the community or neighborhood in which he is located. When an apothecary shop is opened, the proprietor tacitly, if not verbally, announces that he has prepared himself with the knowledge, skill, and material required to perform the responsible duties that appertain to his vocation: each family around him has a direct interest in the truthfullness of this annunciation as, sooner or later, all may be brought to the necessity of testing it practically. The nature of this knowledge and material is but obscurely understood by them; the pure and the impure, the inert and the poisonous, the true and the genuine, may be taken by each family in the confidence they repose in the ability and honesty of their dispenser. Gentlemen, mark this beautiful relationship! Reflect on the almost child-like reliance which sends the family messenger to you for aid for its afflicted member! How priceless is the value of a pharmaceutical reputation, when exalted by knowledge and skill adorned with conscientiousness and integrity; and with what jealous care it should be tended that its brightness be not tarnished (1).

These remarks, made by William Proctor to a graduating class of the Philadelphia College of Pharmacy over 125 years ago, are characteristic of exhortations to professionalism made every spring in commencement addresses to new cadres of fledgling pharmacists. The process of becoming a professional begins even earlier, of course, when students first enter a school of pharmacy. They are encouraged to dress professionally, think professionally, and act professionally. The socialization process includes joining and supporting the Student American Pharmaceutical Association, as well as other professional organizations and fraternities. At many schools academic discipline is in the hands of students, governed by an honors code that is analogous to the code of ethics that will guide professional conduct in practice through self-regulation.

The curriculum itself is a major factor in the development of professionalism. Here students are given the specialized knowledge that will set them apart both from laymen and other health professionals. The curriculum is based on agreed upon expectations of competencies needed in practice (2). During the preclinical years, students move together through the same courses, sharing the same faculty, and seldom mixing with students in other programs. During the clinical years, interaction with patients and other health professionals is carefully supervised by faculty preceptors or docents. At graduation, the class is further bonded by accepting the Pharmacist's Oath, thereby publicly professing dedication to the ideals of the profession:

> At this time, I vow to devote my professional life to the service of mankind through the profession of pharmacy.
> I will consider the welfare of humanity and relief of human suffering my primary concerns.
> I will use my knowledge and skills to the best of my ability in serving the public and other health professionals.
> I will do my best to keep abreast of developments and maintain professional competency to my profession of pharmacy.
> I will obey the laws governing the practice of pharmacy and will support enforcement of such laws.
> I will maintain the highest standards of moral and ethical conduct.
> I will take these vows voluntarily with the full realization of the trust and responsibility with which I am empowered by the public.
> American Association of Colleges of Pharmacy

Now graduates are further tested for competence and acceptance into the profession by sitting for the board of pharmacy examination, authorized by society through state law, but very much a pharmacy-controlled experience. The profession develops the major portion of the examination through the National Association of Boards of pharmacy, and the local state board augments and administers it. Although state boards often include consumer members, pharmacists usually hold a clear majority. The state board examination serves not only to ensure standardization of training and competence, but it is a symbol of the power and control of the board over the practice of pharmacy and the pharmacy practitioner in society.

The Importance of Professionalism

It is not only pharmacy that is concerned with professionalism. Many occupations besides the traditionally accepted ones—medicine, law, the ministry—strive to have their status as professions endorsed by society. Workers such as airline pilots, teachers, accountants, nurses, and engineers often are preoccupied with the extent of their professional status.

The advantages of being accorded professional status are clear from the occupation's point of view. The professions have more control over their work. They determine, in large part, who will be admitted to practice, in what quantity, and under what conditions. Individual practitioners have considerable autonomy in practice, are respected by society, and often make more money than nonprofessionals.

Why is this so? What does society expect in return for the privileges granted? What needs are fulfilled by granting some occupations professional status?

The professions have developed around the provision of services that have three general characteristics (3):

1. They are central to important human values and are important services (e.g. health, education, religion, or welfare).
2. They require knowledge and skills that the typical user does not have (e.g. ability to diagnose disease, fly a plane, or defend against a lawsuit).
3. They are personal services that must be adapted to the needs of individual clients; they are unstandardized (e.g. surgery, pastoral counseling, or tax advice).

In the absence of professionalism, individuals who need services with these characteristics might be at the mercy of incompetents or charlatans. Not only would they not have the knowledge necessary to evaluate the performance of the provider, but the circumstances of seeking the service likely would place the clients at a disadvantage because of emotional distress over the problem requiring the service. Persons who are ill or who have an ill child are vulnerable and need assurance that the services offered to help them are appropriate and of suitable quality.

The solution of society has been to foster professions. If laymen do not have the requisite specialized knowledge to evaluate professional behavior, they must turn to the profession itself to guarantee the integrity of its members. Since the services rendered by professionals are tailored to the needs of individual clients, it is not possible to monitor every professional–client interaction. An implicit "covenant of trust" (4) must be established between the professional and the client to ensure an appropriate relationship. The professions are charged with developing the circumstances that will permit clients to enter into covenants of trust with confidence.

The professions do this by reaching agreement in their associations on the specific responsibilities and functions of their members; an example is the statement of standards of practice for the profession of pharmacy adopted by the American Association of Colleges of Pharmacy and the American Pharmaceutical Association (see Chapter 6). Training programs are established and operated by the professions to ensure that entrants into the field receive standardized curricula that will enable them to perform the agreed upon functions. Licensure and certification programs ensure that applicants who do not meet the professions' standards will be prohibited from practicing. Professional boards monitor practice and discipline practitioners violating accepted standards. And since much professional practice is carried out between individual client and individual practitioner in private, socialization and indoctrination to professional norms are essential to guarantee that standards are met even when no outsider will know if a lapse occurs.

Thus, by granting professions the advantages discussed earlier, society expects a great deal in return. Only when expectations are met in full will professional recognition and respect be the outcome.

Professions and Professionalism

The terms "profession" and "professionalism" are used in such widely varying contexts it is difficult to produce definitions that are relevant and widely accepted. The *Dictionary of the Social Sciences* defines professions as:

> . . . occupations which demand a highly specialized knowledge and skill acquired at least in part by courses of more or less theoretical nature and not by practice alone, tested by some other authorized institution, and conveying to the persons who possess them considerable authority in relation to "clients" (5).

Another approach to clarifying the meaning of profession is to select an occupation generally accepted as a profession and enumerating those elements that seem to contribute to its professional status. Medicine is often the prototype chosen. The following elements emerge as characteristics of an occupation considered to be a profession:

1. Provides socially necessary and important functions
2. Encompasses a body of specialized knowledge and skills requiring advanced theoretical training
3. Renders an individualized, unstandardized service directly to clients
4. Provides autonomy for the definition, organization, and performance of work
5. Internally controls the behavior of its practitioners

6. Has a formal organization, a code of ethics, and licensure requirements

Many occupations may have one or two of these characteristics, but professional status and the ability to exert recognized professional authority require that most or all be present. Occupations can influence many of these elements themselves, and thus the professional status of specific occupations may change over time. Professionalization has been referred to as a "dynamic process whereby many occupations can be observed to change certain crucial characteristics in the direction of a 'profession,' even though some of these may not move very far in this direction" (6). In an effort to determine a standard time sequence for professionalization, one author described the:

> ... typical process by which the established professions have arrived; men begin doing the work full time and stake out a jurisdiction; the early masters of the technique or adherents of the movement become concerned about standards of training and practice and set up a training school, which, if not lodged in universities at the outset, makes academic connection within two or three decades; the teachers and activists then achieve success in promoting more effective organization, first local, then national—through either the transformation of an existing occupational association or the creation of a new one. Toward the end, legal protection of the monopoly of skill appears; at the end, a formal code of ethics is adopted (7).

The Pharmacy Profession

Events in the history of pharmacy have followed the general sequence presented above:

1. 1646—Became a full-time occupation
2. 1821—First United States training program established
3. 1821—First local professional association established
4. 1850—Formal code of ethics established
5. 1852—First national professional association established
6. 1868—First university-based educational program established
7. 1874—First state licensure law established

In several ways, however, pharmacy has fallen short of attaining full professional status and authority. For one thing, it only shares authority over drug use with prescribers, often leading to conflict and inability to act unilaterally in areas of presumed expertise. Even in settings where pharmacists and physicians work closely together in the care of patients, i.e. hospital wards, ambulatory clinics, and HMOs, areas of responsibility and authority must be negotiated individually. Professional recognition often depends as much upon the pharmacist's interpersonal skills as it does on the inherent characteristics of pharmacy.

Sociologists Denzin and Mettlin have argued that pharmacy has failed to achieve full professional status because of a "failure to gain control over the social object [the drug]" (8). Viewing the drug as a product rather than an object toward which their services are directed forces pharmacists to violate some of the basic rules of being professional. Pharmacists become agents through which the drug may be obtained rather than individuals who contribute greatly needed professional service.

Pharmacists have not been vigorous in their efforts to gain this control even when the opportunity arises. Although organized pharmacy has been overwhelmingly successful in achieving the legal right to select the source of prescription drugs available from multiple sources (i.e. generics), empirical evidence indicates that community pharmacists exert this authority in a very small proportion of cases. This behavior is inconsistent with that of other occupations, which typically seize every opportunity to gain further professional autonomy.

Balanced against the evidence showing a certain reluctance toward an expanded role in drug therapy must be the official positions taken by the professional associations representing pharmacy. Among the generally "progressive" steps taken have been the following:

1. Change in the Code of Ethics of the APhA to eliminate the restriction against "counter prescribing" (recommending a nonprescription drug for a common ailment)
2. Change in APhA policy which has been interpreted to mean that pharmacy now views its public health role to encompass *any* activities "necessary to fulfill pharmacists' professional responsibilities to the patients they serve" (9).

On the other hand, official policies of segments of the profession do not always agree. When the American Association of Colleges of Pharmacy considered expanding pharmacy education to a mandatory Doctor of Pharmacy (Pharm.D.) degree, this move was supported by the APhA and American Society of Hospital Pharmacists, but opposed by the National Association of Retail Druggists as well as the organizations representing drug manufacturers and wholesalers.

Such diversity within the ranks almost certainly slows developments more than would a unity of purpose. It is not necessarily unexpected, however. Denzin and Mettlin note "that contrary to current functionalist arguments, professions are not homogeneous, static institutions or groupings of persons sharing the same title. They are, rather, moving, shifting, splitting, assimilating bodies of persons held together at one point in time by a common name or label" (8, p 357). That this observation is true for pharmacy is attested to by the findings and conclusions of the Study Commission on Pharmacy in the United States. One of these conclusions reads as follows:

> . . . a pharmacist must be defined as an individual who is engaged in *one of the steps of a system called pharmacy*. We cannot define a pharmacist simply as one who practices pharmacy. Rather, he must be defined as one who practices a *part* of pharmacy which is determined by the activities carried on in one of the subsystems of pharmacy. A pharmacist is characterized by the common denominator of drug knowledge *and the differentiated additional knowledge and skill* required by his particular role (10).

The Commission concluded further: "Pharmacy is today, and will be in the future, a differentiated profession." There are three categories of such differentiation:

1. Minimal differentiation without appreciable difference in pharmacy knowledge and skill. The setting of practice and the associated differences in activities may be the sole distinction (e.g. staff pharmacist in a general hospital vs. staff pharmacist in a nursing home).
2. Substantial difference in the *character* of pharmacy knowledge and skill, i.e. both may be highly competent, perhaps with advanced training, but in different areas of specialization (e.g. nuclear pharmacist vs. drug information pharmacist).
3. Significant differences in the *amount, complexity, and sophistication of total professional knowledge and its consequent skills* (e.g. Pharm.D.-trained pharmacist vs. B.S.-trained pharmacist) (10, pp 108–109).

Another frequently debated issue related to pharmacists' professional status is the commercial setting in which much of pharmacy is practiced. The business and professional concerns of the pharmacist may often conflict, and these conflicts can cause ambiguity in the way clients view pharmacists. Francke places the blame for this problem squarely on the modern United States retail drugstore:

> The public can associate neither the drugstore nor the pharmacist in it as serving the health needs of society. It cannot esteem a man who works in such an environment; he may sell a health-related product—but he is not accepted as a member of a health profession. Rather, such pharmacists stand outside the boundary of the

profession—theirs indeed is a marginal profession—made marginal by the environment in which they practice. It is the drugstore which debases the profession of pharmacy in America (11).

More specific examples of potential and real professional-business conflicts surround the product lines carried by pharmacies. Individual pharmacists have generated considerable publicity by discontinuing to sell cigarettes or other products deemed inconsistent with the health role of the pharmacist. The very fact that such decisions prompt extensive coverage in the press is evidence that the professional role of the pharmacist is not fully accepted by society.

Health Professions—A Special Case?

A word or two might be devoted to the issue of whether the health professions are somehow *special*, i.e. requiring behaviors and values from their members which are unique. Dr. Edmund Pellegrino, an eminent physician philosopher, argues forcefully that this is indeed the case (12). His arguments, summarized, are as follows:

1. The health professions exist because there is illness.
2. The "ill" person suffers an attack on his "wholeness," his humanity, often his very identity.
3. Voluntarily or not, because of a lack of knowledge and skills necessary to effect a cure, the patient is forced to place himself under the care of another (the health professional) who has these skills, but who may also do harm.
4. This vulnerability is unique in that a lack of health robs the individual of the ability to deal with his other vulnerabilities, e.g. loss of freedom.
5. Health professionals *profess*. They "declare aloud" that they have the requisite skills, can heal or help, and will do so in the patient's best interest.
6. All health professionals, including pharmacists, make this profession when they graduate, enter practice, and, most importantly, in each patient encounter.

Given these arguments, health professionals (pharmacists) have three basic obligations:

1. To *be* competent, since they have professed to be
2. To use this competence in the best interests of the patient
3. To ensure that the patient has adequate information to inform the professional what those interests are

Professionals in Organizations

In the early days most pharmacists, as well as other professionals, worked as solo practitioners, in total control of their own work. As time progressed, more and more professionals began to work for organizations, and today the majority of workers in many professions are employees. Examples include engineers, airline pilots, college teachers, and attornies. In many instances these organizations are not just partnerships or group practices but very large organizations such as hospitals, industrial corporations, nationwide drug chains, or the federal government. Even medicine, the last bastion of private practitioners, has changed dramatically. Physicians increasingly are found practicing in organizations such as HMOs, free-standing urgent visit clinics, and corporate, for-profit hospital chains.

Pharmacy has become a profession of employees. A clear majority of pharmacy practitioners now are employed by chain or large independent community pharmacies, hospitals, academia, or industry. The era of the corner drugstore—owned and operated by the proprietor alone —has long passed.

Since a hallmark of the professional is autonomy—the ability to control one's own work—why do professionals choose to join organizations that may limit or attempt to limit autonomy? Why have so many pharmacists given up the freedom of operating their own pharmacies to become employees of larger organizations? There are many reasons. A solo practitioner may not have the resources to practice independently. The cost of opening a new pharmacy is high, as is the risk. Tasks may be involved in operating independently that a professional does not wish to undertake. A pharmacist may wish to devote full time to working in a prescription department and not spend time managing the front end of a typical pharmacy. In addition, large organizations may help professionals obtain clients, as well as provide the opportunity for collaboration with colleagues. Continuing education and interchange of ideas are other motivating factors (13).

Organizations employing large groups of professionals must realize that a special bureaucratic structure is required to avoid conflict between professional goals and organizational objectives. As Blau points out, "research indicates that a professional orientation toward service and a bureaucratic orientation toward disciplined compliance with procedures are opposite approaches toward work and often create conflict in organizations" (14).

These conflicts arise in pharmacy organizations such as chains and hospitals when management attempts to redefine professional activities, such as dispensing, as purely technical activities that can be organized in an assembly line fashion. Measuring output only by counting prescriptions dispensed per day is a frequent bone of contention between managers and practicing pharmacists. The pharmacy profession especially is vulnerable to this sort of approach because of its involvement with a product—the drug—that is costly to the organization and demands control. Thus, formulary decisions and inventory management decisions tend to be made centrally, often without consulting the pharmacists who must deal with patients and physicians.

It is little wonder that many employee pharmacists are frustrated in their jobs, especially with those functions technical in nature. Some of these frustrations have been articulated in a recent Viewpoint column in American Pharmacy (15).

When functions that involve professional judgments are concerned, however, there is relatively little that the organization can do to control professional autonomy totally. Professionals, by definition, are in the best position to carry out their unstandardized work. Those characteristics of a professional, such as the possession of specialized, advanced knowledge and skills, and the necessity of applying that knowledge in individual client situations combine to give professionals more control over their activities than most employees in large organizations. If the organization tries to limit the professional's autonomy too much, or inappropriately, the skills are usually in enough demand to permit the employee to move to another position. This is one of the effects of the ability of professions to control entry into the profession through licensure. When the supply of manpower is low, salaries will be higher and individual professionals will have more control of their work situation, whether or not it is with a large organization.

Problems of Professions

All occupations, including the professions, face a variety of problems that affect their members and strain the fabric of the occupation. These problems include interprofessional jurisdictional disputes, changes in societal views of the profession, the impact of technology, and internal strains due to the evolution of practice and the resultant differences in education, skills, and attitudes within the same profession. Each of these problems will be discussed in the context of the profession of pharmacy.

Interprofessional Disputes

It was stated earlier that pharmacy often gets into jurisdictional disputes with other occupations over the control of drugs. The function of drug prescribing is fiercely guarded by physicians, even in the face of evidence that under some conditions pharmacists can do it better. Although the law permits pharmacists to select the product dispensed from among generic equivalents, many physicians believe that they should be the ones to designate the specific product dispensed. This view is shared by the Pharmaceutical Manufacturers Association and by many pharmacists.

Selection of therapeutic alternatives is a related issue that is receiving increased consideration. This proposal would permit pharmacists not only to select from among generically equivalent products, but also from among drugs with essentially similar therapeutic effects. That is, if a physician were to prescribe cephalexin, the pharmacist would be able to substitute a different cephalosporin, or even another type of antimicrobial, if deemed appropriate. Needless to say, this proposal has created much controversy between medicine and pharmacy.

Jurisdictional disputes can work in the other direction. As the supply of physicians increases and the competition for patients increases, some physicians have taken to dispensing many of their own prescriptions. Physicians now can obtain the drugs they most frequently use in prepackaged, unit-of-use sizes that require only a label before dispensing to a patient. Pharmacy argues that to combine prescribing with dispensing is to create a conflict of interest not in the best interest of the patient.

Changing Societal Views

Changes in the way in which society views the professions can have an impact on the professions' structure and functioning. Whereas much of the power of the professions flows from the willingness of society to give it up, society can reclaim part of the power if it wishes. The consumer movement of the 1970s and the self-care movement of the 1980s are examples of society desiring a share in decision making, once considered the exclusive domain of medicine and pharmacy. Modern patients are better educated than ever before and are more knowledgeable about the drugs they take. They seek more information about their therapy from physicians and pharmacists and often seek a larger role in decision making about their treatment. This often can be threatening to physicians and pharmacists, especially older pharmacists trained in the days when giving the patient information actually was proscribed by the code of ethics.

Today, consumers are often represented on boards of pharmacy, and drug manufacturers routinely take their messages directly to patients through the mass media. Even prescription drugs now are being advertised directly to consumers, and the *Physicians' Desk Reference* is a bestseller in the nation's bookstores.

Some critics have challenged the notion that professions should be permitted to regulate themselves. They believe that more harm than good has come from the practice and that self-regulation does more to stifle competition and remove incentives for quality than the reverse. In a recent book Gross cites an extensive bibliography to support his case that professional licensure does not improve the quality of services rendered or protect the public health (16). Noted economist Milton Friedman has advocated abolishing professional licensure and permitting the market system to drive incompetent practitioners from the professions (17). In 1967 economist Marion Fletcher published an entire book cataloging the ways he believed professional control of individual and business licensing in pharmacy contributed to restraint of trade (18).

The Impact of Technological Change

Technological change can wreak havoc on any occupational group not prepared to deal with it, and has been responsible for complete extinction of some. Certainly, the functions of pharmacy have undergone significant change during the last 40 years, largely because of a revolution in the manufacture and distribution of drugs; a massive expansion in the number, range of uses, and potency of drugs; and an explosion of information about drug therapy coupled with the arrival of computer technology to help deal with it.

Much of the craft of pharmacy, that is, the art of compounding individual dosage forms for individual patients, has largely disappeared. Fewer than 2% of outpatient prescriptions are compounded today; most drug products reach the consumer in dosage forms prefabricated by the manufacturer. Even the packaging functions that once consumed much of pharmacist's time have been almost eliminated. The old saw of "count, pour, lick, and stick" is as outdated as last year's catchphrase. Counting and pouring have been eliminated by unit-of-use packaging or Coulter Counters, and licking and sticking (and even typing) have been eliminated by computer-generated, self-sticking prescription labels. It is no wonder that some practitioners are concerned about these changes!

Advances in the biomedical sciences have laid the groundwork for hundreds of new drugs with potential for a major impact on health and disease. Aiding physicians and patients in the proper selection and use of these agents is a significant and challenging role for the profession of pharmacy. As the Study Commission pointed out in the quote cited earlier in this chapter (reference 10), pharmacy is now defined by its application of drug knowledge, not only by its craft in manufacturing drug products.

Along with the advances in drug products and therapy comes an explosion of information needs about both the products and the patients who will use them. Modern pharmacists have witnessed an astonishing increase in the amount of information they are expected to be able to use and apply. They must cope not only with the complexity of the information itself, but also with the computer technology that makes it available. Pharmacists now can access extensive data bases through the same microcomputer that maintains their patient records and prints their labels. Cable television and a proliferation of new journals add to the information flow.

Internal Strains on the Profession of Pharmacy

The changes discussed above must be absorbed and dealt with by a profession made up of pharmacists of widely varying educational backgrounds and orientations. Practicing pharmacists today may have completed college educations from 2 to 7 or more years. These individuals have chosen pharmacy for widely differing reasons and practice in a multitude of occupational environments. Many pharmacists have entered pharmacy to be small businessmen (or big businessmen) without much of a commitment to professional ideals. Others may have difficulty coping with almost incomprehensible changes in the field.

One way professions deal with changes of this magnitude is to differentiate internally, that is, form specialties within the profession. This has been true of pharmacy. Groups of pharmacists with similar duties and interests have formed organizations and developed requirements and competencies for membership or practice in certain areas. These arrangements are informal and do not include legal sanctioning through licensure.

The most formal process for achieving specialty status within pharmacy was established by the APhA in 1977. APhA's Board of Pharmaceutical Specialties has developed criteria for defining specialties and reviews petitions from groups of pharmacists desiring specialty recognition. To date, nuclear pharmacy is the only specialty to receive formal recognition.

Some of the efforts at specialization resemble the professionalization process itself and may one day result in the creation or splitting off of new professions. For example, pharmacists graduating recently with Doctor of Pharmacy degrees and practicing a type of pharmacy focused on patient and physician consultation on drug use, usually in institutional settings, are taking on some of the hallmarks of a new profession.

These practitioners define a set of functions distinct from traditional dispensing and require an education program with a different focus. An organization, the American College of Clinical Pharmacy, has been formed, and it is preparing a petition for specialty status for the Board of Pharmaceutical Specialties. Compare these steps with those discussed earlier in the chapter as characteristic of the development of a profession.

The existence of subgroups within pharmacy, both by area of specialization and across generations, has resulted in strains on the profession as a whole. Many specialized organizations vie for the membership of individual pharmacists and are devoted to pursuing specific aims that are frequently at odds with each other. Society often is given the impression that pharmacy is a profession of fragmented goals and positions. While this is true, it is a situation that is shared to a great extent by most professions, especially during periods of turbulent change.

Laypersons' Views of Professions and Pharmacy

Laypersons do not look at occupations from a scientific, sociological viewpoint, trying to categorize them as professions by applying a complex set of criteria. The layperson's view is more of a "folk concept," a set of popularized conceptions of what an occupation has to do to be given the honorific symbol of "profession." Sociologist Becker defines this symbol as:

> . . . a set of ideas about the kind of work done by a real profession, its relations with members of other professions, the internal relations of its own members, its relations with clients and the general public, the character of its own members' motivations, and the kind of recruitment and training necessary for its perpetuation (18).

It is the nature of such a folk concept that its elements are seldom vocalized by the layperson except in protest against "unprofessional activities." Further, because adherence by an emerging profession to professional guidelines by definition lacks public visibility, the response of laypersons in recognizing such adherence lags behind the performance itself. Thus, professionals often are frustrated by a lack of recognition by laypersons.

The most important way in which the views of laypersons can be influenced is their personal experiences with pharmacists. If in their day-to-day dealings with patients pharmacists demonstrate technical expertise and provide services consistent with the patients' views of professional services, the pharmacists will be deemed professional. In other words, it is the collective judgment of laypersons that, in the final judgment, determines whether or not an occupation is a profession.

Some evidence of how the public views pharmacy is offered by public opinion polls conducted by Gallup in the 1980s. Over 1500 adults were asked to rate 25 occupations with regard to honesty and ethical standards. Pharmacists placed second only to clergymen in three separate polls (see Table 5.1).

Summary

From well before the time when its students first graduated from a college-level program to the complex times of today, pharmacy has been fascinated with its professional status. Such a fascination is not uncommon since the benefits of being professional are significant—power, authority, respect, control, and autonomy. The responsibilities also are significant—achieving and maintaining a high level of technical knowledge and expertise, and applying those skills in the best interest of their clients. The health professions must take these responsibilities especially seriously.

Most modern pharmacists are not independent practitioners, but rather are employees of large organizations. This need not be a major disadvantage since the nature of professional activities requires a different form of bureaucratic organization. Standardized training and socialization to the norms of the profession are more important to the maintenance of quality than direct supervision.

All occupations, including pharmacy, are faced with a variety of problems affecting their members and causing strain on the occupation itself. The most important for pharmacy include interprofessional jurisdictional disputes with medicine, the impact of technological changes, changing societal views, and internal conflicts leading to splintering.

In the final analysis, it is the public that decides if an occupation is a profession. In the case of pharmacy, the decision rests on the quality of each individual patient-practitioner interaction.

Table 5.1.
Honesty and Ethical Standards Ratings of 25 Occupations[a]

Honesty and Ethical Standards

	Very high, high			Average			Low, very low			No opinion		
	'85	'83	'81	'85	'83	'81	'85	'83	'81	'85	'83	'81
Clergymen	67%	64%	63%	26%	27%	28%	4%	4%	6%	3%	5%	3%
Druggists, pharmacists	65%	61%	59%	30%	33%	33%	3%	4%	5%	2%	2%	3%
Medical doctors	58%	52%	50%	33%	35%	38%	8%	11%	10%	1%	2%	2%
Dentists	56%	51%	52%	37%	41%	38%	5%	5%	7%	2%	3%	3%
College teachers	54%	47%	45%	35%	38%	36%	5%	5%	8%	6%	10%	11%
Engineers	53%	45%	48%	37%	39%	35%	3%	3%	5%	7%	13%	12%
Policemen	47%	41%	44%	41%	45%	41%	10%	11%	13%	2%	3%	2%
Bankers	37%	38%	39%	51%	49%	47%	9%	9%	10%	3%	4%	4%
TV reporters, commentators	33%	33%	36%	48%	47%	45%	15%	15%	15%	4%	5%	4%
Funeral directors	31%	29%	30%	45%	43%	41%	15%	19%	19%	9%	9%	10%
Journalists	31%	28%	32%	47%	47%	44%	17%	17%	15%	5%	8%	9%
Newspaper reporters	29%	26%	30%	52%	52%	49%	16%	16%	16%	3%	6%	5%
Lawyers	27%	24%	25%	40%	43%	41%	30%	27%	27%	3%	6%	7%
Business executives	23%	18%	19%	54%	55%	53%	18%	20%	19%	5%	7%	9%
Senators	23%	16%	20%	53%	55%	50%	21%	30%	25%	3%	6%	5%
Building contractors	20%	18%	19%	53%	48%	48%	21%	23%	27%	6%	6%	6%
Congressmen	20%	14%	15%	49%	43%	47%	27%	38%	32%	4%	5%	6%
Stockbrokers	20%	19%	21%	51%	45%	46%	10%	11%	7%	19%	25%	26%
Local political officeholders	18%	16%	14%	53%	49%	51%	24%	29%	30%	5%	6%	5%
State political officeholders	15%	13%	12%	55%	49%	50%	24%	31%	30%	6%	7%	8%
Realtors	15%	13%	14%	49%	52%	48%	31%	28%	30%	5%	7%	8%
Labor union leaders	13%	12%	14%	35%	35%	29%	45%	44%	48%	7%	9%	9%
Advertising practitioners	12%	9%	9%	42%	42%	41%	39%	39%	38%	7%	10%	12%
Insurance salesmen	10%	13%	11%	49%	49%	49%	38%	34%	36%	3%	4%	4%
Car salesmen	5%	6%	6%	32%	34%	33%	59%	55%	55%	4%	5%	6%

[a]Data obtained from Gallup polls. As presented in *Pharmacy Times* 51(10):1, 1985.

REFERENCES

1. Proctor W, Jr.: Advice to young pharmacists. *J Am Pharm Assoc* NS13:316, 1962.
2. Standards of practice for the profession of pharmacy. *Am Pharm* NS19:136–145, 1979.
3. Larsen MS: *The Rise of Professionalism*. Berkeley, CA, University of California Press, 1977.
4. Hepler CD: Pharmacy as a clinical profession. *Am J Hosp Pharm* 42:1298–1306, 1985.
5. Gould J, Kobb WL: *A Dictionary of the Social Sciences*. New York, The Free Press, 1964, p 542.
6. Vollmer HL, Mills DL: *Professionalization*. Englewood Cliffs, NJ, Prentice-Hall, Inc., 1966, pp vii–viii.
7. Wilensky HL: The professionalization of everyone. *Am J Sociol* 60:145–146, 1964.
8. Denzin NR, Mettlin CJ: Incomplete professionalization: The case of pharmacy. *Soc Forces* 46:357, 1968.
9. Report of the policy committee on professional affairs. *J Am Pharm Assoc* NS18:37, 1978.
10. Study Commission on Pharmacy: *Pharmacists for the Future*. Ann Arbor, MI, Health Administration Press, 1975, p 140.
11. Francke DE: Let's separate pharmacies and drugstores. *Am J Pharm* 141:161–176, 1969.
12. Pellegrino EE: Toward a reconstruction of medical morality: The privacy of the act of profession and the fact of illness. *J Med Phil* 4:46, 1979.
13. Mintzberg H: The professional bureaucracy. In *The Structuring of Organizations*. Englewood Cliffs, NJ, Prentice-Hall, Inc., 1979, pp 357–358.
14. Blau PM: The hierarchy of authority in organizations. *Am J Sociol* 63:453–467, 1967.
15. Viewpoint: Frustrations of an employee pharmacist. *Am Pharm* NS24:234–235, 1984.
16. Gross SJ: *Of Foxes and Hen Houses: Licensing and the Health Professions*. Westport, CT, Quorum Books, 1984.
17. Blockstein WL: Reassessing the need for licensure of health professionals. *Am J Hosp Pharm* 42:2060–2069, 1985.
18. Fletcher FM: *Market Restraints in the Retail Drug Industry*. Philadelphia, University of Pennsylvania Press, 1967.

CHAPTER 6

Pharmacy Settings and Types of Practice

All we do is count pills. Count out twelve on the counter, put'em in here, count out twelve more. . . . Today was a little out of the ordinary. I made an ointment. Most of the ointments come already made up. This doctor was an old-timer. He wanted something with sulfur and two other elements mixed together. So I have to weigh it out on the scale. Ordinarily I would just have one tube of cream for that.

Doctors used to write out their own formulas and we made most of these things. Most of the work is now done in the laboratory. The real druggist is found in the manufacturing firms. They're the factory workers and they're the pharmacists. We just get the name of the drugs and the number and the directions. It's a lot easier. In the old days you filled maybe twenty, twenty-five prescriptions a day by hand. Nowadays you can fill about 150. This time of the year they're most antibiotics, because people are having colds.

In the old days we just used simple drugs, simple ointment base like Vaseline, lanolin and mixed them together. They didn't have the properties that you find today. You're really an order filler now.(Laughs.)I'm not knockin' the pharmacist, but it's got so highly developed. . . . We just dispense, that's all.

I like it better this way. If you had to make up everything and the physician had to write down a prescription with all the ingredients, you could hardly exist in this economy. Everything is faster, it's better. People wouldn't get relief out of medicine in them days like they get today.

*Pharmacist Nino Giudici
in* Working, *by Studs Terkel*[1]

Methods of Drug Distribution

Prescription Drugs

The system of distribution of prescription drugs is both very simple and very complex. In its most rudimentary form this distribution finds the drug manufactured by the pharmaceutical firm, sold directly to the pharmacist, and, following the physician's prescription, dispensed to the patient. A more traditional form of drug distribution places the wholesaler as an agent between the manufacturer and the pharmacist. As simple as these channels of distribution appear, the relationships among them have grown quite complicated.

The manufacturers, wholesalers, and pharmacists have all traditionally

---

[1] Terkel S: *Working: People Talk About What They Do All Day and How They Feel About What They Do.* New York, Pantheon Books, a Division of Random House, Inc., 1974, p.313. Reprinted with permission.

119

been thought of as one loosely connected "pharmaceutical industry." Conversely, the manufacturers and wholesalers have, equally traditionally, been considered an integral part of "pharmacy." In recent years, partly because of major changes in the complexion of the drug manufacturing component and the drug wholesalers and partly because of changes within pharmacy practice, the old "all for one, one for all" atmosphere seems to be disappearing.

The United States Census of Manufacturers reports that there are nearly 1000 manufacturers of prescription drugs in the United States. The Pharmaceutical Manufacturers Association, which numbers something over 200 members, refers to itself as "representing pharmaceutical companies that produce more than 95 per cent of U. S. prescription drugs." What this means, of course, is that a small number of the drug manufacturers in the country supply by far the majority of the products dispensed in the country. This also means that hundreds of drug manufacturers must be quite small and that they must divide rather sparsely the remaining sales dollars. This concentration among a small percentage of firms is enhanced by the numbers of mergers and acquisitions continually taking place in the pharmaceutical industry.

Quite a number of the drug manufacturers were started by pharmacists in pharmacies. Among these are Eli Lilly & Company, E. R. Squibb Company, and others. Their alliance with and their allegiance to pharmacy was thus both natural and rather strong. With the growth of these companies, however, the injection of new leadership often without such roots in pharmacy practice, some of the old ties have become loosened.

The drug wholesaler has an important history in the development of pharmacy. Reference was made earlier to the fact that "the place of the wholesaler in the channel of distribution was traditional." In spite of this, the role of the wholesaler in prescription drug distribution has been by no means completely secure. In recent years numbers of drug manufacturers have changed their distribution policies to bypass the wholesaler and deal directly with the pharmacist. Faced with such loss of business, drug wholesalers have explored new ways of maintaining their viability. Among these have been the manufacture of their own line of prescription drugs, development of new forms of services including computer analysis, pharmacy modernization, and others, as well as consolidation of operations, mergers, and acquisitions.

The Study Commission on Pharmacy (Millis Commission) has pointed out that "pharmacy is still the compounding and dispensing of drugs" (1). Their "two parts" of pharmacy has been described as consisting of the following series of steps, which obviously involve *all* aspects of the drug industry.

1. Compounding
   a. Discovery or invention
   b. Formulation
   c. Safety
   d. Efficacy
   e. Manufacture

2. Dispensing
   a. Product distribution
   b. Prescription filling
   c. Delivery to patients
   d. Drug administration

Pharmacy differs from most of the professions in that, until recently, the two major types of practice have been identified more often in terms of their physical setting than by the nature of the activities performed. Thus we have "retail druggists" and "hospital pharmacists." There are some changes underway in the nomenclature of pharmacy practice but, as we shall see in this chapter, the change is by no means complete.

A major effort has been underway in recent years to replace the term "retail druggist" with "community pharmacist" and "drugstore" with "pharmacy," and indeed to eliminate the use of the term "druggist" completely. While some progress has been made in this direction, large portions of the lay public continue to use this terminology, and the two major trade organizations in pharmacy refer to themselves respectively as the National Association of *Retail Druggists* and the National Association of Chain *Drug Stores*.

Although they are difficult to quantify, there are probable advantages to these proposed changes in nomenclature, and we use them generally in this text. Much more important, of course, are the changes in the nature and types of practice of pharmacy regardless of the name or setting. Some of these changes are being brought about within pharmacy and result from efforts toward the professionalization process. Others are reflections of changes elsewhere in the health care system.

It has been stated that it is no longer possible for a single medical practitioner operating a solo practice to provide comprehensive medical care for his patients. It seems apparent that the days of medicine as a lifetime relationship between one general practitioner and one patient are over. The physician who works alone is increasingly an anachronism. More and more he depends upon other health professionals for assistance in total patient care. The combined effects of these changes in the system have ranged from salutary to disastrous for pharmacy, depending upon who is evaluating the changes. The same reorganization of medical care that is upsetting the physician-pharmacist-patient relationship of the past, for example, is also placing the pharmacist (sometimes in new settings) in positions of greater responsibility and control.

One practicing pharmacist, Eugene White of Virginia, sees great opportunities for the community pharmacist in the changes taking place.

The new community pharmacist (preferably, the new family pharmacist) of the future will step up and into a new position of professional competence and importance. As the specialist in drug therapy, he will assume a comprehensive and continuing responsibility for *all* of the drug requirements of his patient. When the need arises for any drug therapy, the family physician, family dentist, or other specialist will refer his patient to the patient's pharmacist. Major responsibility in patient care is, for a time, transferred to another specialist, the pharmacist. He will follow through to the termination of drug therapy, being completely responsible for prescribing the drug of choice for the particular diagnosis by the physician, maintaining constant surveillance over the drug action and application to ensure the desired effect, and being directly responsible for toxic or adverse drug reactions. In addition, the drug specialist will be the primary source of information in the drug experience reporting system.

The family pharmacist, by the very nature of his new function and role on the health care team, will know the complete drug history of his patient and his hypersensitivities or idiosyncrasies. This vital knowledge must not be restricted by the threshold of his office. If the family physician recommends hospitalization and drugs are required, the patient's family pharmacist will continue his team role at the hospital or extended care facility. He will work cooperatively with the physician, intern, medical specialist, and, perhaps, a specialist in a pharmacy field (2).

Pharmacist White's predictions, made during the mid 1960s, have yet to gain widespread application, yet each of them has now been tried, at least experimentally. All give promise of acceptance in the 1980s and 1990s.

Community Pharmacy Practice

Independent Practice

The stereotype of pharmacy practice held in the first half of the twentieth century was surely that of the "corner drugstore." It would be a shame to lose our recollection of that institution, yet it certainly constitutes a vanishing minority of independent community pharmacies. The somewhat mixed emotions that memories of the corner drugstore evoke were well summarized in a 1984 article in the *Journal of the American Medical Association*. It is reprinted here in its entirety.

The day of the "corner drugstore" is past. In some ways that's too bad. The drugstore was a pleasant place to visit. The graceful glass containers filled with red, green, and lavender liquid gave promise of the mysterious syrups and elixirs that were dispensed. As we entered yesterday's apothecary, our noses were greeted with indescribable aromas, medicinal and therefore curative. The friendly druggist, known to the townspeople as "Doc," was always ready to dispense pills, potions, and kindly advice.

Old Doc had an air of mystery about him. He was able to decipher your physician's Latin scrawl, which he would study intently. Then he'd nod his head knowingly and retire to his inner sanctum to concoct the lifesaving medicament. If we chose to wait while the druggist worked his legerdemain, we would hear a scraping sound as pestle greeted mortar, or the gurgle of liquid as it was decanted into bottles, then the rustle of papers, as "powders" were folded into single-dose packets.

We knew not what these bottles or packets contained, nor did we wish to know. Part of the magic lay in our blind faith that what the doctor prescribed and the druggist compounded would promptly effect a cure.

This was the "corner drugstore." It was a haven for the sick and the disabled. On the shelves were neat rows of wide-mouthed jars containing peculiar labels—from arnica to orrisroot, from pepsin to nux vomica. The walls were hung with crutches and canes, trusses and back braces, and, oh yes, enamelware bedpans and urinals.

Out front there was a marble-countered soda fountain from which a smiling, chubby young boy or girl would dispense double-thick chocolate malts, priced 15 cents, or a new 5-cent drink called Coca-Cola, stirred to a creamy foam in a glass with that distinctive slender waist.

Now the corner drugstore is gone. Today's counterpart is most often located not on a corner, but in a shopping mall or in a variety store, surrounded by all manner of merchandise, from foodstuff to garden hose. Because the word *drug* has earned an unsavory flavor, the drugstore now is a "pharmacy." The name and the location have changed—indeed, the personality of the place is totally different.

There are no mortar and pestle, no beaker and pipette. Little if any compounding is ever done. Just as peanut butter, crackers, and pickles are no longer dispensed from vats and barrels, so too the shelves of the modern pharmacy bear no bulk items but instead are lined with prepackaged, presealed, prelabeled pills and capsules, creams and ointments. Some of the medicinal mystery is gone, but there is a lot more scientific honesty.

The person behind the counter has also changed. Old Doc, the druggist of yesteryear, was often held in low esteem by the physician who wrote the prescription. It was common knowledge that the druggist learned his trade through a short apprenticeship, his knowledge limited to a cookbook of folksy pharmaceutical recipes. It was smilingly whispered around town that Doc probably tippled the stuff ordinarily used to make tinctures.

The pharmacist of today is a completely different person. Often young, often female—a highly trained professional, the product of an intensive course in an accredited school of pharmacy. Moreover, here is the physician's full partner in caring for the ill, one who has been given top rating in the public opinion polls.

As the complexity of the pharmaceutical repertoire has increased, and as the *Physician's Desk Reference*, with its listings of adverse reactions, drug interactions, complications, and contraindications, has burgeoned to over 2,000 pages, we, as physicians, have gained a new respect for pharmacists and have learned to depend on their specialized knowledge.

We know all too well that the pharmacist can catch a mental lapse on a written prescription, that he can spot the potential problem of a drug interaction, and that he can tip off the physician should there be misuse or overuse of a medication, or a lack of patient compliance. He can be our partner in patient education.

Faced with an almost daily barrage of fresh pharmaceuticals, each one more exotic than the last, physicians cannot escape the ever-increasing weight of responsibility concerning our prescribing practices. We need all the help we can get.

Yes, the colorful corner drugstore is a thing of the past. That's good (3).

The large majority of pharmacists still are practicing their profession in the community pharmacy setting, and these pharmacies are descendents of the corner drugstore of years past, although many bear little resemblance to that institution. Some "corner drugstores" remain, of course, particularly in the smaller towns. Today's independent community pharmacy is more likely to be a large, well-illuminated, busy place, with a number of employees and with annual receipts in the hundreds of thousands of dollars. Some idea of the growth that has taken place in the community pharmacy can be gained from the comparison of selected sales volumes shown below for the years 1969 and 1983. (These data are taken from the Annual Drugstore Sales Surveys of *Drug Topics* magazine.)

	1969	1983	Change
Prescriptions	$4,425,800,000	$16,705,982,000	+277%
Nonprescrip- tion drugs	1,696,360,000	4,250,850,000	+151%
Foot products	59,240,000	172,271,000	+191%
Baby needs	191,380,000	755,486,000	+295%
Feminine needs	160,200,000	356,127,000	+122%
First aid	126,100,000	568,295,000	+351%

Some interesting insights into the overall character of the drug store also can be gained from the following figures, which represent the 1983 average sales per drugstore in the specified categories.

Foods and beverages	$106,166
Photo products	41,520
Tobacco products	34,011
Magazines and books	31,034

The community pharmacies vary in size and apparently in philosophy of practice. The variety of merchandise, much of it completely unrelated to drugs or even to health care, in the pharmacy has been the subject of considerable humor in the past several years (see Fig. 6.1). Similarly, the soda fountain so dominated the image of the pharmacy at one point that comedians suggested students attend pharmacy school to learn how to prepare grilled cheese sandwiches.

Considerable non-health-related merchandise is offered still for sale in many independent pharmacies, although the soda fountain is no longer the hallmark that it once was. The real importance of the independent pharmacy lies in the ready availability of prescription and nonprescription drugs making its existence possible throughout the country. The real function of the pharmacist here must be, of course, meeting the drug and appropriate other health needs of the public.

Some pharmacists, in the face of criticism of the variety of merchandise offered for sale, have maintained that the so-called "front end" products must be sold in order that they might economically provide real pharmaceutical services. Critics have countered that if this argument is true, then there are simply too many pharmacies. Indeed, there may be too many in some places.

Brodie has described the status of the community pharmacist as:

> ... clouded because of commercial intrusions that have entered the community practice of pharmacy ... and the indulgence of pharmacists in nonprofessional activities. This dichotomy has caused many pharmacists who own pharmacies, by act and admission, to

Figure 6.1. "Grandpa, why do they call this a drug store?"

identify themselves as businessmen. Rarely can a man wear with distinction the hat of a professional one day and that of a business-man the next. As a result, the pharmacist is frustrated in trying to serve two masters, and the public must, at times, have difficulty in accepting professional health service in a commercial environment totally unrelated to health (4).

The dichotomy of business interests and professional pursuits (Fig. 6.2) results in many pharmacists spending substantial portions of time in nonpharmacy activity. It is to be hoped that the younger, clinically trained pharmacists will insist on spending the majority of their time in the practice of pharmacy.

Pharmaceutical Centers

That independent community pharmacy practice is possible without the sale of non-health-related merchandise is provided by the success in some locations of the pharmaceutical center concept. The pharmaceutical center was pioneered by E. V. White (5) in Virginia, and, with the encouragement of the APhA and wholesale drug firms, it has achieved acceptance in scores of communities.

In the pharmaceutical center only health-related items are stocked and no merchandise is displayed. Among the services provided are a complete file of all of the medication a patron or his family uses and ready advice for the family or its physician on the drug history of the family. A working library of current journals and basic reference books is maintained and provides the basis for a broad range of drug information services provided by the pharmacist.

Some 5 years after the pharmaceutical center was introduced, more than 200 were in operation. Each of these incorporates professional standards laid down by the APhA, including: no merchandise on display, a patient-pharmacist direct relationship, a family record system, a family health information center, a professional library and extensive reference files, institutional advertising only, a professional fee system, and a completely professional atmosphere (5).

In spite of the professional appeal of the pharmaceutical center concept, it is fair to say that the overall impact on the physical appearance of community pharmacy nationwide has been small. It is also fair to say, however, that the impact has been considerable on the nature of practice, especially with regard to patient medication profiles and counseling.

Evidence of this was provided by a 1984 research study by Macko-wiak and Manasse. In a study comparing office-based practice with traditional drug stores, they found that clients of the office practice had

Figure 6.2.   The pharmacist's dichotomous role.

Table 6.1.
Ten Years of Chain[a] Drug Growth[b]

| Year | Drugstore sales | | | Chain drug | | | Average |
	Chain	Non-chain (billions)	Total	Annual gain (%)	Share of market (%)	No. of units	sales per chain unit (thousands)
1983	$22.8	$16.9	$39.7	11	58	15,969	$1,427.8
1982	20.5	15.7	36.2	11	57	16,347	1,254.1
1981	18.5	14.9	33.4	12	55	14,664	1,261.6
1980	16.4	13.9	30.3	16	54	14,815	1,107.0
1979	14.2	13.0	27.2	17	52	15,110	939.8
1978	12.1	12.2	24.3	16	50	24,709	822.6
1977	10.4	11.7	22.2	14	47	14,530	715.8
1976	9.2	11.3	20.5	14	45	13,918	661.0
1975	8.1	10.7	18.8	14	45	13,705	591.0
1974	7.1	9.9	17.0	11	44	13,034	544.7

[a]Definition of chain is four or more stores.
[b]From: *Drug Store News* 6(10): April 30, 1984.

higher expectations of and higher levels of satisfaction with their pharmacy services. They also reported more frequent consultation with the pharmacist (6).

Chain Drugstores

No honest look at community pharmacy practice can ignore the growing importance of the chain organization. Table 6.1 provides some idea of the growth trend of the chain as a factor in the total volume activity in "retail" pharmacy.

Various definitions have been given for a chain, but reference by this term usually is made to multiple pharmacy, corporately owned organizations. It is also appropriate to refer to them as chain "drugstores" because this is how they refer to themselves and because as a general rule the image, appearance, and philosophy of the chains are better typified by the term "store" rather than "pharmacy." Many of the drugstore chains are owned by nonpharmacy individuals and corporations. Jewel Tea, Kroger, and J. C. Penney are a few of the organizations with substantial interest in drug chains. What has attracted these organizations to pharmacy? What is their approach to pharmacy? Here are the views of one chain executive.

At Revco, we have always felt that prescriptions are what brings people to a drug store. As a result, we have transformed prescriptions into both a professional and promotional category.... It's smart to treat pharmacy as a professional and promotional category. Moreover, we believe there's nothing wrong in this approach—provided that, in the process, we don't lose sight of the fact that the merchandise being sold is sold by a professional and, as such, is sold with professional advice, councel, and service, and in the professional environment that such products call for (7).

This quote highlights a major problem for pharmacy *vis-a-vis* the chains. The business/professional dichotomy is a structural part of the chain operation with the apparent attempt, often cited by chain executives, to both have the cake and eat it, that is, to somehow preserve the professionalism in pharmacy in an obviously, some might say blatantly, mass merchandising environment. Prescriptions have for many years accounted for less than one-fifth of the total dollar volume in chain pharmacies.

In preparing this edition of this book, the authors wrote letters to each of the 25 largest drugstore chains asking for copies of their policies relative to the practice of their pharmacy employees. Only two of the corporations replied, with Payless Drug Stores providing the only detailed response. Their statement on pharmacy ("The Pharmacy Profession") is reproduced here:

Pay Less Drug Stores is dedicated to supporting and advancing the profession of pharmacy. The effectiveness on the Nation's health care delivery system depends upon the growth of the pharmacy profession and its continued integration with the other health functions.

The pharmacist should gladly offer assistance as requested by prescribers and other health professionals as well as performing as a consultant to the individual customer. Pay Less pharmacists must become the focal point of drug information for all who are concerned with the utilization of their medications.

The profession of pharmacy is the cornerstone of Pay Less Drug Stores. Attention to the continued development of the pharmacist as a professional is not only a societal but also an economic necessity. Active membership and participation in local and State associations is urged of Pay Less pharmacists.

It is probably a mistake to view chain pharmacy operations as some sort of insidious encroachment aimed at destroying an honorable profession, although similar views have often been expressed by opponents of chain pharmacy. It is much more realistic to view the chains for what they are—corporate entrepreneurs (often but by no means always pharmacists) for whom the pharmacy department offers a financial opportunity. This view is supported by ventures by the chains into the professional fields of dentistry and optometry. Indeed, it has been suggested that the chains will look next at podiatrists, audiologists, clinical laboratories, and even physicians (8). One can scarely resist the temptation to use terms such as "McDruggist" and "McDoctor."

Recalling the earlier criticism of the "business" orientation of community pharmacy, it is well to examine Provost's view that "it is grossly unfair to equate 'commercialism' with chains and 'professionalism' in the independent practice of pharmacy." He cites as those responsible, "some educators who have failed to instill the professional ethic, chain executives and independent pharmacy owners who have degraded the profession, and employee pharmacists in all practice settings who have allowed themselves to become professionally subservient" (9).

Hospitals

The hospital has always held a great deal of popular fascination. In the early days when a hospital was simply the place where people went to die, it was a horrible fascination. Today it is one of wonder and perhaps awe. The hospital is the site of the heart transplant, of cobalt therapy, of kidney dialysis.

Hospitals have basic characteristics of organization which can affect pharmacy practice there. Among these are:

1. The nonprofit motive which characterizes the majority of hospitals (though that may be changing)
2. The interaction among a high concentration of professional, paraprofessional, and administrative personnel
3. The influence of external governing boards
4. The quality of authority (10)

These are some of the environmental factors enabling the hospital to perform its four basic functions:

1. A workshop for the physician
2. An education center
3. A center for medical research
4. A center for community health, care of ambulatory patients, and home care (11)

There are more than 20,000 pharmacists now employed full time in hospitals. In addition, many thousands more serve as consultants on a part-time basis for smaller hospitals.

Hospital pharmacists may provide drugs for patients within their institutions as well as for ambulatory patients through "outpatient pharmacies." Both of these are growing in importance in the total pharmacy picture.

The American Society of Hospital Pharmacists has adopted Guidelines on the Competencies Required in Institutional Pharmacy Practice in which it is stated that:

> ... the professional staff of the pharmacy department must have the ability to carry out collectively the following service functions:
> 1. Effective administration and management of a pharmacy department in an institution;
> 2. Assimilation and provision of comprehensive information on drugs and their actions;
> 3. Development and conduct of a product formulation and packaging program;
> 4. Conduct of and participation in research;
> 5. Development and conduct of patient-oriented services;
> 6. Conduct of and participation in educational activities;
> 7. Development and conduct of a quality assurance program for pharmaceutical services (12).

These competencies, described in detail in the Guidelines, define a comprehensive service model of professional pharmacy.

Whereas in the early days much of hospital pharmacy was characterized by inadequate physical facilities, little physician contact, and practically no involvement with the patient, this is no longer the case. Not only is the hospital the primary site for most of the current clinical training of pharmacy students, but hospital pharmacists are very much involved today in clinical pharmacy *practice* (13).

Other Types of Practice

The Consulting Pharmacist

Many pharmacists have found it possible to combine community and institutional practice via the role of consulting pharmacist. The Medicare regulations require that some pharmacy services be available, at least through the efforts of a consulting pharmacist, in many institutions which previously operated without such professional services. Many consulting pharmacists practice in the nursing home.

The American Society of Consultant Pharmacists has suggested that the pharmacist consulting with the nursing home should provide the following services:

1. General supervision of the facility's procedures for the control and accountability for all drugs and biologicals throughout the facility and that such drugs and biologicals shall be approved and dispensed in compliance with federal and state laws and the facility's own policies and procedures.

2. Supervision of the records of receipt and disposition of all controlled drugs and the maintenance of such records in sufficient detail so as to allow an accurate reconciliation.
3. Monthly reviews of the drug regimen of each skilled care patient with reports of any irregularities to the nurse in charge and/or the attending physician, and if no appropriate action is taken, he shall report it to the advisory physician and the facility administrator.
4. Supervision of the labeling of all drugs and biologicals to insure that such labeling is based on currently accepted professional principles and includes the appropriate accessory and cautionary instructions as well as the expiration date when applicable.
5. Recommendations, plans for implementation, and continuing assessment through dated, signed reports, which are given to and retained by the administrator for follow-up action and evaluation of performance.
6. Written reports at least quarterly to the pharmaceutical service committee on the status of the facility's pharmaceutical service and staff performance.
7. An active membership in the pharmaceutical services committee and the infections control committee of the facility.
8. Provision, when requested by the administrator, of programs for in-service education for professional staff of the facility that would enhance the effectiveness of the pharmaceutical service; said in-service education to be conducted by the consultant pharmacist or his designees.
9. All other responsibilities required of a qualified or consultant pharmacist as set forth in any federal or state laws, statutes, or regulations as enacted or as may be enacted or amended (14).

Many pharmacists now limit their practices to this setting.

Health Maintenance Organizations

Earlier in this chapter we referred to group practice as one method of community pharmacy organization. Other pharmacists are now practicing in yet another "group" environment: the health maintenance organization (HMO).

An HMO consists of four basic elements:
1. An organized health care delivery system
2. An enrolled population
3. Prepaid comprehensive benefits
4. A managing organization

Currently there is great interest in HMOs from all segments of the health care community and the general public. It is generally agreed that HMOs can help meet today's challenge of providing high quality, comprehensive health care services at a reasonable cost. The HMO presents a method of delivery as well as a method of financing health care. According to official government publications, operating HMOs are organized along two predominant lines. The first, the group practice model, includes physicians of various specialties practicing at a single physical facility or in close proximity to each other. These physicians have the opportunity to consult with one another on patient problems and to maintain common medical records for all patients available to all physicians in the group practice. Normally such physicians are paid on salary basis, and their services usually are not related to a specific fee for each patient service rendered. The other organizational form, the foundation model, involves individual physicians who agree to care for patients enrolled in a prepaid health care plan with reimbursement on a fee for service basis for each patient service rendered. This is essentially a financial mechanism rather than a physical model (15).

There are many ways in which HMOs may arrange to have pharmacy services provided to their patients. Included among these are "inhouse" or contract pharmacies and "out of plan" pharmacy systems. In the latter system the arrangements are essentially financial. In the inhouse pharmacy the pharmacist is an employee of the HMO and operates essentially as an institutional pharmacist for that purpose.

Hospice Practice

An especially challenging type of pharmacy practice is that of the hospice. As Murphy has noted, "pharmacists' principal tasks as members of a hospice care team are likely to revolve around preparing and administering compounds to alleviate pain and assure sound nutrition" (16). In fact "full service" hospice pharmacy assumes a capacity on the part of the pharmacist to cope with the kinds of issues, stresses, and emotions likely to affect both the terminally ill patient and his or her family and friends.

Mail-Order Pharmacy

It is difficult to determine the size of the mail-order practice of pharmacy with any accuracy. It is known that the Veterans Administration (about 20 million prescriptions annually), the American Association of Retired Persons (5 million) and National Pharmacies (2 million), and scores of others still represent less than 3% of all prescription volume (17). Nevertheless, these millions of prescriptions are filled in establishments which are, by definition, incapable of rendering a full range of pharmacy services.

How do they survive? Clearly, the client sees advantages (usually price) or at least no disadvantages. Even the president of one of the larger mail-order pharmacy organizations admits that the slightly lower cost of mail order is not enough to offset the inconvenience of a 10-day wait for drug delivery, combined with the patient's attachment to a local pharmacist with whom he has a good relationship (17). Thus, large price differentials emerge, or the local pharmacist is unsuccessful in maintaining a good client relationship.

Future Developments

Mention should be made of the fact that the borders between some of these practice sites may blur in the future. One of the most dramatic of these may result from joint efforts between the corporate hospital industry and the corporate chain drug industry. In 1984 two hospital groups joined the National Association of Chain Drug Stores (NACDS). Kushner, viewing this development, quoted NACDS President Robert Bolger as seeing as a critical future development the "increasing out-patient hospital pharmacy business in competition with retail pharmacy" (18). It is clear that much of pharmacy practice in the future will be corporate. What is not clear is what kinds of corporations will be involved.

Specialties in Pharmacy Practice

One issue now facing pharmacy that has faced other health occupations in recent years is that of the development of practice specialties.

There has been a general view that hospital pharmacy represents the first rather informally constituted specialty. As noted elsewhere, however, there are numbers of pharmacists who practice both community and hospital pharmacy either simultaneously or sequentially. Also, the practice setting is not the *usual* basis for specializations in other occupations. Provost has pointed out that various authors have identified several specialties of pharmacy practice (19). Included among these are the following: administration and management, drug distribution and control, drug information and "bedside" clinical practice, compounding and manufacturing, assay and quality control, radiopharmacy, clinical and scientific research and product development, and in-service education and teaching.

Provost raised one caution, however:

> ... although the availability of specialists will undoubtedly create an increased demand, there is still a danger of training too many super specialists for the number of positions that are likely to be

Table 6.2.
Pharmacies and Pharmacists[a]

State	Pharmacies						Total	Pharmacists
	Community	Chain	Hospital	Clinic	Nursing home	All others[b]		
Grand Totals	39,377	15,723	5,189	1,553	751	2,371	64,964	160,188
Alabama	873	309	60	24	12	40	1,318	2,786[c]
Alaska	56	24	21	0	3	1	105	256
Arizona	240	259	73	44	3	77	696	2,385[c]
Arkansas	592	116	82	5	4	12	811	1,377
California	3,377	1,196	519	175	5	195	5,467	13,561
Colorado	449	146	51	26	1	52	735	2,661[c]
Connecticut	584	147	1	4	0	0	736	2,093
D.C.	91	71	4	2	0	5	175	410
Delaware	47	69	16	2	2	0	138	407[c]
Florida	1,543	975	258	103	319	195	3,393	5,901
Georgia	1,215	510	182	49	26	73	2,058	4,488[c]
Hawaii	74	34	15	11	0	1	135	302
Idaho	189	53	40	6	3	11	302	703
Illinois	2,183	634	198	82	19	87	3,203	6,749
Indiana	693	574	126	21	10	22	1,446	4,565[c]
Iowa	539	197	26	44	7	22	835	2,200[c]
Kansas	515	125	145	23	2	25	835	1,556
Kentucky	723	273	114	27	12	28	1,177	2,465[c]
Louisiana	819	353	160	31	4	41	1,408	3,355[c]
Maine	155	109	4	1	1	0	270	506
Maryland	435	368	62	12	2	23	902	3,648[c]
Massachusetts	989	349	19	8	0	1	1,366	5,199[c]
Michigan	1,564	472	222	50	10	104	2,422	6,346
Minnesota	674	192	151	38	5	53	1,113	3,494[c]
Mississippi	675	156	118	30	54	5	1,038	1,815

Missouri	890	336	107	45	4	39	1,421	3,845[c]
Montana	166	47	63	8	4	5	293	727
Nebraska	381	73	17	13	4	15	503	1,741[c]
Nevada	84	73	19	4	0	20	200	515
New Hampshire	127	68	32	1	8	1	237	623[c]
New Jersey	1,320	416	89	12	9	10	1,856	6,297[c]
New Mexico	186	85	41	50	2	97	461	883[c]
New York	3,180	767	321	67	69	158	4,562	13,424
North Carolina	953	589	132	24	13	56	1,767	2,573
North Dakota	157	18	54	14	2	4	249	788[c]
Ohio	1,471	998	77	42	11	141	2,740	7,737[c]
Oklahoma	738	210	52	32	0	50	1,082	2,097
Oregon	443	118	58	21	5	10	655	2,050[c]
Pennsylvania	2,095	848	263	25	60	31	3,322	8,601[c]
Puerto Rico	1,019	92	46	8	0	17	1,182	887
Rhode Island	133	78	17	2	1	2	233	710
South Carolina	475	338	59	25	5	30	932	2,514[c]
South Dakota	173	17	60	20	4	7	283	504
Tennessee	944	349	166	43	7	54	1,563	2,850
Texas	2,378	1,208	317	114	3	363	4,383	8,668[c]
Utah	229	100	33	9	0	37	408	1,047[c]
Vermont	93	39	18	1	1	1	153	271
Virgin Islands	0	0	0	0	0	0	0	21
Virginia	583	518	119	39	6	38	1,303	3,042
Washington	648	249	126	38	6	37	1,104	3,459
West Virginia	324	156	86	21	2	14	603	1,308[c]
Wisconsin	802	199	121	55	15	38	1,230	3,059
Wyoming	88	23	29	2	0	10	152	429
Pacific Islands	0	0	0	0	0	0	0	5
APO/FPO, foreign	3	0	0	0	0	0	3	284

[a]Includes 1140 department stores and 540 grocery stores.
[b]82,528 newly licensed or relicensed R.Ph.'s, May 1984.
[c]From: Official list of the NABP and NCPDP. *Business Mailers, Inc.* March 1983.

available, leaving unmet the continued need in community hospitals for well grounded general practitioners (19).

Formal attention to the specialty problem has been given by the APhA. Through a Task Force on Specialties in Pharmacy, it recommended the creation of a Board of Pharmaceutical Specialties authorized to recognize, approve qualifications of, certify, and recertify specialists in pharmacy. The Task Force identified seven criteria for specialty recognition, as follows.

Criterion 1—The area of specialization in the practice of pharmacy rests on a specialized knowledge of pharmaceutical sciences, which have their basis in the biological, physical, and behavioral sciences, and not on the basis of managerial, procedural, or technical services, nor on the basis of the environment in which pharmacy is practiced.

Criterion 2—The area of specialization shall be one for which specially trained practitioners are needed to fulfill the responsibilities of the profession of pharmacy in improving the health and welfare of the public, which responsibilities may not otherwise be effectively fulfilled.

Criterion 3—The area of specialization shall represent an identifiable and distinct field of practice that calls for special knowledge and skills acquired by education and training and/or experience beyond the basic pharmaceutical education and training.

Criterion 4—The area of specialization shall be one in which schools of pharmacy and/or other organizations offer recognized education and training programs to those seeking advanced knowledge and skills in the area of specialty practice so that they may perform more competently.

Criterion 5—The area of specialization shall be one in which there is an adequate educational and scientific base to warrant transmission of knowledge through teaching clinics and scientific and technical publications immediately related to the specialty.

Criterion 6—The area of specialization shall be one in which there exists a significant and clear health care demand to provide the necessary public reason for certification.

Criterion 7—The area of specialization shall be comprised of a reasonable number of individuals who devote most of the time of their practice to the specialty area (20).

The only specialty recognized to date by these criteria has been nuclear pharmacy.

Summary

Pharmacy has been characterized by its tendency to identify the practitioner in terms of the setting in which he practices. The apparent stereotype of the friendly neighborhood druggist is no longer adequate to describe even the majority of pharmacy practitioners. In the community setting, pharmacies differ by size, by ownership (see Table 6.2), by method of operation, and by type of goods and services offered. In addition to the community practice of pharmacy, there is considerable growth in the institutional component, including practice in hospitals, nursing homes, extended care facilities, and some of the new types of practice settings. In addition, there is growing interest in the activities of the pharmacist in such areas as industry, government, teaching, and research.

It remains to be seen, of course, how the practice of pharmacy will evolve. Standards of contemporary practice have been set, however, and agreed upon by the APhA and the American Association of Colleges of Pharmacy. These appear as an appendix to this chapter and deserve serious study by anyone seeking an appreciation for the nature and scope of pharmacy practice.

REFERENCES

1. *Pharmacists for the Future.* Ann Arbor, MI, Health Administration Press, 1975.
2. White EV: Conceptual design of pharmaceutical practice in the community. In Deno RA (ed): *Pharmacy, Medicine, Nursing Conference on Health Education.* Ann Arbor, MI, The University of Michigan, 1967, pp 71–72.
3. Fox ERW: The corner drugstore. *JAMA* 252(8), 1984.
4. Brodie DC: *The Challenge to Pharmacy in Times of Change.* Washington, D.C., American Pharmaceutical Association, 1966, p 48.
5. Professional acceptance and economic success of the pharmaceutical center (special advertising insert). *Southeast Drug J* 45, June 1971.
6. Mackowiak J, Manasse H: Expectations for ambulatory services in traditional and office-practice pharmacies. *Am J Hosp Pharm* 41:1140, 1984.
7. Dworkin S: The era of promotional pharmacy. *Chain Store Age* 43:88, 1975.
8. Kushner D: On the drug chains' 1980's agenda: Major expansion in the health field. *Am Drug* 180:3, 1979.
9. Provost GP: Commercialism in pharmacy—who's responsible? *Pharm Management* 151:147, 1979.
10. Hayes JH: quoted in Somers HM, Somers AR: *Doctors, Patients and Health Insurance.* Washington, D.C., The Brookings Institute, 1961, p 64.
11. Sith HL: Two lines of authority: The hospital's dilemma. In Jaco EG (ed): *Patients, Physicians, and Illness.* Glencoe, IL, The Free Press, 1958, pp 468–477.
12. Guidelines on the competencies required in institutional pharmacy practice. In Smith MC, Brown TR: *Handbook of Institutional Pharmacy Practice.* Baltimore, Williams & Wilkins, 1985.
13. Stolar M: National survey of hospital pharmaceutical services—1982. *Am J Hosp Pharm* 40:963, 1983.

14. American Society of Consultant Pharmacists: Consultant Pharmacist Retainer Agreement.
15. *Inclusion of Pharmaceutical Services in Health Maintenance and Related Organization, A Review of Supplemental Benefits.* Rockville, MD, U.S. Department of Health, Education and Welfare, 1974.
16. Murphy D: The delicate art of caring. *Am Pharm* NS24:388, 1984.
17. Glaser M: Mail-order RXs: Separating facts from fiction. *Drug Topics* 128:42, 1984.
18. Kushner D: Profit-seeking hospitals and drug chains. *Am Drug* 126:1, 1984.
19. Provost G: Specialization and general practice. *Am J Hosp Pharm* 27:531, 1970.
20. APhA Task Force on Specialties in Pharmacy. *J Am Pharm Assoc* NS14:619, 1974.

Standards of Practice for the Profession of Pharmacy

Source: *American Pharmacy*, NS 19:21ff (1979)

Section I.
General Management and Administration of the Pharmacy

Selects and supervises pharmacists and nonprofessionals for pharmacy staff; establishes a pricing structure for pharmaceutical services and products; administers budgets and negotiates with vendors; develops and maintains a purchasing and inventory system for all drugs and pharmaceutical supplies; initiates a formulary system. In general, establishes and administers pharmacy management, personnel, and fiscal policy.

Responsibility No. 1: Establishes and/or implements written policies and procedures for pharmacy operations.

Tasks:

1. Identifies each specific pharmaceutical function performed.

2. Within each functional area develops specific policies and procedures consistent with legal, institutional, and/or professional guidelines.

   (a) Assures that the format of each policy or procedure is uniform.

   (b) Uses sufficient detail to express each concept or topic.

   (c) Clearly states circumstances, conditions, and personnel that are covered by (or subject to) each policy and/or procedure.

   (d) Clearly states where performance of a procedure is limited to certain personnel.

   (e) Assures that policies and procedures are consistent with established job descriptions.

   (f) Assures that the policies and procedures do not duplicate or conflict with one another.

3. Organizes policies and procedures to allow a quick and logical method for reference.

4. Subjects policies and procedures to appropriate review process.

5. Generates and distributes policies and procedures to appropriate personnel.

(a) Identifies where and to whom copies of policies and procedures are to be distributed.

(b) Updates distribution list when appropriate.

6. Educates the staff regarding scope and content of the policies and the proper use of policies as a reference and/or job aid.

(a) Orients new employees.

(b) Provides periodic in-service and/or refresher training for current employees.

7. Periodically reviews and updates policies and procedures.

Responsibility No. 2: Plans or assists in the design and the layout of physical facilities for pharmacy.

Tasks:

1. Evaluates the functions to be performed in the practice setting.

2. Plans for reasonable physical space for each function unit in coordination with physical arrangement to give the best work flow.

3. Plans for the comfort and convenience of the patient and/or personnel.

4. Creates an environment conducive to patient/pharmacist and health professional/pharmacists interaction.

5. Develops a good traffic flow pattern where applicable.

6. Periodically re-evaluates space allocations.

Responsibility No. 3: Reviews operations of the pharmacy for compliance with local, state, and federal laws and regulations.

Tasks:

1. Maintains current copies of all regulations.

2. Reviews all regulations on a periodic regular basis.

3. Conducts physical inspection of pharmacy facilities to insure compliance.

4. By observation, verifies that personnel in the pharmacy are performing their responsibilities in compliance with regulations.

Responsibility No. 4: Develops and implements an appropriate pharmacy security system to prevent theft and/or drug diversion.

Tasks:

1. Evaluates practice site history and setting to determine overall security needs.

2. Establishes a secure physical environment.

3. Establishes internal controls and procedures as indicated.

4. Periodically reviews security needs and makes adjustments in physical environment and internal procedures as indicated.

Responsibility No. 5: Establishes a pricing structure for pharmaceutical services and products.

Tasks:

1. Establishes a pricing structure based on sound management principles which would provide a "fair and reasonable" return on investment.

2. Periodically reviews pricing structure and revises as indicated.

Responsibility No. 6: Initiates a formulary system to meet the needs of patients and practitioners.

Tasks:

1. Determines whether informal (unwritten) or formal (written) formulary system is appropriate.

2. Determines patient and practitioner population to be served by formulary system.

3. Determines guidelines for inclusion in the formulary.

   (a) Determines manufacturing source(s).

   (b) Determines whether drug has potential for inequivalence.

   (c) Determines cost differential for different sources.

   (d) Determines manufacturer reliability.

   (e) Determines whether there is a great difference in formulation among products (e.g., taste, ointment/cream base).

   (f) Determines allergenicity of product.

   (g) Inspects product for defects. (Further quantification of these elements may be found in Section II, Responsibility No. 6: Selects the manufacturing source of drug(s)/ product(s) to be dispensed for a prescription order written in generic terminology; Tasks 1,2,4,5,6,7, and 8.)

4. Implements and administers the formulary.

   (a) Educates health care practitioners of formulary system.

   (b) Develops procedures for handling addition to or deletion from the formulary.

   (c) Initiates procedures for obtaining nonformulary drugs.

5. Periodically reviews formulary, revising as necessary.

Responsibility No. 7: Establishes and maintains an ongoing cost analysis program.

Tasks:

1. Implements an effective accounting system.

2. Identifies cost centers: prescription, nonprescription (e.g., sundries, cosmetics).

3. Develops cost information retrieval system.

4. Utilizes and evaluates the information generated.

Responsibility No. 8: Maintains and reconciles accounts receivable from various third-party payors.

Tasks:

1. Maintains a record system for third-party receivables.

2. Completes appropriate billing process.

3. Reconciles differences between charges submitted and payments received.

4. Corrects and resubmits claim.

Responsibility No. 9: Prepares and/or participates in the preparation of the budget and its controls in providing for pharmacy services.

Tasks:

1. Reviews previous budget to evaluate adequacy in meeting needs.

2. Projects changes in budget for previously budgeted items.

3. Determines additions and/or deletions with justifications to previous budget.

4. Establishes procedures for periodically reviewing and evaluating performance with respect to budget.

Responsibility No. 10: Reviews and/or prepares periodic reports of pharmacy's fiscal performance in relation to budget.

Tasks:

1. Establishes frequency of periodic reports.
2. Collates fiscal and budgetary data.
3. Evaluates performance against budget.
4. Prepares fiscal/budget reports.

Responsibility No. 11: Develops and maintains an inventory system for all drugs, pharmaceutical supplies, etc., in active and inactive storage areas.

Tasks:

1. Establishes inventory goals.
2. Selects appropriate method of inventory control.
3. Develops method for maintaining optimal stock levels.
4. Periodically reviews inventory goals, method of inventory control, and optimal stock levels.

Responsibility No. 12: Establishes and monitors a system to insure proper storage conditions for perishable pharmacy items.

Tasks:

1. Identifies all items requiring special storage.
2. Establishes equipment necessary to meet storage requirements in all drug storage areas.
3. Establishes receiving procedures for the handling of special storage drugs.
4. Establishes procedures to monitor the proper storage of special storage drugs.
5. Establishes procedures to monitor the operation of special storage drug equipment.

Responsibility No. 13: Develops and maintains a system for the regular removal from storage areas of all pharmaceutical items that are outdated or whose manufacture has been discontinued.

Tasks:

1. Regularly reviews professional literature for recalled and/or discontinued items.
2. Systematically reviews dating on all dated items in stock.
3. Disposes of removed items in an appropriate manner.

Responsibility No. 14: Assists in design or implementation of computer systems for use in the pharmacy (e.g., patient records, inventory control, drug utilization).

Tasks:

1. Determines feasibility of using a computer to meet pharmacy needs.
2. Defines the functions the computer is to perform.
3. Defines format of output necessary to meet pharmacy needs.
4. Determines cost/benefit ratio of alternative systems.
5. Insures that operators use the system competently.
6. Monitors system for efficiency.

Responsibility No. 15: Establishes drug quality specifications for drugs to be purchased.

Tasks:

1. Determines manufacturing sources.
2. Determines manufacturer reliability.
   (a) Assesses quality control data.
   (b) Reviews recall records.
   (c) Inspects product for defects.
3. Develops list of criteria for identifying potential inequivalence.
   (a) Consults references which rate potential inequivalence (e.g., FDA information).
   (b) Determines whether drug has low water solubility.
   (c) Determines whether condition being treated needs high or critical serum levels.
   (d) Determines whether drug has narrow therapeutic index.
   (e) Determines whether formulation is designed for delayed absorption.
   (f) Assesses bioavailability data, if available.
4. Develops quality specifications for evaluating differences in formulation among products (e.g., taste, ointment/cream base).
5. Inspects products for defects.

Responsibility No. 16: Determines primary and alternate vendors for pharmaceutical supplies.

Tasks:

1. Determines buying policy.
2. Evaluates vendor programs.
3. Institutes buying program to maximize cost effectiveness.

Responsibility No. 17: Prepares and/or reviews purchase orders (both routine and emergency).

Responsibility No. 18: Negotiates with vendors regarding cost, delivery schedule, etc.

Responsibility No. 19: Verifies that purchases received from vendor conform to the specifications on the original purchase order and authorizes payment.

Tasks:

1. Compares items ordered with items received.
2. Compares invoiced items with items received and marks according to established policy.
3. Verifies correctness of prices.
4. Verifies correctness of invoice extension and total.
5. Approves payment.

Responsibility No. 20: Establishes, administers, and interprets personnel policies and procedures.

Tasks:

1. Develops and promulgates written employee policies and procedures.
2. Explains personnel policies to all employees.
3. Administers policies and procedures.
4. Establishes feedback apparatus to evaluate policies.
5. Evaluates compliance with policies and procedures.
6. Where necessary, counsels with employees.

Responsibility No. 21: Prepares written job descriptions for pharmacists and nonpharmacists on pharmacy staff.

Tasks:

1. Develops an organizational chart.
2. Prepares job descriptions.
   (a) States title, duties, and responsibilities.
   (b) States any limitations.
   (c) Identifies the department and the immediate supervisor.
3. Consults with each employee to insure understanding of the job duties.
4. Develops a mechanism for revision of job descriptions as circumstances and personnel needs dictate.

Responsibility No. 22: Recruits, interviews, selects, and hires pharmacists and nonpharmacists for pharmacy staff.

Tasks:

1. Establishes a continuous recruitment program using multiple channels and methods (e.g., newspapers, employees, schools, other referrals).
2. Uses a selection process (interviews, tests, evaluation of training and experience) which identifies able prospective employees and conforms to legal guidelines.
3. Maintains appropriate records (sex, race, etc.) on applicants and selected employees required by legal guidelines.

Responsibility No. 23: Instructs and trains pharmacist and nonpharmacist staff in carrying out assigned responsibilities.

Tasks:

1. Evaluates employee performance against established standards of performance.
2. Determines individual and group needs for training.
3. Trains and/or refers employees for appropriate training.

Responsibility No. 24: Supervises and evaluates job performance of pharmacy staff.

Tasks:

1. Establishes procedure for evaluating job performance of pharmacy staff consistent with legal guidelines.
2. Reviews or supervises review of evaluation of employees.

Responsibility No. 25: Schedules work hours for pharmacy staff.

Responsibility No. 26: Institutes disciplinary action and/or discharges pharmacy staff for cause.

Tasks:

1. Notes violations of rules or procedures and/or identifies inadequate performance.
2. Discusses situation with employee and records results of discussion.
3. Decides whether to counsel, institute discipline, or discharge.
4. Records and documents course of action taken consistent with legal guidelines.

Responsibility No. 27: Administers wage, salary, and benefit programs for pharmacy staff.

Tasks:
1. Establishes wage and benefit (e.g., pay, discounts, insurance, vacation, sick leave, holidays) policies consistent with competitive factors, legal requirements, and budgetary constraints.
2. Assists employees in understanding and utilizing the wage, salary, and benefit program.
3. Determines salary adjustments to the wage and benefit package, based on evaluation of employee performance, in a fair and equitable manner.

Section II.
Activities Related to
Processing the Prescription

Verifies prescription for legality and physical and chemical compatibility; checks patient record before dispensing prescription; measures quantities needed to dispense prescription; performs final check of finished prescription; dispenses prescriptions.

Responsibility No. 1: Determines necessity of immediately handling the preparation and delivery of the medication to the patient (emergency or stat).

Tasks:
1. Receives a request for an immediately needed drug.
2. Screens prescription order to determine priority of handling prescription.
   (a) Determines therapeutic category of prescription medication(s).
   (b) Determines regulatory responsibilities.
   (c) Determines route of administration.
3. Gathers additional information about the situation to determine immediacy of the need.
   (a) Observes the patient condition.
   (b) Questions patient or patient's agent to determine:
      (i) Patient complaint.
      (ii) Whether problem is of an acute nature.
      (iii) Whether patient received starter or "stat" dose.
   (c) Questions other appropriate sources where necessary.

Responsibility No. 2: Verifies prescription order for completeness and legality.

Tasks:
1. Checks prescription order to verify that it can be legally filled. Verifies that order is written by a person authorized to prescribe, checking the following items:
   (a) The prescriber is identified.
   (b) The prescriber is licensed/authorized to prescribe by the appropriate agency.
   (c) The prescriber has ordered medication that is within his/her legal privileges.
   (d) The prescription is not forged.

(e) The date of the prescription order is within legal limits.

(f) Other legal requirements of the prescription have been met (e.g., name, address).

2. Checks for completeness of prescription order. Checks to see that the following are legibly included on the prescription:

(a) Name of medication.

(b) Number of dosage units to be dispensed (when appropriate).

(c) Dosage form and strength.

(d) Complete directions that insure rational drug usage.

(e) Item described is allowable under formulary, where applicable.

(f) Route of administration delineated.

(g) Third-party payor identification number.

3. Obtains additional information necessary to make prescription order complete and legal.

(a) Interviews patient for additional information.

(b) Calls prescriber to obtain necessary information.

(c) Calls appropriate person(s) and/ or agency to obtain additional information.

Responsibility No. 3: Verifies prescription order for amount per dose, appropriate route, frequency, and duration of therapy.

Tasks:

1. Evaluates the dose.

(a) Verifies dose as falling within therapeutic ranges.

(b) Verifies dose as nontoxic.

(c) Determines that dose is practical to measure and administer.

(d) Determines physical availability of dosage.

2. Evaluates route of administration.

(a) Verifies dose as falling within therapeutic ranges.

(b) Verifies dose as nontoxic.

(c) Determines that dose is practical to measure and administer.

(d) Determines physical availability of dosage.

3. Evaluates the frequency of dosage administration.

(a) Checks that the total daily dose (amount/dose × frequency) is therapeutic and nontoxic.

(b) Obtains information from patient and other sources regarding disease state being treated.

(c) Evaluates whether frequency of administration is consistent with disease state being treated.

(d) Evaluates whether frequency of administration is consistent with the drug and dosage form characteristics.

(e) Evaluates the duration of therapy for inappropriateness.

4. Consults with prescriber to provide suggestion for alteration(s) of order.

Responsibility No. 4: Verifies prescription order for physical and chemical compatibility.

Tasks:

1. Verifies that quantity of vehicle (diluent, IV fluid) is appropriate to the drug(s).

(a) Confirms that drug(s) is (are) soluble in ordered quantity of vehicle.

(b) Confirms that drug(s) is (are) stable in ordered quantity of vehicle.

2. Verifies that concentration of vehicle is appropriate to the drug(s).

(a) Confirms that drug(s) is (are) soluble in ordered quantity of vehicle.

(b) Confirms that drug(s) is (are) stable in ordered quantity of vehicle.

3. Verifies that type of vehicle is appropriate to the drug(s).

(a) Confirms that pH of vehicle is compatible with drug(s).

(b) Confirms that drug(s) is (are) soluble/miscible in ordered type of vehicle.

(c) Confirms that drug(s) is (are) stable in ordered type of vehicle.

4. Verifies that order contains no drug-drug incompatibilities.

(a) Checks that pHs of drugs are compatible.

(b) Checks that mixture will not chelate.

(c) Checks that mixture will not precipitate.

(d) Checks that drugs will not inactivate each other.

5. Verifies that preservative(s) is (are) compatible with order.

Responsibility No. 5: Checks patient record for pertinent patient information before dispensing prescription medication.

Tasks:

1. Verifies that records pertain to the correct patient.

2. Checks prescription order against patient drug sensitivities/allergies.

3. Checks compatibility of prescription order with current patient diagnosis.

4. Checks prescription order against patient profile data for presence of interactions.

(a) Drug-drug interaction.

(b) Drug-diet interaction.

(c) Drug-lab interaction.

(d) Drug-disease interaction.

(e) Inappropriate concurrent prescribing.

5. Checks patient statistics to determine whether any factors will affect response to drug.

(a) Weight.

(b) Age.

(c) Race.

(d) Sex.

(e) Occupation.

Responsibility No. 6: Selects the manufacturing source of drug(s)/product(s) to be dispensed for a prescription order written in generic terminology.

Tasks:

1. Determines manufacturing source(s) of generic order.

2. Determines whether the order contains any drug(s) which has (have) potential for inequivalence.

(a) Consults reference(s) which rate(s) potential inequivalence (e.g., FDA information).

(b) Determines whether drug has low water solubility.

(c) Determines whether condition being treated needs high or critical serum levels.

(d) Determines whether drug has narrow therapeutic index.

(e) Determines whether formulation is designed for delayed absorption.

(f) Assesses bioavailability data, if available.

3. Determines whether patient has taken specific brand of drug before or chronically.

(a) Refers to patient record.

(b) Communicates with patient or practitioner.

4. Determines cost differential for different sources.

5. Determines manufacturer reliability.

(a) Assesses quality control data.

(b) Reviews recall records.

6. Determines whether there is a great difference in formulation among products (e.g., taste, ointment/cream base).

(a) Ascertains whether patient/condition needs certain formulation.

7. Determines whether patient is allergic to nondrug components of product.

(a) Selects brand which is allergen free.

8. Inspects product for defects.

9. Communicates change or choice of brand to patient/practitioner if legally or ethically indicated.

10. Makes notation on prescription order indicating specific drug product and manufacturer selected.

Responsibility No. 7: Selects the manufacturing source of drug(s)/product(s) to be dispensed for a brand name prescription order in those cases where legally authorized.

Tasks:

1. Determines manufacturing source(s) of generic order.

2. Determines whether the order contains any drug(s) which has (have) potential for inequivalence.

(a) Consults reference(s) which rate(s) potential inequivalence (e.g., FDA information).

(b) Determines whether drug has low water solubility.

(c) Determines whether condition being treated needs high or critical serum levels.

(d) Determines whether drug has narrow therapeutic index.

(e) Determines whether formulation is designed for delayed absorption.

(f) Assesses bioavailability data, if available.

3. Determines whether patient has taken specific brand of drug before or chronically.

(a) Refers to patient record.

(b) Communicates with patient or practitioner.

4. Determines cost differential for different sources.

5. Determines manufacturer reliability.

(a) Assesses quality control data.

(b) Reviews recall records.

6. Determines whether there is a great difference in formulation among products (e.g., taste, ointment/cream base).

(a) Ascertains whether patient/condition needs certain formulation.

7. Determines whether patient is allergic to nondrug components of product.
  (a) Selects brand which is allergen free.
8. Inspects product for defects.
9. Communicates change or choice of brand to patient/practitioner if legally or ethically indicated.
10. Makes notation on prescription order indicating specific drug product and manufacturer selected.

Responsibility No. 8: Measures quantities needed to dispense the prescription.

Tasks:

1. Measures and counts oral dosage forms.
  (a) Selects and cleans appropriate equipment.
  (b) Observes usual precautions for proper drug handling.
  (c) Measures out or counts appropriate amount.
2. Measures appropriate substances needed for extemporaneous compounding.
  (a) Selects, cleans, and calibrates needed equipment.
  (b) Observes usual precautions for proper drug handling.
  (c) Measures out or counts appropriate amount.
  (d) Performs appropriate calculation.
3. Annotates on prescription order the calculations made.
4. Selects prepackaged unit-of-use item.
  (a) Removes non-patient-oriented labels and inserted materials.
  (b) Checks for completeness of product (e.g., inserter with vaginal products).
  (c) Checks quantities in prepared sizes.

Responsibility No. 9: Compounds the prescribed ingredients according to prescription formula or instructions.

Tasks:

1. Selects appropriate equipment and environment.
2. Cleans preparation area before and after compounding.
3. Mixes ingredients in proper sequence.
4. Performs the steps necessary to produce a pharmaceutically elegant product.
5. Follows aseptic techniques where necessary.

Responsibility No. 10: Reconstitutes lyophilized or powdered pharmaceuticals into a dosage form suitable for administration.

Tasks:

1. Prepares a pharmaceutical product for reconstitution by loosening powder.
2. Selects and adds proper diluents; shakes to insure complete mixing.
3. Checks for complete solution or suspension.

Responsibility No. 11: Performs packaging and labeling functions to promote product stability.

Tasks:

1. Selects appropriate package for medication.
  (a) Package will be of appropriate size.
  (b) Package meets storage requirements.

(c) Package meets legal requirements.

(d) Package meets patient requirements.

2. Transfers measured number of dosage units to prescription container.

3. Closes/seals prescription container(s).

4. Selects proper storage labeling.

5. Notates on prescription order if non-child-resistant container was dispensed.

Responsibility No. 12: Selects appropriate labeling for prescription container and includes patient instructions.

Tasks:

1. Prepares primary label.

(a) Meets all legal requirements.

(b) Contains clear, concise, and comprehensive instructions to patient.

(c) Is legible and professional in appearance.

2. Chooses appropriate auxilliary labels reinforcing or supplementing instructions on primary label.

3. Affixes appropriate (proper) label(s) to product.

4. Makes notations on prescription order to insure consistent future labeling.

(a) Notes what labeling instructions used.

(b) Notes size and type of container used.

Responsibility No. 13: Performs a final check of the finished prescription to insure that each of the steps has been accomplished accurately.

Tasks:

1. Checks prescription label for accuracy against prescription order.

(a) Verifies patient name is correct.

(b) Verifies directions are correct.

(c) Verifies medication and dosage form are correct.

(d) Verifies expiration date of medication.

(e) Verifies dispensing date.

(f) Verifies prescriber.

(g) Initials prescription label if necessary.

2. Checks medication for accuracy against prescription order.

(a) Verifies correct medication.

(b) Verifies correct dosage form.

(c) Verifies correct strength.

(d) Verifies correct manufacturer.

(e) Verifies correct quantity dispensed.

(f) Returns bulk container to storage area.

3. Checks auxiliary label instructions.

(a) Reviews special storage requirements.

(b) Reviews special administration requirements.

(c) Reviews special preparation requirements.

4. Determines price of prescription.

5. Initials and/or signs prescription.

Responsibility No. 14: Develops and maintains an inventory system for all drugs, pharmaceutical supplies, etc., in active and inactive storage.

Tasks:
(See Section I, Responsibility No. 11.)

Responsibility No. 15: Establishes and monitors a system to insure proper storage conditions for perishable pharmacy items.

Tasks:
(See Section I, Responsibility No. 12.)

Responsibility No. 16: Develops and maintains a system for the regular removal from storage areas of all pharmaceutical items that are outdated or whose manufacture has been discontinued.

Tasks:
(See Section I, Responsibility No. 13.)

Responsibility No. 17: Maintains a record file of current prescription orders including pertinent patient information and renewal data.

Tasks:
1. Complies with legal requirements for filing prescription orders.
    (a) Records in proper form.
    (b) Records stored to provide proper access and preservation.
    (c) Appropriate retention policies in effect.
2. Reviews prescription order for completeness before filing.
    (a) Checks prescription to determine that all legal requirements have been met.
    (b) Checks that all necessary notations on labeling and container used are posted.
    (c) Checks that prescription order is signed or initialed.

Responsibility No. 18: Maintains a record of controlled substances and poisons received, stored, and dispensed by pharmacy.

Tasks:
1. Complies with legal requirements for processing prescription orders for controlled substances.
2. Complies with legal requirements for maintaining record of over-the-counter controlled substances and poisons.

Responsibility No. 19: Prepares and/or reviews purchase orders (both routine and emergency).

Tasks:
(none)

Section III.
Patient Care Functions

Clarifies patient's understanding of dosage; integrates drug-related with patient-related information; advises patient of potential drug-related conditions; refers patient to other health care resources; monitors and evaluates therapeutic response of patient; reviews, and/or seeks additional drug-related information.

Responsibility No. 1: Reviews and/or seeks additional drug-related information (e.g., cost, pharmacokinetic characteristics, bioavailability, common adverse effects) to identify potential problems regarding drug therapy.

Tasks:

1. Collects subjective and objective data to further clarify the situation.
2. Determines what type of information is needed, if any.
3. Retrieves and reviews information from appropriate sources.
4. Evaluates information obtained.

Responsibility No. 2: Reviews patient-related information for potential problems regarding drug therapy (e.g., socioeconomic factors, compliance habits, disease influences).

Tasks:

1. Screens existing information on patient.
   (a) Reviews prior and present medical problem(s).
   (b) Reviews drug usage (including OTC and prescription).
   (c) Reviews patient compliance with drug regimen.
   (d) Reviews drug allergies or sensitivities, i.e., date, route of administration, type of reaction.
   (e) Reviews list of health care practitioners consulted.
   (f) Reviews laboratory and physical examination results.
2. Collects additional information from appropriate sources if necessary.
3. Evaluates information obtained.

Responsibility No. 3: Interviews the patient or his/her representative to obtain information for entry into patient record, patient profile, or family health record.

Tasks:

1. Identifies patient.
2. Uses effective communication techniques in accomplishing the following:
   (a) Obtains history of prior and present medical problem(s).
   (b) Obtains history of drug usage (including OTC and prescription).
   (c) Obtains history of patient compliance with drug regimen.
   (d) Obtains history of drug allergies or sensitivities, i.e., date, route of administration, type of reaction.
   (e) Obtains list of health care practitioners consulted.
   (f) Verifies patient health information where possible.

Responsibility No. 4: Integrates drug-related with patient-related information in order to determine appropriate course of action (e.g., timing of dosage schedule, advising patient of possible adverse effects).

Tasks:

1. Determines whether patient is predisposed to side effect because of disease state(s).
2. Determines whether potential exists for a significant drug interaction.
3. Determines whether patient manifests signs and/or symptoms of potential problems.
4. Assesses significance of potential problem(s) regarding drug therapy.
5. Determines alternative(s) to present regimen.

Responsibility No. 5: Confirms and further clarifies patient's understanding of medication dosage, dosage frequency, and method of administration.

Tasks:

1. Assesses level at which to communicate with patient.
2. Determines whether patient understands how to use medication.
3. Ascertains from patient and/or records factors affecting compliance. Determines:
    (a) Life style (e.g., sleeping hours, working hours, eating schedule).
    (b) Compliance history.
    (c) Attitude toward disease and medication.
    (d) Physical and/or mental impairments.
    (e) Socioeconomic constraints.
    (f) Living conditions.
4. Determines whether potential compliance problem exists.
5. Determines appropriate dosing regimen based on prescription directions, drug's characteristics, and patient's schedule, consulting with physician when necessary.
6. Explains dosing regimen to patient.
    (a) Suggests time of administration.
    (b) Explains or demonstrates method of administration.
    (c) Asks whether there are questions.
    (d) Has patient describe dosing regimen.

Responsibility No. 6: Advises patient of potential drug-related or health-related conditions which may develop from the use of the medication for which patient should seek other medical care.

Tasks:

1. Determine indication for drug use if possible.
2. Assesses patient's level of anxiety regarding the prescription/disease.
3. Assesses benefit vs. risk of explaining side effect and/or expected response.
4. Explains possible effects of drug use to patient.
    (a) Explains to patient how to recognize the signs and/or symptoms that indicate:
    (i) Therapeutic response.
    (ii) Therapeutic failure.
    (iii) Pertinent side effects.
    (b) Advises patient what to do if signs and/or symptoms occur.
    (c) Advises patient how to minimize side effects.
    (d) Assesses whether patient understands explanation.
  5. Notifies practitioner of pharmacist/patient interaction if indicated.

Responsibility No. 7: Updates the patient's history in the patient's record from information obtained by recurring patient interviews.

Tasks: None.

Responsibility No. 8: Consults with patient to properly identify symptoms in order to advise patient for self-medication.

Tasks:

 1. Identifies patient.

2. Uses effective communication techniques in identifying major symptoms of patient:
   (a) Onset of symptom.
   (b) Duration of symptom.
   (c) Severity of symptom.
   (d) Description of symptom.
   (e) Location of symptom.
   (f) Other associated symptoms.
   (g) Relief of symptom.
   (h) Self-treatment history.
3. Through interview, further defines symptom complex.
4. Obtains information on other medical problems, drug therapy (including OTCs), drug allergies, and sensitivities.
   (a) Through patient interview.
   (b) Through patient record.
5. Observes patient when feasible or obtains information from patient's agent.
6. Performs physical assessment (e.g., inspection of wound.)
7. Makes professional judgment as to patient's condition and need for referral (See Responsibilities No. 4 and 1).
8. Recommends a product, no treatment, or other treatment or refers to appropriate health care professional (See Responsibilities No. 6, 9 and 13).
9. Educates patient as to proper use of medications, dosage and precautions, etc. (See Responsibilities No. 5 and 6).
10. Arranges for follow-up, if necessary.
11. Makes appropriate entry into patient's record (See Responsibility No. 7).

Responsibility No. 9: Refers patient to other health care providers and/or health resources where indicated.

Tasks:
   1. Determines need for referral.
   2. Recommends appropriate professional/agency for referral based on needs and severity.
   3. Selects most appropriate method to facilitate meeting of patient's needs.

Responsibility No. 10: Provides information, treatment, and/or referral in emergency cases involving ingestion of toxic substances.

Tasks:
   1. Maintains information system for dealing with emergency situation (e.g., poison control center, antidote chart, references).
   2. Obtains information to further define the ingestion situation.
   3. Evaluates information and recommends treatment or referral.

Responsibility No. 11: Continuously evaluates and monitors therapeutic response of patient to prescribed medication.

Tasks:
   1. Determines appropriate clinical parameters to monitor:
   (a) Progress/status of disease state and its complications.
   (b) Effectiveness of therapy.
   (c) Patient compliance with all aspects of therapeutic plan.
   (d) Toxicity/adverse effects of therapeutic regimen.

2. Collects appropriate subjective and objective data in order to evaluate parameters.

3. Evaluates the data collected.

4. Recommends therapeutic regimen modification where necessary.

5. Enters evidence of monitoring and evaluation into appropriate patient record.

Responsibility No. 12: Upon request, reviews and interprets medication history to the physician, patient, or other persons involved with patient's care.

Tasks: None.

Responsibility No. 13: Makes recommendations regarding drug therapy to the physician, patient, or other persons involved with patient's care.
Tasks:

1. Makes alternate recommendations for treatment plan after evaluating data base.

2. Documents recommendations made.

Responsibility No. 14: Monitors patient records for indications of drug abuse or misuse.

Tasks:

1. Develops procedures for identifying drug misuse and a method for communicating information to relevant individuals.

2. Utilizes procedures to monitor patient and patient's records for signs and symptoms that might indicate abuse or misuse.

3. Institutes appropriate corrective action.

Responsibility No. 15: Participates in emergency patient care activities.

Tasks:

1. Assesses needs for pharmacist's involvement in emergency care activities in the practice setting.

2. Actively participates in certain emergency situations (e.g., CPR team, emergency prescription service).

3. Supports services for emergency activities (e.g., provides supplies for rescue squad and civil defense planning).

Responsibility No. 16: Advises patients on personal health matters (e.g., smoking, drug abuse).

Tasks:

1. Maintains pharmacist's availability to patients.

2. Makes available health care information.

Responsibility No. 17: Instructs patients in the use of medical or surgical appliances (e.g., inhalers, colostomy bags, trusses).

Tasks:

1. Possesses expertise in medical and surgical appliances and services offered by the pharmacy.

2. Maintains a private fitting room if applicable.

3. Instructs patient in the use and care of medical and surgical appliances.

Responsibility No. 18: Publicizes and/or participates in mass screening programs (e.g., hypertension, diabetes, TB, VD).

Tasks:

1. Determines the need for pharmacist participation in mass screening programs.

2. Determines pharmacist's degree of participation in the program.

3. Participates in the organization, promotion, and operation of mass screening programs (e.g., publicity, mechanics of program, materials, equipment).

Section IV.
Education of Health Care
Professionals and Patients

Organizes, maintains, and provides drug information to other health care professionals; organizes and/or participates in "in-pharmacy" education programs for other pharmacists; makes recommendations regarding drug therapy to physician or patient; develops and maintains system for drug, distribution and quality control.

Responsibility No. 1: Continuously evaluates and monitors therapeutic response of patient to prescribed medication.

Tasks:

(See Section III, Responsibility No. 11).

Responsibility No. 2: Makes recommendations regarding drug therapy to the physician, patient, or other persons involved with patient's care.

Tasks:

(See Section III, Responsibility No. 13).

Responsibility No. 3: Participates in emergency patient care activities.

Tasks:

(See Section III, Responsibility No. 15).

Responsibility No. 4: Develops and implements systems for drug distribution and drug administration in institutional settings (e.g., nursing homes, hospitals).

Tasks:

1. Determines need for type of drug control system (e.g., unit dose, specialized drug administration system).

2. Examines available resources (e.g., personnel, space).

3. Develops appropriate drug control system including written policies and procedures.

4. Obtains necessary resources (e.g., space, equipment, personnel).

5. Trains personnel.

6. Operationalizes system.

7. Monitors and evaluates performance of system.

8. Implements necessary changes.

Responsibility No. 5: Initiates a formulary system to meet the needs of patients and practitioners.

Tasks:

(See Section I, Responsibility No. 6).

Responsibility No. 6: Develops and maintains quality control records for drugs that are prepackaged, bulk compounded, sterile product formulated, etc.

Tasks:

1. Identifies drugs which need quality control records (e.g., inspection, chemical analysis, lot number control, microbiological analysis).

2. Determines standards and ranges of acceptability for each drug.

3. Documents and maintains records of quality control activities.

Responsibility No. 7: Prepares and/or reviews purchase orders (both routine and emergency).

Tasks:

(None)

Responsibility No. 8: Participates in appropriate community educational programs relating to health care and drugs (e.g., drug abuse, alcoholism, hypertension).

Tasks:

1. Maintains pharmacist's availability for community educational programs.

2. Defines areas of participation.

Responsibility No. 9: Provides drug information to other health care professionals in a formal setting (e.g., organizes in-service educational programs, lectures, seminars, exhibits).

Tasks:

1. Determines drug information needs to be met.

2. Organizes drug information into program.

3. Evaluates program.

Responsibility No. 10: Participates in utilization reviews, medical audits, and medical care evaluations (e.g., as a member of medical care evaluation committee or in peer review).

Tasks:

1. Promotes pharmacy representation in quality assurance activities.

2. Participates in development of criteria and standards.

3. Participates in collection and evaluation of data.

4. Participates in initiating measures to improve the quality of patient care.

Responsibility No. 11: Assists in establishing, executing, tabulating, and evaluating clinical studies regarding drugs.

Tasks:

1. Participates in the design and/or conduct of studies.

    (a) Identifies questions to be studied or problems to be solved within various practice settings (e.g., community, academic, institutional).

    (b) Conducts studies recognizing the limitations of practice settings.

    (c) Disseminates findings.

Responsibility No. 12: Organizes and/or participates in "in-pharmacy" education programs for other pharmacists.

Tasks:

1. Identifies education/training needs.

2. Organizes training.

(a) Identifies resources and screens for appropriateness.

(b) Develops material, where necessary.

3. Administers training/education program.

4. Evaluates results.

Responsibility No. 13: Selects, evaluates, organizes, and maintains a current library of drug information for use of pharmacy personnel in their training and conduct of their day-to-day operations.

Tasks:

1. Identifies any special areas of need based on legal requirements and practice setting.

2. Identifies sources available (e.g., textbooks, journals, subscription services, retrieval systems, phone numbers of drug information/poison centers) and evaluates materials for completeness, reliability, currency, ease of use, etc.

3. Obtains and organizes sources and places in a convenient location.

4. Orients and/or trains employees.

5. Periodically updates materials.

Responsibility No. 14: Serves as a member of governmental health boards (e.g., mental health board, health systems agencies).

Tasks:

1. Maintains pharmacist's availability.

2. Competently performs tasks expected of board member.

CHAPTER 7

Pharmacists

Today there are over 235 million people in the United States. Less than one-tenth of 1% of them are pharmacists. Despite their rather insignificant numbers, they play a vital role in the health of the remainder, for whenever anyone in the United States becomes ill, the odds are very high that a pharmacist will be involved with the drug therapy that sick person will very likely receive.

But what is a pharmacist? And what is pharmacy? Although all of us have had contact with pharmacists and pharmacies, it would be useful to develop a more precise understanding of the meanings of these terms. A logical place to start is the dictionary; Webster defines pharmacy as "the art or practice of preparing, preserving, compounding and dispensing drugs" (1). In its own peculiar logic, the dictionary goes on to define pharmacist as "one engaged in pharmacy."

This dictionary definition is not very helpful. There are many other aspects to pharmacy besides the four factors mentioned, and there are many persons other than pharmacists who are involved in preparing, preserving, compounding, and dispensing drugs. In fact, most drug products today are manufactured in large industrial firms that employ many nonpharmacists.

The Study Commission on Pharmacy has noted that it is no longer possible to define a pharmacist as someone who practices pharmacy. Rather, it defined pharmacy as both a health service and a knowledge system, or, more specifically, "a system which renders a health service by concerning itself with knowledge about drugs and their effects on men and animals." It further defined a pharmacist as "an individual who is engaged in one of the steps of a process called pharmacy" (2).

Rather than attempting to come up with a concrete definition of our own of the terms pharmacy and pharmacist, we will be content to state some operational terms which are used in this text. Later in this chapter we will go into much more detail on the functions of different kinds of

161

pharmacists and attempt to shed light in this way on a more full meaning of the term. In one sense it is the purpose of this entire book to define modern pharmacy in the context of American society.

Operational Definitions

In this book a pharmacist is defined as someone who has graduated from a school of pharmacy. At this time, the entry-level degree in the United States is either a 5-year baccalaureate or a 6-year Doctor of Pharmacy. In order to practice pharmacy, the graduate must also be licensed by a state board. Thus, a second definition is that of a licensed pharmacist. This is a legal definition that refers to any pharmacist licensed by one or more of the states to practice pharmacy. In order to become licensed, graduates of a school of pharmacy are required in all states to complete a practical experience requirement and to pass an examination administered by the State Board of Pharmacy. Only properly licensed pharmacists may perform certain restricted activities that are defined by the law and regulations of each state. For example, all states restrict the dispensing of prescriptions and the supervision of prescription departments to pharmacists licensed in that state. A summary of state pharmacy laws is available from the National Association of Boards of Pharmacy.

There is another way we can define pharmacist which may be useful in further discussion. This continuum can be termed the "distance of the pharmacist from the specific patient." At the extreme left of the continuum is the pharmacist who dispenses drugs or gives advice to or for a specific patient. He is most directly involved in the health care of specific individuals. As we move farther to the right on the continuum, the "distance" from the specific patient increases. The drug consultant who discusses a specific patient's drug therapy with a physician is not much farther down the continuum. He is still concerned with the health of an individual patient. If this pharmacist were giving general information about a class of drugs without reference to a specific patient, he would be still farther down the line. Pharmacists who are involved in research, laboratory work, or control activities in a manufacturing plant or hospital laboratory are, of course, pharmacists performing pharmaceutical functions but not with reference to specific patients. At the extreme right of the continuum are those pharmacists performing activities that not only are unrelated to specific patients but do not involve health care services at all. For purposes of our discussions in this book, we refer to pharmacists who are primarily involved in functions dealing with specific patients as *practicing pharmacists* or *practitioners*. The largest number of pharmacists in the United States are practicing pharmacists, and it is with this group that this book deals primarily; however, it should be remembered that there does exist a significant group of pharmacists who do not engage directly in professional practice, and their functions, goals, and values may be considerably different from those of practitioners.

Functions of Practicing Pharmacists

In learning about pharmacists, a good place to start, and an obvious one, is with what they do. We have already distinguished between practicing pharmacists and other sorts of pharmacists; it will be convenient to discuss the functions of each separately.

Types of Functions

From common knowledge of what goes on in a typical pharmacy, we know that practicing pharmacists do many things, some of which are directly connected with their position as pharmacists, others of which are not. We will classify the functions of practicing pharmacists in the following manner, realizing that not all things a pharmacist might do are included.

1. Professional functions—include cognitive, judgmental, and affective functions related to the control of the use of drugs in medical care.
2. Technical functions essential to practice—may or may not be restricted to pharmacists.
3. Administrative, supervisory, and managerial functions—as related to professional functions and nonprofessional functions.
4. Entrepreneurial functions—related to the investment of capital and ownership of pharmacies.

Professional Functions. In Chapter 5 we discussed the characteristics of a profession. It is clear that pharmacy embodies many, if not all, of these characteristics. It should be noted that the definition of a profession requires that all elements be present in concert. It is not enough for an individual to be oriented only toward the welfare of others or only to have a grasp of a significant body of knowledge. Only when all elements are combined is the definition of a profession fulfilled.

Professional functions, therefore, demand cognitive skills based upon years of education and experience, and responsible judgments based upon a value system that holds the patient's interests and well-being paramount. The cognitive component is easily grasped and understood; advanced formal education is its hallmark. Professional judgments must be based on a sure understanding of the relevant knowledge. But knowledge alone is not enough for the professional. Unlike the scientist, who deals with knowledge for the purpose of understanding and adding to it, the professional seeks to apply that knowledge to the problems of those in need of his services. To do this requires not only objective information but also a subjective feel for the needs of the patient. This is termed the *affective* component.

The affective component cannot be taught very easily, if at all, yet the true professional has it. It is the ability to recognize a patient's anxieties and to calm them with appropriate words and actions. It is a pharmacist recognizing intuitively that the patient has forgotten or not clearly understood the physician's instructions, and tactfully resolving the problem. It is, simply, *patient orientation*, a hallmark of clinical pharmacy.

Note that both cognitive and affective elements are present in professional functions. They are naturally intertwined. All available knowledge will not help to solve an unrecognized problem, nor will incorrect advice, however perceptive and sympathetic, be of much help to a physician in need of information. You cannot have one without the other and call the result professional.

We now turn to a more specific discussion of some of the professional functions performed by practicing pharmacists.

Dispensing Prescriptions. The function of dispensing is the most common of the typical pharmacist's workday. Over 1.5 billion prescription orders are dispensed annually from community and hospital pharmacies. The commonness of the function does not reflect upon its significance. Each of those billion-plus prescriptions was intended as a tailor-made course of therapy for a specific individual, and it was the pharmacist's responsibility to see that the order was carried out properly. Although it is true that well over 98% of the prescriptions dispensed today are prefabricated, the professional functions necessary to proper dispensing are numerous. A special task force of the APhA has described six steps in dispensing (3).

1. Receiving a prescription. If the prescription is received orally, its receipt is a professional function to be performed only by a pharmacist, inasmuch as judgment is often required. If the prescription is written, its receipt does not require a professional.

2. Certifying the prescription order. Professional judgment is required to determine, among other things, the legality and completeness of the prescription, the appropriateness of the

medication as judged from the patient's drug history (which contains, besides previous prescribed drugs, notations of allergies, idiosyncrasies, etc.), and the correctness of the dose. This function must be performed by a pharmacist.

3. Preparing the prescription. For most prescriptions, this involves counting or pouring prefabricated dosage forms. Obviously, the physical act of counting or pouring is not a professional function, but its supervision is. Extemporaneous compounding does require professional skills and must be done by a pharmacist.

4. Labeling the prescription. The formulation of clear, explicit instructions is a key element in dispensing that requires professional expertise. Studies have shown that large proportions of patients at all levels of education consistently misinterpret label instructions, and pharmacists have a responsibility to attempt to improve this situation.

5. Certifying the finished prescription. This step is analogous to step 2. Here, final checks and rechecks are made of the original prescription, its preparation, and labeling. Information about the prescription is added to the patient's drug history. This is primarily a professional function.

6. Issuing the prescription to the patient. This is a vital link in the chain of professional functions involved in dispensing. More than simply handing out a package, this step offers the opportunity for the pharmacist to ensure that the client understands how to use and store the drug product and how to avoid its improper use. This is a key professional function and should not be delegated.

It is necessary to pause here to point out that the functions described in this section are being defined logically and not empirically. In other words, a function is not being labeled professional because it is usually performed by a pharmacist. We realize, of course, that many pharmacists type prescription labels and that many clerks issue finished prescriptions to patients. By understanding the logical distinction between professional and other functions, however, we will be in a better position to strive for a situation in which the division of functions may be optimal. If nonprofessional functions are performed by professionals, we have waste to society; if professional functions are performed by nonprofessionals, we have potential harm to society.

Dispensing OTC Products.   In addition to dealing in prescription drugs, the pharmacist is also knowledgeable about and distributes nonprescription drugs. The distinction between these classes of drugs is an arbitrary but legal one, based largely upon judgments of safety for use by laymen. Because these products may be obtained without formal contact with a physician, the pharmacist can function professionally by offering appropriate advice on the selection and use of nonprescription drugs.

The importance of self-medication to medical care and the significance of the pharmacist's role should not be underestimated. Pharmacists should be involved directly in decisions related to the selection of OTC products to be carried by pharmacies and the accessibility of these products to consumers. Although there is, at present, no legislation mandating a class of drugs to be sold only by pharmacists, pharmacists do have the authority to determine how and where OTC products are to be displayed and sold in their pharmacies. Thus, pharmacists can exert control over the sale of OTCs in their pharmacies (4).

Some idea of the importance of self-medication to the consumer can be gained from an examination of Table 7.1. These data were obtained by personal interviews in 1200 rural Mississippi households and show the proportions of people treating selected symptoms through self-medication.

Providing Professional Advice. One of the pharmacist's most important professional functions is to provide information and advice in his area of expertise. This advice may be required by clients, physicians, other health practitioners, government, or private groups. It requires professional knowledge and skills to provide needed information that is appropriate in scope, content, and level to the needs of those seeking assistance.

Pharmacists practicing in the community will find numerous opportunities to provide professional advice to laymen. As the nation's most accessible health professionals (people see pharmacists far more frequently than they see physicians or nurses) pharmacists can fill a vital role as a point of entry to the health care system.

We have already mentioned the tremendous potential of the pharmacist as a source of information about OTC drug products. In addition, it is imperative that patients receive thorough instructions in the use of prescription medications. In the more general area of health education, information can be distributed and patients can be counseled on a wide variety of health problems. Drug abuse education, immunization programs, and diabetes detection efforts are but a few examples of how pharmacists can contribute. Contraceptive counseling is one area of special potential (5).

The need for drug information by physicians has been well documented. While the drugs marketed in this country are invariably safe and generally effective, the quality of their use by prescribers is uneven.

Table 7.1.
Selected Symptoms and Proportions with Self-Medication[a]

Symptom description	% self-medication	Total number reporting symptoms
Serious "gas"	44.0	116
Hemorrhoids	40.3	134
Bad stomach cramps	37.2	43
Frequent "loose bowels"	31.9	47
Painful or swollen joints	30.7	101
Sinus trouble	29.1	467
Serious daily headaches	27.9	86
Arthritis/rheumatism	26.7	371
Hay fever	25.0	120
Chronic vomiting	23.3	43
All symptoms	15.9	5205

[a] From: *Journal of Clinical Pharmacy* 4: 150, 1979.

Pharmacists can play a major role in improving this situation by providing and interpreting drug information for physicians.

Pharmacists practicing in hospitals have been particularly successful in helping to meet this need. Drug information centers utilizing extensive library and elaborate computer information retrieval systems to provide ready access to the drug literature have been established in many locations. Similar approaches to tapping a vast literature have been used by poison information centers and drug abuse crisis centers, often organized and staffed by pharmacists.

The rapid development of clinical pharmacy in larger hospitals demonstrates the need and demand for pharmacists with the ability to analyze therapeutic problems and work with physicians to construct optimal drug therapy for specific patients. Such pharmacists practice on the wards, obtain drug histories from patients, and advise the prescriber at the time and place that drug use decisions are made. Such clinically oriented pharmacists also are involved in monitoring drug therapy, detecting and treating adverse drug reactions, and counseling patients on appropriate drug use upon discharge.

Many pharmacists have become actively involved in conducting drug prescribing review studies and medical audits aimed at improving prescribing practices.

Selecting Products for Inventory. As anyone who has examined a pharmacy's shelves or thumbed through drug catalogs is aware, literally thousands of drug products are available commercially. Although the pharmacist has no choice but to carry single-source prescription drugs ordered by physicians, considerable opportunity exists to select specific suppliers of multiple-source drugs and specific nonprescription drug products. Pharmacists also, of course, have influence over prescribing through advice and counsel with physicians; this influence is formalized in hospital pharmacy and therapeutic committees, where drug selection decisions are made for the entire hospital. Because many drug products are available in most therapeutic categories, a choice has to be made as to which are to be stocked. This decision should be made based upon professional knowledge and judgment and not solely on market demand or whim.

Technical Functions Essential to Practice.   In addition to those functions requiring cognitive and affective professional judgments, there exists a large variety of manipulative or mechanical tasks that must be carried out during the course of practice. These are called *technical functions.* Although these functions often are performed by practicing pharmacists, particularly in smaller practices where assistants are not available, it is possible to differentiate them from professional functions. Judgments about technical functions may be made by the pharmacist separately from the physical task itself, thus permitting nonprofessional personnel to be involved (under professional supervision). Some examples of types of technical functions follow.

Functions Indirectly Related to Dispensing.   These include such tasks as stocking shelves, cleaning up after the pharmacist, and so on. These clearly are not professional tasks.

Functions Carried Out As a Prerequisite to Dispensing.   These include the prepackaging of multiple and unit dose packages of drugs and their labeling. In large practices bulk compounding is often carried out by a technical staff. Professional judgments must be made before these activities, with procedures and checkpoints carefully established and implemented by the pharmacist.

Functions Directly Involved with Dispensing.   These include counting or pouring prefabricated medications, reconstituting dry powders, and preparing labels, all under the direct supervision of a pharmacist.

The reader undoubtedly can think of other manipulative tasks requiring only physical skills and the ability to follow directions which can be classified as technical functions. Those discussed above are common and are functions that can be performed safely by nonpharmacists.

Administrative, Supervisory, and Managerial Functions.   Most modern pharmacists are involved to some degree in administration. Even the employed practicing pharmacist with no direct managerial responsibility has administrative duties related to practice. These include proper prescription record keeping, pricing procedures, maintaining patient drug histories, and so on. With proper planning, such tasks, along with others such as inventory control, personnel scheduling, and payroll, may be delegated to clerks, but a supervisory responsibility remains. In recent years the growth of third-party programs, with their attendant paperwork, has greatly increased the administrative chores of pharmacists.

Because most pharmacy practices are relatively small, that is, involve only a few pharmacists, a large proportion of pharmacists are involved in the management of a prescription department or practice. In community pharmacies pharmacists usually manage the entire operation, either because they have an ownership interest in it or because they are the most educated employees.

In any event it is not uncommon for pharmacists to be thrust into the position of managing a business operation, a set of functions for which they are not very well prepared. The importance of these functions should not be underestimated. If the goal of management is the effective and efficient operation of practice, it is congruent with the best interests of the pharmacy's patients. Should, however, the goal become profit maximization either explicitly or implicitly, it may come into direct conflict with the patient's needs in some situations. Thus, the professionals' determination that patient needs take precedence may hinder their performance as managers (and vice versa), depending on the criteria used. In fact, for optimal professional practice, managerial policy related to practice must be determined by pharmacists.

The problem of managing a practice is shared with most other professions, including medicine, law, and dentistry. It is perhaps more apparent in pharmacy because the usual commercial setting of pharmacy makes it more salient. Excessive or predominant concern with managerial functions may divert pharmacists from mainline professional functions. While this is not necessarily bad, it should be done self-consciously so that its consequences, such as failure to keep up with the pharmacy field, may be assessed.

There is another aspect of management that more pharmacists ought to be getting into, and that is the overall management of the nature and direction of the pharmacy profession. The health care system of the United States is changing and becoming more institutionalized, which means a higher degree of organization at all levels. This organization may be reflected by third-party financers such as insurance companies or increased federal involvement through programs such as Medicare and Medicaid. The development of these ventures into pharmacy is often managed by nonpharmacists. To its displeasure, pharmacy frequently has found that pharmaceutical services and drug distribution in third-party programs are being determined by insurance men, government officials, or union organizers. It is essential to public health that high quality pharmaceutical services be made available through public and private third-party programs. Individual pharmacists must become more involved in managing not only their own practices but also the course of pharmaceutical services in the nation as a whole.

Entrepreneurial Functions.   Many pharmacists choose to practice as independent professionals, establishing their own practice by investing personal and borrowed funds. Thus, they take the financial risk that they may not succeed in hopes of a greater financial and/or personal reward if they are successful. They are dependent directly upon their own skills as professionals and as managers rather than on a salary paid by others.

The entrepreneurial function assumes greater significance in pharmacy than in the other health professions since it often requires much more capital. It also often involves a significant investment in nonhealth merchandise because the typical American pharmacy is an emporium. The possibility of conflicts between professional and entrepreneurial goals, values, and activities is obvious. Although it has been argued that independent practitioners are directly responsive to the desires of their clients, these clients usually are not in a position to evaluate professional services wisely.

Thus, practicing pharmacists who become entrepreneurs must be cognizant of the often subtle conflict situations which may arise in the course of daily practice and must take steps to see that they are resolved professionally.

Job Analysis of Practicing Pharmacists

In 1978 a national study of the practice of pharmacy was published which identified elements of the work of the practicing pharmacist. This study, jointly sponsored by the APhA and the American Association of Colleges of Pharmacy, was the result of a national survey of more than 1600 pharmacists. In the following list the activities identified in four major functional areas of practice are enumerated. Examination of this list will provide a functional outline of the contemporary practice of pharmacy (6).

I. GENERAL MANAGEMENT AND ADMINISTRATION OF THE PHARMACY

Description

Institutes disciplinary action and discharges pharmacy staff for cause.

Recruits, interviews, selects, and hires pharmacists and nonpharmacists for pharmacy staff.

Establishes, administers, and interprets personnel policies and procedures.

Schedules work hours for pharmacy staff.

Administers wage, salary, and benefit programs for pharmacy staff.

Supervises and evaluates job performance of pharmacy staff.

Prepares and/or participates in the preparation of the budget and its controls in providing for pharmacy services.

Negotiates with vendors regarding cost, delivery schedule, etc.

Determines primary and alternate vendors for pharmaceutical supplies.

Establishes a pricing structure for pharmaceutical services and products.

Reviews and/or prepares periodic reports of pharmacy's fiscal performance in relation to budget.

Establishes and maintains an ongoing cost analysis program.

Develops and implements an appropriate pharmacy security system to prevent theft and/or drug diversion.

Prepares written job descriptions for pharmacists and nonpharmacists on pharmacy staff.

Plans or assists in the design and the layout of physical facilities for pharmacy.

Establishes and/or implements written policies and procedures for pharmacy operations.

Verifies that purchases received from vendor conform to the specifications on the original purchase order and authorizes payment.

Establishes drug quality specifications for drugs to be purchased.

Reviews operations of the pharmacy for compliance with local, state, and federal laws and regulations.

Instructs and trains pharmacists and nonpharmacist staff in carrying out their assigned responsibilities.

Develops and maintains an inventory system for all drugs, pharmaceutical supplies, etc., in active and inactive storage areas.

Prepares and/or reviews purchase orders (both routine and emergency).

Maintains and reconciles accounts receivable from various third-party payors.

Establishes and monitors a system to ensure proper storage conditions for perishable pharmacy items.

Develops and maintains a system for the regular removal from storage areas of all pharmaceutical items that are outdated or whose manufacture has been discontinued.

Assists in design or implementation of computer systems for use in the pharmacy (e.g. patient records, inventory control, drug utilization).

Initiates a formulary system to meet the needs of patients and practitioners.

II. ACTIVITIES RELATED TO PROCESSING THE PRESCRIPTION

Performs a final check of the finished prescription to ensure that each of the steps has been accomplished accurately.

Verifies prescription order for amount per dose, appropriate route, frequency, and duration of therapy.

Verifies prescription order for completeness and legality.

Compounds the prescribed ingredients according to prescription formula or instructions.

Selects appropriate labeling for prescription container and includes patient instructions.

Verifies prescription order for physical and chemical compatibility.

Measures quantities needed to dispense the prescription.

Determines necessity of immediately handling the preparation and delivering the medication to the patient (emergency or stat).

Performs packaging and labeling functions to promote product stability.

Reconstitutes lyophilized or powdered pharmaceuticals into a dosage form suitable for administration.

Establishes and monitors a system to ensure proper storage conditions for perishable pharmacy items.

Maintains a record of controlled substances and poisons received, stored, and dispensed by pharmacy.

Selects the manufacturing source of drug(s)/product(s) to be dispensed for a prescription order written in generic terminology.

Develops and maintains a system for the regular removal from storage areas of all pharmaceutical items that are outdated or whose manufacture has been discontinued.

Checks patient record for pertinent patient information before dispensing prescription medication.

Maintains a record file of current prescription orders including pertinent patient information and renewal data.

Selects the manufacturing source of drug(s)/product(s) to be dispensed for a brand name prescription order in those cases where legally authorized.

Prepares and/or reviews purchase orders (both routine and emergency).

Develops and maintains an inventory system for all drugs, pharmaceutical supplies, etc., in active and inactive storage areas.

III. PATIENT CARE FUNCTIONS

Advises patient of potential drug- or health-related conditions which may develop from the use of the medication for which patient should seek other medical care.

Confirms and further clarifies patient's understanding of medication dosage, dosage frequency, and method of administration.

Integrates drug-related with patient-related information in order to determine appropriate course of action (e.g. timing of dosage schedule, advising patient of possible adverse effects).

Consults with patient to properly identify symptoms in order to advise patient for self-medication.

Interviews the patient or his/her representative to obtain information for entry into patient record, patient profile, or family health record.

Updates the patient's history in the patient's record from information obtained by recurring patient interviews.

Refers patient to other health care providers and/or health resources where indicated.

Reviews patient-related information for potential problems regarding drug therapy (e.g. socioeconomic factors, compliance habits, disease influences).

Advises patients in personal health matters (e.g. smoking, drug abuse).

Upon request, reviews and interprets medication history for the physician, patient, or other persons involved with patient's care.

Monitors patient records for indications of drug abuse or misuse.

Continuously evaluates and monitors therapeutic response of patient to prescribed medication.

Reviews and/or seeks additional drug-related information (e.g. cost, pharmacokinetic characteristics, bioavailability, common adverse effects) to identify potential problems regarding drug therapy.

Instructs patients in the use of medical or surgical appliances (e.g. inhalers, colostomy bags, trusses).

Makes recommendations regarding drug therapy to the physician, patient, or other persons involved with patient's care.

Provides information, treatment, and/or referral in emergency cases involving ingestion of toxic substances.

Publicizes and/or participates in mass screening programs (e.g. hypertension, diabetes, tuberculosis, venereal disease).

Participates in emergency patient care activities.

IV. EDUCATION OF HEALTH CARE PROFESSIONALS

Provides drug information to other health care professionals in a formal setting (e.g. organizes in-service educational programs, lectures, seminars, exhibits).

Assists in establishing, executing, tabulating, and evaluating clinical studies regarding drugs.

Participates in utilization reviews, medical audits, and medical care evaluations (e.g. as a member of medical care evaluation committee or in peer review).

Organizes and/or participates in "in pharmacy" education programs for other pharmacists.

Develops and implements systems for drug distribution and drug administration in institutional settings (e.g. nursing homes, hospitals).

Initiates a formulary system to meet the needs of patients and practitioners.

Develops and maintains quality control records for drugs that are prepackaged, bulk compounded, sterile product formulated, etc.

Prepares and/or reviews purchase orders (both routine and emergency).

Serves as a member of governmental health boards (e.g. mental health board, health systems agencies).

Selects, evaluates, organizes, and maintains a current library of drug information for use by pharmacy personnel in their training and conduct of their day-to-day operations.

Participates in appropriate community educational programs relating to health care and drugs (e.g. drug abuse, alcoholism, hypertension).

Functions of Other Pharmacists

More than 10% of all active pharmacists do not meet our definition of practicing pharmacist; that is, they are not engaged in providing pharmaceutical services directly to patients. They are, however, engaged in important functions related indirectly to practice. These include the development, production, and distribution of drugs; teaching and research in academic institutions; legal and regulatory functions with regard to drugs and pharmaceutical practice; public health functions; association work; and pharmaceutical journalism. Each of these areas requires skills beyond those normally taught in colleges of pharmacy; thus, those pharmacists working in these areas must acquire skills either through additional education or by experience and on-the-job training. In all cases pharmaceutical knowledge provides a strong base for diversification.

Development, Production, and Distribution of Drugs

The drug products required by over 98% of the prescriptions dispensed through community pharmacists today are supplied in prefabricated dosage forms by the pharmaceutical industry. Over 6500 pharmacists are employed in the industry, most in nonpractice positions that do not require licensure. Pharmacists in industry work both in technical areas such as research and development, production, and quality control, and in nontechnical areas such as sales, marketing, and administration.

Research and Development. The United States pharmaceutical industry is one of the most research intensive of all industries. The success or failure of major drug firms depends on a consistent stream of significant new therapeutic agents; therefore, a large percentage of the profits from the sale of existing drugs is poured into research. Unlike some other industries such as defense, almost none of the drug industry's research funding comes from the government.

Scientists engaged in drug research have a variety of backgrounds. Many have professional degrees in pharmacy coupled with advanced training in pharmaceutics, pharmacology, or medicinal chemistry. The preponderance, however, are nonpharmacist chemists, biologists, microbiologists, or physicians. As a result of the diverse training directed toward an understanding of therapeutic agents and their mode of use, the pharmacist is ideally suited for product development work in the pharmaceutical industry. As part of an effective pharmacy research group, these scientists are busy with many basic and applied problems. Expressed in broad terms, the following areas best illustrate their role:

1. Establishment of those physiochemical properties of drug substances and dosage forms that will influence potency, uniformity, stability, and bioavailability.
2. Preparation of Clinical Materials for the study of safety and effectiveness.
3. Development of the final formulations and full-scale manufacturing processes and controls for all products, regardless of the route of administration.
4. Improvement of existing preparations and processes from the standpoint of absorption, activity, and safety; cost or product elegance; and quality.
5. Scientific investigation of product stability, including the making of recommendations for storage conditions and setting of expiration dates for old and new products.
6. Evaluation of new raw materials and their specifications—colors, flavors, excipients, solvents, preservatives, etc—with

respect to potential value in pharmaceutical and toiletry formulations.

7. Scientific evaluation of new equipment and new or improved processes, and the determination of their effect on product quality prior to routine use in pharmaceutical production.
8. Investigation into the suitability and possible improvement of proposed packaging materials and containers.
9. Development of information from the foregoing for submission to the FDA and other regulatory agencies (7).

Analysis and Control.   Because prefabricated drug products must be dispensed confidently by pharmacists, it is vital that the drug manufacturer see to it that each dosage unit of every product distributed contains the product intended in proper form. Pharmacists and others working in analysis and control are concerned with developing and implementing methods to establish and maintain such quality assurance.

Today, pharmaceutical analysts must devise techniques that will measure accurately drug molecules at the microgram level in finished medications and impurities at the nanogram or picogram levels. To do this, analytical researchers must be able to use mass spectroscopy, X-ray crystallography, high pressure liquid chromatography, and electron microscopy (7).

Other control personnel are engaged in carrying out day-to-day qualitative and quantitative checks on raw materials, intermediate and finished products, and packaging components such as glass vials for injectables and plastic containers. Chemists often are preferred for the laboratory functions required, whereas graduate pharmacists are preferred in administrative control activities such as liaison with government regulatory agencies, reviewing control procedures, and auditing results.

Production.   Pharmacists frequently function in industry in such production areas as manufacturing, production planning, and inventory control. Because of their technical knowledge, they are often responsible for supervising these increasingly sophisticated activities.

The potency of modern drug substances permits no laxity in the technical control of manufacturing operations; cross-contamination must be prevented and unit-to-unit and batch-to-batch uniformity must be kept within extremely narrow limits. Manufacturing procedures must be meticulously followed, and the reliability and reproducibility of a process can be ensured only by clear understanding of the principles involved and the absence of deviation from prescribed controls. During the course of their education and training, pharmacists are imbued with a strong sense of responsibility concerning the handling of drugs and the absolute necessity for concentration and accuracy.

Marketing.   Once manufactured, drug products must be sold, and the marketing department functions to see that products are properly distributed, priced, and promoted. Numerous pharmacists have reached managerial positions in this area, both because of their technical knowledge and their understanding of the pharmaceutical market.

Most pharmacists who enter marketing with a professional degree start as medical sales representatives or detail men. They are responsible for personally visiting prescribers and pharmacists to sell their products in a professional manner. The drug's indications and side effects must be presented in a fair manner, and the representative must have the scientific knowledge to respond intelligently to the physician's inquiries. Since drugs are a technical product requiring expertise to promote properly, pharmacists are favored as sales representatives. However, because pharmacists often can earn more money as practitioners, pharmaceutical sales positions frequently are filled with persons trained in the chemical or biological sciences, bolstered by sophisticated company training programs.

Teaching and Research

Over 2000 pharmacists are engaged in teaching and research in the nation's pharmacy schools. An advanced degree—either a Ph.D. or a Pharm.D—is a general requirement for an academic career, although many pharmacists are involved in teaching as preceptors in internship and externship programs.

As pharmacy schools have become larger and, in many cases, associated with universities and/or medical centers, many have assumed significant research functions. Although academic research in many ways parallels industrial research, in general it tends to be less goal oriented and frequently more basic in nature.

Legal and Regulatory Functions

Because pharmacy is a complex scientific and technical field, its regulation must be carried out by persons with technical and/or science backgrounds. As a result, many pharmacists are engaged in regulatory activities. For example, state boards of pharmacy are made up almost exclusively of pharmacists. Federal agencies such as the FDA and the DEA utilize pharmacists in many areas.

These pharmacists must be familiar with the law and regulations with which they work. Thus, they work closely with attorneys and officials of the court. It is not unusual to find pharmacists who have themselves gone to law school and obtained a law degree.

Other Functions

Pharmacists perform a variety of other health-related functions. Some have become administrators or planners of various types of public health programs, including those related to health promotion and disease prevention (8), while others are functioning as executives of local, state, and national pharmaceutical associations. Still others are engaged in medical or pharmaceutical communication, such as editing drug- or pharmacy-related publications.

It is apparent that the relatively small proportion of pharmacy graduates who have not chosen to practice their profession directly are engaged in functions which contribute greatly to the nation's health and welfare.

Supply and Distribution of and Demand for Pharmacists

Pharmaceutical functions have been discussed from the point of view of the individual pharmacist, so far in an absolute sense. In a society such as ours, the individual is free to choose among alternative employment opportunities and also, to a more limited extent, to perform different functions within the same type of job. Thus, the pharmacist may choose to practice or not to practice, to work in a community pharmacy or in an institution, to settle in the east or west, urban or rural, and so forth. Within the practice setting he or she may choose to enhance his ability through continuing education, to manage or own a practice, or to become a preceptor to pharmacy interns. In the aggregate, these individual decisions produce the characteristics, distribution, and productivity of the profession. These characteristics are covered in this section.

Supply of Pharmacists

In 1982 the U.S. Bureau of Health Professions estimated that there were about 150,000 pharmacists actively employed in the nation. This compares with about 440,000 civilian physicians, 127,000 dentists, and 1.4 million registered nurses in the same year. Pharmacy is therefore the third largest health profession.

The supply of health professional manpower usually is related to the size of the population for planning purposes. Figure 7.1 illustrates the relative stability of pharmacist-population ratios between 1960 and 1980 and shows the dramatic increase in physician supply during that time

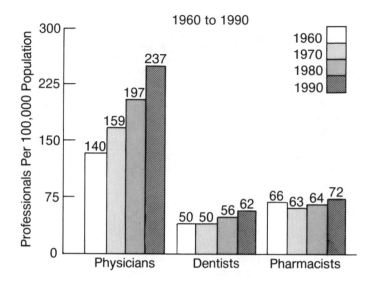

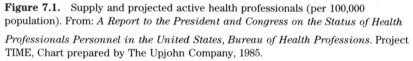

Figure 7.1. Supply and projected active health professionals (per 100,000 population). From: *A Report to the President and Congress on the Status of Health Professionals Personnel in the United States, Bureau of Health Professions.* Project TIME, Chart prepared by The Upjohn Company, 1985.

period. The illustration provides national averages; there is considerable variation from state to state in pharmacist-to-population ratios. These ratios tend to be simplistic, failing to take into account such factors as type of practice, degree to which practice is full time, and prescription volume at the place of employment.

Well over 90% of current pharmacy practitioners have a minimum of a 4-year baccalaureate program as a first professional degree. This became mandatory in 1932. Table 7.2 illustrates the wide variety of career opportunities available to pharmacists today. Although a clear majority continues to work in community pharmacy settings, the number of pharmacists working in hospitals is substantial, as is the number employed in nonpractice settings.

Women in Pharmacy

The number of women choosing pharmacy as a profession is thought to have important implications for the supply of pharmaceutical services. The number of female pharmacy graduates has increased from 12% of the total in 1960, to 19% in 1970, and to 48% in 1984 (9). When this increase began to become apparent in the 1970s, a number of articles appeared in the pharmacy literature expressing concern because of the

Table 7.2.
Career Options for Pharmacy Graduates—A Macro View[a]

Estimated number of pharmacy graduates employed as pharmacy practitioners, by major type of employment setting, United States, December 1983

Independent community pharmacy	62,200
Large chain community pharmacy	29,400
Small chain community pharmacy	19,000
Clinic or medical building pharmacy	6,500
Other facility serving primarily ambulatory patients (department store, mail order, HMO, etc.)	2,200
Government facility—nonhospital	400
Private hospital	20,400
Government hospital (VA, military, state, etc.)	9,800
Nursing home (pharmacy on or off premises)	2,200
	152,100

Estimated number of pharmacy graduates employed as nonpractitioners by major type of occupational area, United States, December 1983

Pharmaceutical manufacturing	6,650
Health care providers[b]	3,800
Educational institution[c]	2,300
Nonpharmacist practitioner/clinician[b]	1,400
Government—state and local[d]	1,260
Government—federal[d]	1,000
Chain drug firm[d]	740
Pharmaceutical wholesaling	680
Law	280
Business firm/consulting	270
Professional association	210
Publishing	40
Third-party insurance (private)	40
All other	30
	18,700
	170,800[e]

[a] Table prepared by T. Donald Rucker, Ph.D. University of Illinois College of Pharmacy, January 1, 1984.

[b] All are employed in the health care delivery system.

[c] The primary appointment of perhaps 175 pharmacists is as a clinician. Hence they really work in the health care delivery system.

[d] A relatively small number of these pharmacists work in the delivery system.

[e] Data derived from NABP records which show that 164,349 pharmacists were employed as of 8/83. Thus more than 6,400 non-licensed pharmacists have been added, primarily in pharmaceutical manufacturing.

perceived employment patterns of women. Rodowskas reported that data on women in practice at that time showed that women tended to have shorter working careers and to work fewer hours per day than men. If those characteristics continued, he argued, proportionally more women must be educated to provide a given quantity of service (10).

Kirk and Ohvall (11) reported that almost 20% of 1344 female respondents to a questionnaire reported that sex discrimination was a serious problem in their employment situation. Kronus (12) predicted that the dramatic change in the sex ratio taking place in pharmacy would cause a significant change in the profession in the near future.

Responding to these issues, in 1979 the APhA appointed a Task Force on Women in Pharmacy. The primary mission of the Task Force was to "address the needs of women in pharmacy, [and] assess the impact of the increasing number of women entering the profession" (13). The Task Force worked for 14 months to carry out its charge, and held an open hearing at the 1980 APhA annual meeting to obtain input. Its report was issued in March 1981 and included 12 recommendations for the Association. Basically, these recommendations called for the APhA to work to encourage greater participation by women in all areas of the profession, including management and administration, industry, higher education, and professional organizations. The Task Force reported findings that two of three women pharmacists were employed full time in 1980, a higher proportion than in 1971 (13).

Demand for Pharmacists

The demand for pharmacists in the United States can be examined from two points of view: the demand for "pharmacists," that is, persons who are pharmacists; and the demand for "pharmaceutical services," that is, the product of the pharmacist's effort. Both are discussed in this section.

The demand for persons who are pharmacists is not related simply to the demand for pharmaceutical services. For example, between 1930 and 1960 the total number of pharmacists remained relatively constant, despite large increases in both the population and the number of prescriptions dispensed. The current high demand for pharmacists and the resultant high starting salaries being commanded by pharmacy graduates seem to be related more directly to the expansion of corporate pharmacy—the chains—and to legal requirements in most states that a licensed pharmacist be on duty at all times a pharmacy is open. Thus, in many instances the demand for a pharmacist can be seen to be a need for a person with a license so that a store can be opened, rather than a demonstrated need for a given quantity of pharmaceutical services in a community.

To get a more accurate picture of the amount of pharmaceutical services needed in the country, analysts have depended primarily upon data related to prescription dispensing, not because this is the only pharmaceutical service but because it is a major service and is easily measurable and projectable. The growth in prescription volume in recent years has far exceeded the growth in the number of pharmacists, but increases in productivity have permitted current pharmacists to meet the demand with no undue strain.

The data indicate that new methods of providing pharmaceutical services, including the use of ancillary personnel and electronic data processing, have helped to meet the increasing demand for these services.

Thus, the pharmacy student of today probably will enter practice at a time when significant changes in methods of practice are underway. Regardless of the precise method by which demand is measured, there is little doubt that, upon graduation and licensure, the well-educated pharmacy student of today will find ample opportunity to apply his professional talents in a variety of settings.

Summary

In this chapter several operational definitions of the pharmacist were offered: a *pharmacist* is defined as any graduate of a first professional program in a school of pharmacy; a *licensed pharmacist* is one who has been licensed to practice in at least one state. A *practitioner* or *practicing pharmacist* is a licensed pharmacist who offers his services directly to patients.

The functions of practicing pharmacists were treated in detail, with special attention given to the professional functions that form the foundation for practice. A careful distinction was made between those functions in the dispensing process requiring professional expertise and judgement and those that are merely manipulative. The functions of pharmacists in the distribution of nonprescription drugs, in the provision of drug information, and in other areas were discussed. Technical, administrative, and entrepreneurial functions also were considered.

The activities of pharmacists in other areas of the field were discussed, including the role of the pharmacist in drug development, production and distribution, teaching and research, legal and regulatory activities, and association work. The chapter closed by providing some summary statistics related to the supply and distribution of and demand for pharmacists and pharmaceutical services. Special attention was given to opportunities for women within the profession.

REFERENCES

1. *Webster's New Collegiate Dictionary.* Springfield, MA, G. & C. Merriam Company, 1974.
2. Study Commission on Pharmacy: *Pharmacists for the Future.* Ann Arbor, MI, Health Administration Press, 1975.
3. Report of the task force ... Practitioner's and subprofessional's roles in pharmacy. *J Am Pharm Assoc* NS9:415–423, 1969.
4. Knapp DA, Beardsley RS: Put yourself into the OTC picture—professionally. *Am Pharm* NS19:549–551, 1979.
5. Smith MC, Wetherbee H, Sharpe TR: A test of knowledge of contraceptive methods: Pharmacists and pharmacy students. *Am J Pharm Ed* 43:19–21, 1979.
6. Rosenfeld M, Thornton RF: *A National Study of the Practice of Pharmacy.* Washington, D.C., American Pharmaceutical Association, 1978.
7. Blake T: Pharmacists in industry. In *Remington's Pharmaceutical Sciences,* ed 17. Easton, PA, Mack Publishing Company, 1985, pp 37 and 38.
8. Bush PJ (ed): *The Pharmacist Role in Disease Prevention and Health Promotion.* Bethesda, MD, ASHP Research and Education Foundation, 1983.
9. Penna RP, Sherman MS: *Pharmacy Degrees Conferred Over Time.* Bethesda, MD, American Association of Colleges of Pharmacy, 1985, Table A.
10. Rodowskas CA: Pharmacy manpower: Current status and future requirements. Paper presented at District I meeting, AACP/NABP, Boston, 1972.
11. Kirk KW, Ohvall RA: Women in pharmacy: Gratification or discrimination? *J Am Pharm Assoc* NS13:610–613, 1973.
12. Kronus CL: Women in pharmacy: Trends, implications, and research needs. *J Am Pharm Assoc* NS17:674–479, 1977.
13. APhA Task Force on Women in Pharmacy: *Summary Report.* Washington, D.C., American Pharmaceutical Association, 1981.

CHAPTER *8*

Pharmaceutical Education

One of the hallmarks of a profession is an intellectual base and possession of a specialized body of knowledge. This knowledge base is passed on to new generations through an elaborate system of professional education and controlled experience requirements. In pharmacy the predominant entry-level degree is a 5-year baccalaureate, although an increasing number of schools require a 6-year Doctor of Pharmacy (Pharm.D.). In addition, 6 to 12 months of practical experience is required in most states before an applicant is eligible to take a board examination for admission to practice. Those desiring more specialized education may spend an additional 1 to 5 years in advanced educational, residency, or fellowship programs.

The highly structured educational system for pharmacy in the United States is relatively new. A baccalaureate degree has been required for less than half a century, and the current 5-year program has been in effect as a requirement only since 1960.

Evolution of Pharmaceutical Education*

In the early days of the United States, pharmacists were trained entirely by the apprenticeship method under the guidance of practitioners. The only formal pharmacy education available was that offered to *medical* students in a few early university programs. During this period, there were no schools of pharmacy, no organized local, state, or national pharmacy groups, and no legal regulation covering the education of pharmacists for practice.

---

*For more complete discussions of this topic see Sonnedecker G: *History of Pharmacy*, ed 4. Philadelphia, J. B. Lippincott Company, pp 226–254; and American Society of Hospital Pharmacy testimony, open hearing: *The Final Report of the Task Force on Pharmacy Education*. Washington, D.C., American Pharmaceutical Association, 1984, pp 13–20.

The need for a better method of preparing pharmacists was one of the prime reasons for the formation of the first local association in the United States. The Philadelphia College of Pharmacy was founded in 1821, and one of the first activities of the group was to offer formal lectures in pharmacy. The word College referred to the association and not to an educational institution; offering lectures was only one function of the group. The school of pharmacy they established, however, has the same name and is still in existence as the oldest and one of the most highly regarded in the United States.

The program offered by the Philadelphia College of Pharmacy was part time; students were pharmacy apprentices who worked full time and attended classes at night. This pattern was followed over the next few decades by a number of other privately established pharmacy schools, most of which were located on the east coast. The number of students was small: during the first 25 years the Philadelphia College of Pharmacy graduated only five or six persons a year. Indeed, by the time of the Civil War, only about 500 pharmacists possessed a diploma.

During the 1870s the Midwest universities began to have a large impact on pharmaceutical education. The University of Michigan was the first state-supported school to offer a course in pharmacy, and the resources of such a state university signaled eventual pre-eminence over the private schools. The program at Michigan consisted of a full-time, 2-year course. For the first time attention was paid to admission requirements. Laboratory work was incorporated into the curriculum, and apprenticeship was not required for graduation (a radical move then, since state boards were not yet in existence to take over supervision from the school). Remember that the "firsts" mentioned are landmarks; general adoption of successful innovation in pharmaceutical education was much slower. For example, a 2-year course did not become a requirement for all students until 1907, over 35 years later.

The establishment of state laws to regulate the licensure of pharmacists proceeded most rapidly during the 1870s and 1880s. The development of state board examinations, which included a component devoted to testing the applicants' practical knowledge, permitted the schools to ease their requirements for apprenticeship as a prerequisite to admission or graduation. At the turn of the century, about 12% of the practicing pharmacists had at least some formal technical training.

By 1907 all schools in what is now the American Association of Colleges of Pharmacy had adopted a 2-year curriculum. In 1925 this was lengthened to 3 years. The first major study of the American pharmaceutical curriculum was begun in 1923 under the direction of W. W. Charters of the University of Pittsburgh. Published in 1927, the Charters' report did not make a specific recommendation about curriculum length, but it did speculate that to educate a pharmacist not only in professional and commercial subjects but also in cultural topics would require at least 4 years (1). A 4-year course of study was adopted in 1932.

Soon after the end of World War II, a major study of the profession of pharmacy and pharmaceutical education was undertaken by the American Council on Education with the support of the APhA, the National Association of Boards of Pharmacy, and the American Association of Colleges of Pharmacy. The Pharmaceutical Survey of 1946 to 1949 was directed by Edward C. Elliott, President Emeritus of Purdue University, and developed into the most comprehensive examination of the profession to that time. The final report included the following recommendation:

> ... the American Association of Colleges of Pharmacy and the American Council on Pharmaceutical Education [should] take the necessary initial steps for the development and establishment of a six-year program of education and training leading to the professional degree of Doctor of Pharmacy (Pharm.D.), this program to include two or more years of general education and basic science training (2).

Pharmacy and pharmaceutical education have been arguing about that recommendation ever since.

In 1954 the American Association of Colleges of Pharmacy agreed to a compromise resolution of the issue, and a mandatory 5-year baccalaureate program became the entry-level degree program for pharmacy beginning with the entering class of 1960. Some schools, however, notably the University of Southern California and the University of California at San Francisco, did embrace the Elliott Report and switched to all-Pharm.D. programs in the 1950s.

In the meantime, by the middle of the twentieth century, many changes had occurred in pharmacy. Virtually all drug products were being prefabricated by industry, and prescriptions requiring compounding dropped to fewer than 2% of all prescriptions dispensed. Although compounding remained (and still remains) a vital professional service in many instances, the time devoted to it by most pharmacists dropped markedly.

Concurrently, the total number of prescriptions ordered was rising rapidly and the possibility of problems with the use of drugs became increasingly recognized. Physicians, whose training traditionally has emphasized diagnosis, needed help with the selection and use of drugs in therapy, and patients needed help in learning more about the drugs they were taking. These societal needs led to a change in the focus of phamaceutical education. In addition to the longstanding emphasis upon the drug as a physical product came an increased emphasis upon the way drugs are used in patients.

Although this aspect of pharmacy was implicit in pharmaceutical education all along, formal clinical components began to be introduced in the 1960s, first in the California schools, with a rapid spread to other schools.

Students were required to rotate through in-patient and out-patient clinical departments in hospitals. They began to interact not only with other pharmacy students and faculty, but also with medical students, practicing physicians, and all of the other personnel who staff the teaching hospital. In the early 1970s the inclusion of a component of clinical pharmacy in the curriculum became a requirement for schools wishing to obtain federal capitation funds in support of pharmaceutical education. Clinical training now is a requirement for accreditation in the latest standards of the American Council for Pharmaceutical Education.

In 1973 the American Association of Colleges of Pharmacy decided that the time was right for another national study of the practice of pharmacy. A distinguished panel was appointed, headed by John S. Millis, a noted medical educator. The Study Commission on Pharmacy deliberated for 2 years and released its final report in Washington, D.C., at the end of 1975 (3).

A sizeable portion of the report of the Study Commission dealt with pharmaceutical education. The Commission defined the pharmacist as an individual engaged in one aspect of a total system called pharmacy. While all pharmacists share a common core of knowledge about drugs, individual pharmacists are characterized by the differentiated additional knowledge and skill required by a particular role. Thus, the Commission offered the following sequential educational objectives for pharmacy education:

a. The mastery of the knowledge and the acquisition of the skills which are *common* to all of the roles of pharmacy practice.
b. The mastery of the additional knowledge and the acquisition of the additional skill needed for those differentiated roles which require additional *pharmacy* knowledge and experience.
c. The mastery of the additional knowledge and the acquisition of the additional skills needed for those differentiated roles which require additional knowledge and skill *other than pharmacy*. (3, p 141).

The Study Commission also endorsed competency-based curricula. That is, it argued that graduates should be evaluated upon their attainment of the competencies necessary for practice rather than upon knowledge gained in individual disciplines. Other recommendations called for an evaluation of "the relative emphasis given to the physical and biological sciences against the behavioral and social sciences in a curriculum for the first professional degree," the development of a limited number of "clinical scientists" who would combine specialized scientific knowledge and practice skills, and the provision of appropriate practice opportunities for those faculty members having clinical teaching responsibilities (3, p 142).

While the Study Commission spoke in general terms about pharmaceutical education, it did not offer specific guidance on two issues which had plagued the profession for years: the name and length of the first professional degree program. In 1975 the American Association of Colleges of Pharmacy initiated discussion on these issues, which quickly reduced to the question of whether schools of pharmacy should continue to offer the 5-year baccalaureate degree as the entry-level degree, or whether all schools should switch to the Pharm.D. as the basic entry-level degree. Three years of intense debate and discussion followed, culminating in a formal vote on the issue at the 1978 meeting of the Association. The question posed to the delegates at that meeting read as follows:

> The interests of society and pharmacy will best be served by:
> A. maintaining the present Bachelor's Degree (B.S. or B.Pharm.) as the minimum entry level degree programs for pharmacy; or
> B. establishment of the Doctor of Pharmacy (Pharm.D.) degree as the minimum entry level degree for pharmacy.
> The results were:
> A. 107, in favor of the B.S. as the entry degree;
> B. 58, in favor of the Pharm.D. as the entry degree; and
> C. 2 abstentions (4).

While the educators were voting to preserve the baccalaureate as the basic entry-level degree, practitioners continued to be impatient with the notion that 5 years of education, plus extensive practical experience, led only to a B.S. degree and the designation of "registered pharmacist." As more and more pharmacists began practicing in settings where they dealt directly with other health practitioners, the professional designation of "doctor" began to take on more importance. In addition, the education required above the traditional 4-year B.S. program seemed to deserve a different degree.

Many pharmacists also believed that the 5-year baccalaureate program was inadequate to provide the level of competence required to practice modern pharmacy. Thus, by the late 1970s practitioner organizations were speaking out on the Doctor of Pharmacy degree issue.

In 1978, the American Society of Hospital Pharmacists' (ASHP) House of Delegates went on record as favoring a single Doctor of Pharmacy degree as the basic prerequisite for pharmacy practice. In 1981 the APhA established a Task Force charged with devising "a plan of action for the most expeditious implementation for the granting, by pharmacy schools, of a uniform doctor of pharmacy degree—this degree to be the sole entry-level degree for the profession" (5).

Some state pharmaceutical associations, led by the Indiana association, decided to circumvent the educational debate over curriculum length and name of degree, and adopted the designation "PD" (Doctor of Pharmacy). Advocates argued that PD was a more appropriate designation for pharmacists than RPh, and several associations and some state boards now use the PD designation on membership certificates and licenses. This action has resulted in what some pharmacists have referred to as a "tempest in a teapot," with educators, APhA, and ASHP feeling obliged to disagree with designations that imply "an academically conferred doctoral degree where none exists" (6, p 69).

The APhA's Task Force on Pharmacy Education presented its final report in 1984. It commented:

> ... Substantial disagreement about the nature of the education and the title of the degree ... exists today ... in the profession. The five year education program leading to a B.S. in Pharmacy, adopted in the mid-1950s as a compromise, ... still stands as the only degree available at 37 schools of pharmacy. Five schools of pharmacy (seven by the fall of 1984) offer the Pharm.D. degree as their only entry-level degree, while 28 (soon to be 29) offer both the B.S. Pharmacy and the Pharm.D. degrees (6).

American Association of Colleges of Pharmacy statistics show that Doctor of Pharmacy degrees accounted for about 6% of all first-professional degrees in pharmacy for the period between 1965 and 1980. The percentage has risen to about 7% in 1984 (7).

APhA's Task Force recommended that "a six-year professional degree with an enhanced professional competency evolve as the desired goal with the intent that it become the sole entry level for the practice of pharmacy" (6, p 28). The Task Force went on to say that the desired goal could not be accomplished immediately because "a majority of present-day colleges lack resources for this move" (6, p 3).

The entry-level degree issue again was raised at the 1985 meeting of the American Association of Colleges of Pharmacy in San Francisco. This time the members of the House of Delegates were presented with the following two choices:

    a. to maintain either the baccalaureate (B.S. or B.Pharm.) degree or the Doctor of Pharmacy (Pharm.D.) degree as the entry level degree programs for the profession of pharmacy or,

    b. to establish the Doctor of Pharmacy (Pharm.D.) degree as the sole entry level degree for the profession of pharmacy (8).

The vote was 76 for choice *a* and 57 for choice *b* (8). Thus, two entry-level degrees remain in pharmacy. In the meantime, the Doctor of Pharmacy degree as a postbaccalaureate degree continues to increase in popularity. The number of such degrees granted annually has almost tripled in the decade ending in 1984, when 331 postbaccalaureate Pharm.D. degrees were granted (7).

Areas of Curriculum

Whereas there continues to be disagreement over the length and title of entry-level degree programs in pharmacy, there is a reasonable amount of agreement on curriculum content. Although different schools organize content areas in different ways, most schools incorporate the following components into their core curriculum (6, pp 23–24):

General education
- Oral and written communication skills
- Social sciences
- Behavioral sciences
- Humanities
- Computer literacy
- Other (non-pharmacy-based) sciences

Basic physical and biological sciences and mathematics
- Mathematics through calculus
- General chemistry
- Organic chemistry
- Physics (emphasis on selected aspects of nuclear physics)
- General biology
- Microbiology

Biomedical sciences
- Anatomy (includes aspects of histology)
- Physiology
- Biochemistry (includes some significant emphasis on nutrition)
- Immunology

- Biostatistics

Pharmaceutical sciences

- Medicinal chemistry (includes natural products)
- Pharmaceutics and pharmaceutical chemistry (includes basic principles of biopharmaceutics, pharmacokinetics, and dispensing)
- Pharmacology (includes clinical toxicology)
- Pharmacy administration (includes management, marketing, laws, and ethical principles pertaining to professional practice and knowledge of the health care delivery system)

Clinical sciences

- Pathophysiology
- Clinical laboratory medicine
- Clinical biopharmaceutics and pharmacokinetics
- Clinical pharmacology and therapeutics
- Physical assessment

Practice experiences

All students

- Drug information and literature evaluation
- Community pharmacy practice (independent and/or chain pharmacy)
- Hospital pharmacy practice (urban and/or rural; secondary or tertiary level care)
- General medicine in an inpatient acute care area

Optional tracking opportunities

- Specialties in contemporary practice (nursing homes, home health care agencies, hospice, long-term-care facilities, nuclear pharmacies)
- Outpatient health care settings (community health clinics, hospital-related satellite clinics, HMOs)
- Medical speciality area (outpatient or inpatient settings)
- Nontraditional settings (industries, wholesale firms, chain management offices, association headquarters, or others)

A rationale for each of these named core curriculum components has been prepared by the APhA Task Force on Education and is presented here as a good overview of the content of an entry-level program in pharmacy:

- The *general education* subject areas are to be understood, clearly, as a part of a total curriculum and not just a set of admission requirements for entry to the professional program.

The accrediting standards brought to bear on the schools and colleges of Pharmacy by the American Council on Pharmaceutical Education call for devoting a minimum of 20% of the total curriculum (PrePharmacy plus the Professional program) to General Education. The Task Force considers this to be a *bare minimum* not an ideal, and encourages honest and ever-present concern on the part of Pharmacy faculties for the dangerous misfortune inherent in our as yet inadequate resolution of the problem of linking, or even integrating, humanistic with professional insights and understanding.

The individual, whatever the degree or compass of his or her specialization, is a member . . . at best a thinking and sensitive member . . . of society. A person is, and let it not be forgotten, *a General Practitioner of Living*. Such a one is a citizen whose knowledge and judgment are brought to bear on decisions important to oneself and to a community that now reaches out from the doorstep to the world. Any attempt to cripple differentiation would be as futile as it would be foolish. The need is to find ways of accommodation, relationship and reconciliation between the liberally educated mind and specialized competence.

Because of the relatively small portion of the curriculum devoted to general education, it is not only desirable but strongly urged that the student have careful and sympathetic guidance by an experienced and understanding faculty academic advisor so that there can be some coherence in course selection.

The Task Force suggests the following subject areas (not to be construed, necessarily, as courses) as being appropriate in satisfying general education requirements.

— written and spoken communication skills
— social and behavioral sciences—including, as examples, economics, history (general and specialized), anthropology, political science, psychology and sociology
— humanities—language, foreign language(s), literature, philosophy, music, art, ethics
— computer literacy
— other science areas, not necessarily pharmacy related: geography, geology, meteorology and astronomy serve as examples

The Task Force would observe that the subject areas in general education, like those in the sections that follow, ought to be under regular and critical analysis by faculty. This section, as is the case with others, should be considered dynamic and evolving.

Additionally, it could be pointed out that the talents needed for the growth of a profession come in various ways and from various preparatory routes. Admission of persons having a broad mix and variety of general education will create a pharmacy student body that can bring growth and enrichment to the profession.

● With respect to *basic physical and biological sciences and mathematics*, it would be well to remember that these areas are fundamental to universal science "general" education. They provide a broad-based foundation for good professional preparation. Moreover, knowledge, skill and, in some areas, competence in these areas are essential both to understanding and to ability to apply numerous concepts important in the health sciences.

● In considering the *biomedical sciences*, it would be well to note that a basic understanding of the normal structure and function of mammalian organ systems is essential to develop a working knowledge of the pharmaceutical and clinical sciences. An understanding of biostatistics is necessary for rational interpretation of important portions of the professional literature. Without question, it is necessary that the practitioner learn how to read, understand and interpret the literature, including reports of the results of clinical trials.

In consideration of the broad area of the basic sciences, it should be emphasized that the faculties will have to determine those areas that will require laboratory practice. It is true, the Task Force believes, that the laboratory can provide a fine opportunity for student-teacher interaction, for developing problem solving skills and for reinforcing didactic information.

● With respect to the *pharmaceutical sciences*, the Task Force suggests the inclusion in the curriculum of the following general areas:

— Medicinal Chemistry
   In order to discharge important responsibilities of professional practice, the practitioner must be able to understand and utilize the relationships that exist between physical and chemical properties of molecules (structure, solubility, etc.) and drug activity. Moreover, to serve as a reliable information source, the practitioner must have a knowledge of drug sources and possess fundamental facility with natural, synthetic and semisynthetic drugs.

— Pharmaceutics and Pharmaceutical Chemistry
   In utilizing pharmaceutics and pharmaceutical, chemistry (including basic principles of biopharmaceutics, pharmacokinetics and dispensing) it is true that a major professional responsibility of practitioners involves their ability to evaluate drug dosage forms. To do this, a working knowledge of the analytical, physical, chemical and mathematical principles in pharmaceutical dose formulation is essential. The traditional dispensing function of pharmacists is and will remain an important responsibility of professional practice.

Practitioners, without exception, must be competent in discharging tasks associated with processing the prescription order, dispensing it correctly and communicating appropriate information to the patient and prescriber.

— Pharmacology and Toxicology
The provision of advice about the rational therapeutic use of drugs requires an understanding of pharmacology and pharmacodynamics, the principles of drug metabolism and the various parameters responsible for drug absorption, distribution and excretion. To discharge professional responsibilities relating to the provision of information, treatment, and/or referral in emergency cases involving ingestion of toxic substances, the practitioner must have a working knowledge of clinical toxicology.

— Pharmacy Administration
Knowledge of pharmacy administration (including management, marketing, laws and ethical principles pertaining to professional practice, and knowledge of the health care delivery system) is important. To maintain an effective practice, pharmacists must understand the basic social and economic factors that influence the health care system. Additionally, numerous professional responsibilities require that they have the ability to establish and administer pharmacy management, personnel and fiscal policies. In this regard, practitioners should be able to utilize computer technology in discharging the several responsibilities of contemporary professional practice. Finally, it is essential that practitioners have a working knowledge of the federal and state statutes and regulations which apply to the profession as well as an appreciation of what constitutes ethical practice and behavior. In the event that a deficiency (resources, personnel, library, computer laboratory) in this subject area exists within a school of pharmacy, that school's faculty is encouraged by the Task Force to seek all possible assistance from cognate faculty and support staff in business schools, computer science departments, or other intrauniversity sources.

● Subject Areas in the *Clinical Sciences*

— Pathophysiology
Knowledge of the pathogenesis of disease is essential to the comprehension and recognition of the signs and symptoms of a specific illness; it is also the basis upon which the pharmacist can promote the rational prescription and use of drugs to alleviate disease. A knowledge of this subject area

is also essential to effective communication with health providers and the public regarding health matters in general and drug therapy specifically.

— Clinical Laboratory Medicine
The ability to interpret commonly performed laboratory tests is essential to an understanding of disease and drug effects and to the selection and dosing of drugs.

— Clinical Biopharmaceutics and Pharmacokinetics
Examples of pharmacists' responsibilities which are based upon comprehension of this subject area include evaluation of bioavailability data from manufacturer's literature and individualization of dosing regimens of drugs for patients with specific medical problems.

— Clinical Pharmacology and Therapeutics
The ability to review drug profiles, evaluate drug therapy, make recommendations regarding the appropriate use of drugs, recommend rational changes in drug therapy, and evaluate the clinical drug literature relies heavily on the pharmacist's knowledge of the clinical use and effects of drugs, including nonprescription medications.

— Physical Assessment
Background information necessary for a basic understanding of this area and the ability to perform selected physical assessment skills enables the pharmacist to read and interpret patient medical records, evaluate self-diagnoses, and monitor the effects of drug therapy. Physical assessment should be taught in tandem with history-taking skills. This information does not suggest the practice of medicine by the pharmacist; it should enable the pharmacist to communicate effectively with the physician or other health professional. The freedom to learn what is necessary to begin pharmacy practice is the justification for the study of physical assessment. This point also applies to other areas: clinical laboratory medicine is another example. To prepare pharmacy students for professional communication, education should assist in creating an environment where good interprofessional relations with physicians, nurses, laboratory technicians and other health professionals can develop.

● Practice Experiences
— Drug Information and Literature Evaluation
— Contemporary Community Pharmacy Practice (community pharmacies, chain store pharmacies)
— Contemporary Hospital Pharmacy Practice
— General Medicine in an Inpatient, Acute-Care Area

As a drug expert, the pharmacist must be able quickly and

effectively to retrieve, interpret and evaluate effectively drug literature and communicate the information to those who need to use it.

There are substantial differences between community and hospital pharmacy practices. Students should be proficient in both since
these are major areas of practice.

The medical problems and management of patients in an acute-
care setting often are entirely different from those experienced in
an ambulatory care setting. The pharmacist must understand the
differences in the continuum of care and be able to function within
the practice limits of each setting. Clinical *practice experience* in
general medicine gives students an opportunity to apply therapeutic principles to patients with a broad spectrum of medical problems. Students are more likely to observe the therapeutic use of a
large variety of drugs and drug classes in this setting. Moreover, to
prepare for professional communication it is incumbent upon
education to assist in creating an environment where good interprofessional relations with physicians, nurses, laboratory technicians and other health professionals can evolve.

There must be opportunities, also, for optional programs, flexible placements, and alternative tracks, as exemplified below.

— Specialty areas in contemporary practice (e.g., nursing homes,
  home health care agencies, hospices, long-term care facilities)
— Outpatient health care settings (e.g., community health
  clinics, clinics associated with hospitals, health maintenance
  organizations)
— Medical specialty areas (outpatient or inpatient settings)
— Nontraditional settings (e.g., industries, wholesale firms, chain
  management offices, association headquarters, or others)

The Task Force wishes to make particular note, with respect
both to subject areas in the *clinical sciences* and to *practice
experiences*, that flexibility in program, student option and sound
faculty advice and counseling will enable tracking to occur within
the core curriculum. This is not to say that the core is an abstract
concept, it is to recognize that time, circumstances, abilities and
interests will require adjustment. This must be abundantly clear at
the outset (6, pp 75–77).

The curriculum content areas were discussed here one by one for
simplicity and convenience. It always should be kept in mind that the
overall objective of including any material is to prepare a better pharmacist. The truly competent professional must be able to integrate
appropriate content from many areas in order to arrive at solutions to
problems faced in practice. Thus, by graduation the student must be
able to breach the lines often drawn around content areas in order to be
able to utilize knowledge and skills successfully in practice.

Professional Experience Requirements

In addition to completing the rapidly evolving pharmacy curriculum, students must complete a professional experience requirement under the supervision of practicing pharmacists before being eligible to take a state licensing examination. The amount of professional experience required varies from about 1000 to 2000 hours, with a majority of states requiring about 1500 hours. In most states the requirement can be met by students prior to graduation. A number of different mechanisms have been developed to achieve experience. These have been defined as follows:

Internship is any experience in a supervised pharmacy practice program with the following characteristics:
1. conducted before or after graduation, but prior to board licensing
2. under the direction and control of the state board of pharmacy
3. no program involvement by a university or college
4. no academic credit granted to the intern

Externship is any experience in a supervised pharmacy practice program with the following characteristics:
1. conducted prior to graduation
2. conducted outside of the classroom in patient-care settings
3. component of a university- or college-based program
4. program sanctioned by the state board of pharmacy while under the direction and control of the college
5. academic credit is granted to the extern
6. extern's experiences are:
    a. patient oriented and
    b. directly related to the distributive and management functions of pharmacy
    c. supervised by a pharmacist/preceptor
    d. under a 1:1 ratio relationship between preceptor and extern.

Clerkship is an academic course conducted in patient-care settings where the student is provided with nonsimulated experiences in patient care with emphasis on all phases of drug therapy relative to the disease states of individual patients. Specifically a clerkship is any experience in patient-care settings where the student's activities can be characterized as:
1. primary involvement with provision of clinical pharmacy services on either an out-patient or in-patient basis
2. peripheral involvement with the distributive and management functions of pharmacy
3. functions are included which may not be presently associated with current standards of pharmacy practice
4. supervising preceptors, selected by the school or college, may or may not be pharmacists

5. a 1:1 relationship between preceptor and student may not be required (9).

The present trend is toward specifying that more and more of the professional experience requirement be met through externship and clerkship programs. The APhA Task Force has endorsed the recommendation of the American Council on Pharmaceutical Education that "the curriculum should contain an externship and a clerkship of such quality and quantity to serve in lieu of the internship requirements." The Task Force would like to see this recommendation implemented by 1990 (6, p 24).

Externship and clerkship programs place responsibility for development and implementation in the hands of schools of pharmacy. This permits greater coordination and integration of the academic portion of the curriculum with the professional experience requirement. Because students participating in externship and clerkship programs receive academic credit, the faculty has more control over the quality and content of the experience than with internships. Controlled experience usually results in a reduction in the total amount of time required to gain licensure.

The assumption of responsibility for the professional experience requirement has placed new demands on schools of pharmacy in terms of staffing, curriculum design, and logistics. Significant scheduling revisions usually are necessary to accommodate externships and clerkships that are often off campus and require large blocks of time. Appropriate sites must be arranged, and preceptors of high quality must be selected, trained, and integrated into the teaching program.

Despite the growth of the role of schools of pharmacy in managing the professional experience requirement of students, responsibility for the state board examination and licensure remains with state boards of pharmacy.

Graduate Education

About 40 schools of pharmacy are involved in a major way in graduate education. Master of Science and Doctor of Philosophy programs produce the scientists, educators, and administrators vital to the future of the profession. High quality graduate programs require an active core of research faculty and the availability of strong supporting departments; therefore, most such programs are found in the larger schools located on university or academic health center campuses.

Because graduate education is discipline based, not all schools offer graduate programs in all areas. In addition to advanced course work in a particular area of study, significant research leading to a thesis or dissertation is required. Although research and graduate study in the pharmaceutical sciences brings to mind the bench sciences of medicinal chemistry, pharmacology, and pharmaceutics, graduate work also is available in the clinical areas, in social and administrative sciences, and in history of pharmacy. Master's degree programs in institutional pharmacy also are available to train the administrators of pharmacy departments in hospitals.

Types of Pharmacy Schools

Many variables affect the kind and quality of pharmaceutical education obtained by a student. A large number of these variables are related to the school of pharmacy in which the student enrolls. All accredited schools meet the minimum standards of the American Council on Pharmaceutical Education, and their graduates meet the education requirements of the state boards of pharmacy, but there remain (and rightfully so) many areas of difference that are often significant. Some are related to the school of pharmacy itself, others to its setting and environment. Examples of both types of factors are discussed in this section.

Factors Related to the School of Pharmacy

Size of Faculty and Student Body. Pharmacy schools vary a great deal in size, although most of the 71 accredited schools tend to be small in comparison with other types of professional schools and even with other university divisions. It is not unusual for many university departments to be larger in faculty size than the entire school of pharmacy. The problem of faculty size can be a critical one because even the smallest school must treat adequately each of the pharmaceutical sciences as well as the professional areas of the curriculum. Overall comparisons of faculty size are difficult to make since consideration must be given to different educational backgrounds, full- of part-time appointments, shared responsibilities with other schools (e.g. pharmacology is sometimes taught by the medical school), and type of appointment (e.g. clinical professors).

Pharmacy student enrollment in the mid 1980s ranges from fewer than 100 in the final 3 years of study to over 700. Total enrollments grew rapidly nationwide in the 1970s, prodded by the financial incentives of national health manpower policy. Enrollment peaked at close to 25,000 in 1975 and declined to a current level of about 20,000 (10).

Curriculum Pattern. Accredited pharmacy schools must offer at least the final 3 years of the curriculum leading to the first professional degree within the school. Earlier years may be offered directly by the schools of pharmacy or may be completed elsewhere by the student. Thus, three types of curricular patterns are available in the 5-year B.S. program: 0–5 (no prepharmacy, all 5 years within pharmacy school), 1–4 (1 year prepharmacy, 4 years pharmacy), and 2–3 (2 years prepharmacy, 3 years pharmacy). Since the first 2 college years consist almost entirely of basic sciences and general education in most curricula, students planning on attending a pharmacy school on the 1–4 or 2–3 systems can take these early years practically anywhere and transfer later to a pharmacy shool. This may mean greater convenience and lower costs if a general college is more accessible than a pharmacy school. The schools operating on these patterns can leave the teaching of basic courses to the general colleges and concentrate their efforts and talents on the strictly pharmacy areas. Some pharmacy schools that are not connected with universities do not have an option: they must offer the total 5-year curriculum within their walls.

There are advantages to the 0–5 pattern, of course. Students feel more a part of a pharmacy educational program from their first day in college, as opposed to students taking basic courses at a multiversity in classes of hundreds of mostly nonpharmacy students. The faculty is also often better able to tailor basic courses to the needs of the pharmacy program. Too much tailoring, however, may result in an overly narrow educational program.

Financial Support. Most schools of pharmacy today are state supported, although several are private or church affiliated. The schools have been established, of course, to train pharmacists, and the bulk of their support is related, at least in part, to the number of students in training. Thus, most schools are motivated to attract more students, which means a larger operating budget, the ability to attract more and better faculty, and the means to develop more programs.

The federal government has been involved significantly in the financing of graduate education and research in pharmacy through research grants and contracts, pre- and postdoctoral fellowships, and training grants, although such funds have been drastically reduced in recent years. Tuition and fees from students are another major source of income, with private contributions playing a small but important role. (In certain institutions private contributions have been very significant.) It is easy to see that the above factors are closely interrelated: funding, faculty, students; and all are in turn connected with a variety of factors outside of the school proper. These are termed environmental factors.

Environmental Factors

Geographic Setting: Urban versus Rural.   This factor affects the overall milieu of the campus rather than the pharmacy school specifically. Preference is largely a matter of personal choice. One major aspect of the pharmacy curriculum that this factor may affect is the provision of adequate clinical facilities. A pharmaceutical education program of any size must have access to patient care facilities (hospitals, nursing homes, pharmacies) to provide the necessary practical experience to students. Schools without such facilities at a convenient distance are relatively handicapped in their efforts to offer a well-rounded program.

Students attending schools located in areas of limited population may find it difficult to obtain professional experience and financial support while attending school. Some authorities would contend that this is an advantage because it prevents the student from working while he should be studying. On the other hand, many students find concurrent practical experience helpful while attending school.

Affiliation of School with Other Academic and Clinical Units.   In addition to geographic location, location of the school of pharmacy within a complex of other academic and clinical units is another important environmental variable. At one extreme the school may be an integral part of a complete university, including a medical center, while at the other extreme the school may exist as an entirely separate entity without formal ties to any other institutions. There are also a number of intermediate degrees of affiliation. Some of these possibilities are discussed below, with examples of schools falling into each classification along the continuum.

1. The school most closely tied with the largest range of supporting units would be one which is a part of a university with a medical center on the same campus. Here the pharmacy school has the best possible opportunity to offer a complete and well-balanced program: basic sciences and general education courses offered by supporting university departments, support in the pharmaceutical sciences both from basic science departments such as chemistry and mathematics and from medical departments such as human anatomy and physiology, and access to medical center facilities for the professional and clinical courses in the latter phases of the 5-year program. Because of available resources, it is usually easier to offer a broader variety of programs in this setting; thus, most but not all schools with the substantially developed graduate programs outlined above will be found in this setting.

2. Some schools of pharmacy are located at universities without medical centers or with the medical center located on another campus. In this situation the school may take advantage of the resources of the university as discussed in no. 1 but must make other arrangements for its clinical and related needs.
3. The reverse of no. 3 may be true, that is, the school of pharmacy may be located with the medical center apart from the main university campus. This situation usually forces the pharmacy school to a 2–3 curricular pattern and makes it difficult to have a close relationship with students during their prepharmacy years. The school would have the possibility of a close working relationship with other units of the medical center.
4. Some pharmacy schools are located on the campuses of small universities that have no medical school. In fact, some of these universities have no other health-related programs. Often they are primarily undergraduate oriented and may be church affiliated. The variety of programs offered by the pharmacy school tends to be more limited. These pharmacy schools often have to work very hard to establish relationships with local hospitals and other educational institutions to meet their needs.
5. Finally, a limited number of pharmacy schools are completely independent of any formal relationship with a larger academic institution. These schools offer complete 5-year professional programs, teaching basic sciences and general education requirements internally. Arrangements are made with convenient and appropriate hospitals and other institutions for clinical experience for their students.

Both the Millis Commission and the APha Task Force on Pharmacy Education have argued that the ideal setting for pharmacy education is in an academic health center. Table 8.1 lists the 28 pharmacy schools in the United States located in such a setting.

Although we have been focusing on a series of variables one by one, it should be remembered that the kinds and quality of education provided by a particular school are a product of the interaction of all of these variables. A pharmacy school cannot be judged by any of these factors alone.

Continuing Education

No discussion of pharmaceutical education would be complete without reference to the importance of continuing education to the practitioner of pharmacy. With the constant acceleration of change in all areas of life, no amount of formal education and externship, no matter how complete or excellent, can totally prepare an individual for a

Table 8.1.
Universities with Schools of Pharmacy Located in an Academic Health Center

University of Arizona
University of Arkansas for Medical Sciences
University of California, San Francisco
University of Southern California
Howard University, District of Columbia
University of Florida
University of Illinois at Chicago
University of Iowa
University of Kentucky
University of Maryland at Baltimore
University of Michigan
Wayne State University, Detroit
University of Minnesota
University of Missouri at Kansas City
University of Nebraska
State University of New York at Buffalo
University of North Carolina at Chapel Hill
Ohio State University
University of Cincinnati
University of Oklahoma
Temple University, Philadelphia
University of Pittsburgh
Medical University of South Carolina
University of Tennessee
University of Utah
University of Washington
West Virginia University
University of Wisconsin at Madison

lifetime of practice. Continuing education is especially important for professionals in a healing field such as pharmacy. They have "professed" their knowledge in the area of drugs and are prepared to use it in the service of patients. But the underlying knowledge base of pharmacy changes so rapidly that specifics learned in school are soon outdated or irrelevant. Thus, a major objective of the formal educational system is to teach students how to learn on their own. This is reflected in one of the standards for accreditation of schools of pharmacy which states: "The need to maintain competency in the profession should be a part of professional development. Colleges or schools of pharmacy should seek to inculcate such an awareness and attitude in students during the undergraduate professional degree program" (11).

Many institutions in pharmacy besides schools are concerned with the problem of continuing education. Recent years have brought not only an increasing schedule of conferences, seminars, and lectures for the pharmacist but also a fascinating array of technologic advances and gadgets designed to make learning faster, easier, and more palatable. Unfortunately, no one has yet devised a way to transfer the actual work of learning from the student! The motivation to keep up with advances in the profession and the concomitant effort must flow from practitioners themselves.

Continuing education has been grasped by the profession as a solution to the issue of maintaining competence in pharmacy. Over the past 10 years, about 35 states have adopted requirements for mandatory continuing education as a prerequisite for licensure renewal. The American Council for Pharmaceutical Education has established procedures for accrediting providers of continuing education and about 200 schools, associations, and other groups now are accredited (6, p 44).

Continuing education has its problems. Many programs are short, on a single topic, and produced on an ad hoc basis. The existence of mandatory requirements has often resulted in programs taken solely to satisfy the law rather than to improve competence. Recently, more effort has been made to take a curricular approach to continuing education, that is, to develop coherent courses of study with defined educational objectives and evaluation to determine whether the objectives are met.

In 1985 the American Association of Colleges of Pharmacy organized and sponsored a conference on post-entry-level education and training (12). Representatives of all major national pharmacy organizations discussed the need for continued professional education and identified a number of avenues being explored to provide such education. In addition to more traditional efforts at continuing education, the conference recognized the importance of the following:

1. Certificate programs—structured educational experiences are designed to meet a specific practice need.
2. External degree programs—academic programs designed to result in a degree (usually the Pharm.D.) obtained through part-time, nontraditional work.
3. Residency programs—organized training experiences obtained in a practice setting while the resident contributes substantially to the work effort of the institution. The most well-developed residencies in pharmacy are those accredited by the American Society of Hospital Pharmacists.
4. Fellowship programs—post Pharm.D. programs involving full-time research activity and training in a clinical area.
5. Mid-career training programs—formal opportunities for professionals to retool or recharge in the middle of their careers. The academic sabbatical is the best example of this.

6. Corporate training programs—usually job-specific, short-term programs designed to meet the needs of a specific company. Trainees are company employees receiving regular salaries.

As can be seen, pharmacy clearly has recognized the need for post-graduate education and training if the profession is to keep abreast of changes in health care. Many options have been developed to meet this need, and current pharmacy graduates can look forward to a lifetime of learning.

Summary

In this chapter we have touched upon a wide variety of topics related to the education of pharmacists. The evolution of education in the United States was traced from the early days of completely empirical training under the apprenticeship method, through the painful struggle to establish formal college-level training programs, to today's highly structured curricula. The modern educational program moves progressively through the basic sciences, the pharmaceutical sciences, and finally to the professional courses, with a leavening of general education throughout. Formal classroom training is supplemented by a structured professional experience program with a strong emphasis on clinical practice.

Emerging Doctor of Pharmacy degree programs were analyzed and other specialized degree programs described. Examples of each were given. Types of schools then were discussed, with attention given to the many factors contributing to a school's individuality. Such factors include the number and type of faculty, the size of the student body, the curricular pattern, and the types of programs offered. Environmental factors include urban or rural setting, the control of the school (state, private, religious), and the university setting and supporting areas.

Finally, the importance of continuing professional education was stressed. To reiterate, the use of continuing education resources lies solely with the pharmacist. Materials and information are readily available throughout the country. Utilization of the resources will increasingly become the hallmark of the successful professional.

REFERENCES

1. Charters WW, Lemon AB, Monell LM: *Basic Material for a Pharmaceutical Curriculum*. New York, McGraw-Hill Book Company, Inc., 1927.
2. Elliott EC: *The General Report of the Pharmaceutical Survey, 1946–49*, Washington, D.C., American Council on Education, 1950.
3. Study Commission on Pharmacy: *Pharmacists for the Future*. Ann Arbor, MI, Health Administration Press, 1975.

4. Goyan JE: The case for the Pharm.D. as the only professional degree in pharmacy. *Contemp Pharm Practice* 3:59–64, 1980.
5. Delegates resolve wide range of policy issues. *Am Pharm* NS21:282, 1981.
6. American Society of Hospital Pharmacy testimony, open Hearing: *The Final Report of the Task Force on Pharmacy Education*. Washington, D.C., American Pharmaceutical Association, 1984.
7. Penna RP, Sherman MS: *Pharmacy Degrees Conferred over Time*. Bethesda, MD, American Association of Colleges of Pharmacy, 1985.
8. Memo from Executive Director of American Association of Colleges of Pharmacy, August 2, 1985.
9. Walton CA: Chair report for the Committee on Academic Affairs. *Am J Pharm Ed* 42:464–473, 1978, p 469.
10. Belmonte AA: Trends in pharmacy education and practice. *Am Pharm* NS23:594–596, 1983, p 594.
11. Cited in Nona DA: Time to focus on an overlooked accreditation standard. *Am Pharm* NS20:23, 1980.
12. *Report of the Post Graduate Education and Training Conference*, Bethesda, MD, American Association of Colleges of Pharmacy, October, 1985.

CHAPTER *9*

Control of the Practice of Pharmacy

The pharmacist in his practice is subject to a wide variety of controls. Some are imposed because he is a pharmacist and a professional. Some are imposed because of the drugs with which he deals. Some controls are imposed by society in the form of laws and regulations as a part of the franchise given to the pharmacist. Some are self-imposed: the ethical constraints with which the pharmacists attempt to control their own professional activities.

In this chapter we deal with both the society-determined and pharmacy-determined rules of conduct in pharmacy practice. Some mention is given to the legal control of the drugs themselves, but a more thorough discussion of this is reserved for a later chapter.

Legal Control

The legal controls on the pharmacist are of many types. He is subject to federal control through the many regulations which apply to the unique commodities—drugs—with which he deals. Regulation of the actual *practice* of pharmacy is reserved by the several states. Much of the legal control imposed on pharmacy is directly related to the drugs and to the special characteristics of the profession. It is well to remember, however, that in the eyes of the law the pharmacist is also subject to all laws and regulations which apply to any businessman in the community. Thus, he is liable to both civil and criminal actions if he violates any of these rules. We are interested primarily in those controls which apply specifically to pharmacy, but some mention of other controls should also be made.

There are several components to the legal structure of the United States.

Constitutional Law

The United States Constitution is the supreme law of the land, and all other law, including the state constitutions, must be consistent with it. Under the Constitution certain powers were given by the states to the federal government with all other powers reserved to the states. The words health and medicine do not appear in the Constitution. Nevertheless, the federal government has developed many important activities related to health through the exercise of constitutional powers to regulate interstate and foreign commerce and to promote the general welfare.

Statutory Law

Laws passed by legislative bodies are termed statutes (or in the case of local law, ordinances). These are compiled in statutory codes. The states pass a wide variety of laws under the inherent "police power" of the sovereign state to take action protecting the general health, safety, and welfare of the public.

Administrative Law

Administrative law encompasses the rules and regulations by which statutes are carried out or implemented by administrative agencies or through which specific regulatory agencies carry out their work. It is administrative law under which the various state boards of pharmacy carry out their functions.

Common Law

Common law is a law that has been developed from court cases based on precedent and custom. It is derived from English common law. Most civil actions—actions taken by one person or group against another—are carried out under common law. Among the types of civil suits that can be brought are those related to contracts (for example, breach of contract) and those involving wrongful acts or torts that involve injury through infringement on personal or property rights. The most frequent and well-known cause for the latter type of civil action in the health field is professional negligence or malpractice.

Federal Control

There is little direct federal control over the practice of pharmacy other than that which prevails over any self-employed professional person or business enterprise, such as those laws and regulations which relate to taxes, price fixing, and unfair business practices. The federal government does, however, impose many restrictions on the sale and distribution of the drugs with which it is pharmacy's function to deal. The inventory requirements, for example, of the DEA restrict the handling of drugs covered under that law as well as the number of prescription refills allowable and the record keeping required for exempt narcotics.

Before discussing some pharmacy-specific federal controls, it may be helpful to review the procedure by which the legislative process results in legislative controls (laws) and by which the regulatory process undertakes to implement (and sometime expand) them.

The Legislative Process

A legislative proposal can be introduced by a representative or senator when Congress is in session. The idea for the proposal may originate with a member or group of members; with the President or head of an executive agency; with a constituent; or with a trade association, consumer group, or other organization.

The proposal takes one of five forms, but only two are important here.

1. A *bill*, generally used for a proposal having wide application, is the most common type of measure. It is designated as "H.R." in the House of Representatives or "S." in the Senate, with the abbreviation followed by a number. Unless it is a rare "private bill," it becomes a public law after it has been passed by both houses of Congress and signed by the President, at which time it is given a public law number.
2. An *amendment*, which is a rider to a bill, joint resolution, resolution, or concurrent resolution, is, if passed, incorporated into the original measure. In the House, an amendment must be germane to the original measure (although there are loopholes); in the Senate, relevance applies only to appropriations bills.

After a measure is introduced, it is referred to one of the 22 standing committees in the House or one of the 15 standing committees in the Senate. Depending upon its "primary emphasis," a health measure is referred to the Energy and Commerce Committee, or the Labor and Human Resources Committee, both of which have health subcommittees, in the House, or the Labor and Human Resources Committee in the Senate. A measure involving taxation, such as Medicare or national health insurance, is assigned to the House Ways and Means Committee or Senate Finance Committee, both of which have health panels.

The membership of each committee is divided between Democrats and Republicans, generally in proportion to their total representation in each body. Customarily, the chairman and ranking minority members of each committee are the members with the greatest committee seniority on each side.

Since only several hundred of the several thousand proposals are acted upon, referral of a measure most often means its languishment during the session and its death at the end of the Congress in which it is introduced. It is at the committee stage that the fate of a bill is almost always determined; if it is introduced by a member of the committee with jurisdiction, it has the best chance of being considered.

Although a bill may be considered initially by a full committee, it usually is referred by the committee chairman to a subcommittee with jurisdiction over its subject matter; for instance, a Senate bill on Medicare benefits is assigned to the Senate Finance Committee's health subcommittee. If it has committee support, it usually undergoes a public hearing at which representatives of the affected executive agency, interest groups, and professional associations, as well as expert witnesses, consumers, and even representatives and senators who are not members of the committee, have the opportunity to present their views. In most cases witnesses are required to submit copies of their testimony in advance and to limit their oral presentations to summaries. They also may substitute written statements for personal appearances, although the latter tend to give more weight to their arguments.

After a bill is heard, it may be reported favorably to the full committee, with or without amendments, or tabled, an adverse action that usually kills it.

Once a bill is reported out of subcommittee to the full committee, it is marked up—amended and/or redrafted if need be—voted upon, and, if approved, reported to the full House or Senate. Each report is designated by number; for example, House Report N. 97–1 designates the first House committee report of the 97th Congress.

Typically, in each house a bill is debated, amended, and voted upon, with approval requiring a majority vote of the members present.

When a bill has passed either the House or Senate, it is sent to the other chamber, where it is most often referred to the appropriate committee, and is subjected to the subcommittee, committee, and floor stages described above. When the two chambers pass different versions of a bill, one body may accept the other's version without a conference. If not, either chamber may ask for a conference, whose members are selected by the Speaker of the House and by the full Senate.

After a bill or conference report has been approved by both chambers, it is sent to the White House for presidential action. The President has 10 days in which to act on the bill. If he either signs or fails to sign it within the 10-day period, while Congress is in session, it becomes law. If he vetoes it, returning it to Congress, it can become law only if a two-thirds majority in each house votes to override the veto. If Congress has adjourned during the 10-day period and the President neither signs nor vetoes the bill, it dies, subject to a "pocket veto." A signed bill is ordinarily assigned a public law number, which indicates the Congress and the order of signing, for example, P.L. 99–1.

Initiation or continuation of funding for a program requires both an authorization and an appropriation. An authorization—contained in a substantive legislative bill—stipulates the maximum amount which can be appropriated; an appropriation—provided in a separate bill, which always has an H. R. number because appropriations originate in the House of Representatives—establishes the actual budgetary figure.

The Regulatory Process

Legislation that has been enacted to establish or modify a federal program becomes the administrative responsibility of the executive agency (or agencies) of jurisdiction, with Congress retaining oversight. In most instances the legislation authorizes, and in some instances directs, the agency to formulate regulations to carry out the purposes of the law. An example of such an agency is the FDA.

Whether the agency must follow specific instructions or can work within a flexible framework, it generally prepares draft regulations that reflect input from various sources. Agency officials may consult representatives and senators, staff members of the congressional committees with jurisdiction, persons within their own agency and other agencies of the executive branch, officials of local and state government, and/or representatives of business and industry, labor, professional associations, or consumer groups.

Once the proposed regulations have been cleared, they are printed in the *Federal Register*, which is published each federal working day.

After the proposed regulations have appeared in the *Federal Register*, interested persons may submit written comments on them. Occasionally, the opportunity for comment may extend to testifying at a public hearing, held on the agency's own initiative or due to a statutory requirement or petitioner's request. Through written comments and/or hearing testimony, concerned individuals and organizations hope to bring to the agency's attention information or opinions on the proposed regulations that the agency may not have taken into account. By presenting views during a period in which the agency's positions are

Table 9.1.
Major Developments in Drug Industry Regulations Since 1900

1906	Federal Food and Drug Act: Established first major federal over drugs.
1914	Harrison Narcotic Act: Provided the basis for control of narcotic and other habit-forming and addicting drugs. Amended since a number of times.
1938	Federal Food, Drug and Cosmetic Act (FDCA): Provided much strengthened control over proof of safety of new drugs prior to marketing.
1951	Durham-Humphrey Amendment to FDCA: Established authority to limit dispensing of legend drugs to dispensing by the pharmacist on prescriptions only.
1962	Kefauver-Harris Amendments to FDCA: Established new controls to ensure safety and efficacy of all drugs, old and new, and provided much stronger regulatory power for the FDA, particularly in drug labeling and promotion.
1965	Drug Abuse Control Amendments: Strengthened the law toward control of illicit traffic in depressant and stimulant drugs.
1970	Drug Abuse Prevention and Control Act
1976	Medical Device Amendments to FDCA
1984	Drug Price Competition and Patent Term Restoration Act: Eased requirements for marketing generic drugs and extended certain patents for time lost in premarketing approval process.

fluid, the public may be able to influence the content of the final regulations. Public comments generally are made available for public inspection by the issuing agency.

Final regulations are adopted only after agency officials have reviewed the public comments, made modifications—if any—to the draft regulations, and conducted further internal review. The final regulations, with a statement of their basis and purpose, usually are published in the *Federal Register* at least 30 days before their effective date of application, although exceptions to the time period are permitted under certain circumstances. Such regulations are subject to amendment or repeal petitions from concerned parties.

It should be pointed out that regulations, once they have been through this process, have the power of law. Table 9.1 contains a list of selected important historical developments in drug regulation.

Federal Controls and Pharmacy

In his comprehensive study of the medical profession, Freidson compares pharmacy unfavorably with optometry in their respective progress toward professional autonomy, stating that "the pharmacist is firmly subordinated to medicine" (1). Freidson points out that the trained optometrist may legally diagnose and prescribe while the pharmacist may not. He cites as authority the earlier work of Denzin and

Mettlin (2), who had described as the reason for the "incomplete professionalization" of pharmacy its failure to gain control of the "social object," the drug.

A major *legal* barrier to pharmacist control over the drug has been the so-called Durham-Humphrey Amendment, an amendment to the Federal Food, Drug and Cosmetic Act passed in 1951. This legislation identified three general categories of drugs which must bear the legend (hence, legend drugs) "Caution: federal law prohibits dispensing without prescription." These categories included hypnotic or habit-forming drugs, drugs not safe for self-medication because of potential harm, and "new drugs" unsafe for self-medication. The result of this amendment was to prohibit the pharmacist from providing patrons with legend drugs on his own accord.

Reaction of organized pharmacy at the time of this legislation was mixed because the bill covered more than just the legend item. Pharmacy leaders have been active in recent years in efforts to have new classes of drugs legally indentified, which would have the effect of giving the pharmacist more control over drug choice.

However, the FDA, from whom such regulation would have to come, has taken the position that it is opposed to the concept of a "third class" of drugs, available without prescription but restricted to sale by pharmacists or in pharmacies. As we have seen in earlier chapters, this is not yet a dead issue.

Many physicians apparently feel that the FDA regulations interfere with their own practice of medicine. In a study conducted by *Medical Times* magazine, 86% of some 3500 responding family physicians indicated that they felt that "the FDA regulations overprotect ... patients and possibly deprive them of important therapeutic drugs." A similar percentage believed that government regulations had deprived them of drugs that they found both effective and safe in their practice of medicine. On the other hand, 62% did feel that FDA regulations had provided important protection to their patients against, for instance, the possibility of a thalidomide disaster (3).

State Control

Traditionally, pharmacy practice has been regulated primarily by the individual states. Each state has some type of state pharmacy act or law that deals with the control of drug distribution in the state and, more importantly, with the nature of pharmacy practice.

The power of the state to regulate the practice of pharmacy comes to it through the so-called police power. Police power may be defined as the right of the state given by its citizens to enact such legislation as is necessary to maintain the health, morals, safety, and welfare of its citizens. It remains the purview of the states rather than that of the federal government under the provisions of the tenth amendment to the Constitution of the United States, that is, it has not been delegated to the federal authorities and therefore remains in the hands of the state governments.

There is considerable variation from state to state in the details of the laws and regulations governing pharmacy practice. Some of this variation arises from tradition and historical development within the state. Additional variation comes from the fact that most of the control of pharmacy practice in the various states is more a function of *regulation* than of *legislation*. Most of the state pharmacy laws have as a major component the establishment of a state board of pharmacy with the power to impose regulations on pharmacy practice. Thus, we have 50 different and relatively autonomous state boards of pharmacy, each with its own different orientation, pressures, and makeup.

The laws, *legislation*, are those requirements set down by the people-elected representatives. *Regulations* may be thought of as the efforts of an administrative agency to implement (and sometimes expand) the law. Loosely defined, it is sometimes possible that an administrative agency may act as a legislative, executive, and/or judicial body within the scope of the relevant law. Because of the potential for broadening the intent of the law, a potential also exists for abuse. Indeed, some abuses have been charged to state boards in the areas of "harrassment" of some types of pharmacy. A charge has also been brought that the state boards have behaved on occasion as though their goal were to protect the pharmacy practitioner rather than the public.

The boards of pharmacy in the various states usually are made up of practicing pharmacists appointed by the governor. In many states the state pharmaceutical association has the prerogative to suggest or nominate pharmacists for appointment to the state board of pharmacy. Also, in many states it has been a tradition that eligibility for membership on the state board includes the ownership or at least the operation of a pharmacy. State boards now are bending toward inclusion of other types of pharmacists, including hospital pharmacists and employee pharmacists. By tradition most state boards have provided no opportunity for membership by faculty of the various schools of pharmacy.

Chief among the powers and obligations of the state boards of pharmacy are:

1. Promulgation of additional regulations or changes, or deletion of unsatisfactory regulations

2. Administration of the state pharmacy law
3. Administration of the pharmacy licensure procedures, including state pharmacy board examinations

The bulk of the day-to-day administration of the affairs of the state board of pharmacy usually falls in the hands of the secretary of the state board. In most cases the secretary is a full-time employee of the board of pharmacy and handles such affairs as setting up dates for licensure examinations, calling meetings of the board, and overseeing the activities of any pharmacy inspectors who might be employed by the state board of pharmacy.

The state boards of pharmacy are members of a national association: the National Association of Boards of Pharmacy (NABP). In addition to affording its members the opportunity to learn the activities and changes of the other states, the NABP maintains a national list of licensed pharmacists by state and works with the various state boards to arrange for a transfer of licensure for pharmacists wishing to move from state to state—the process known as reciprocity. Because the state has its own power to maintain requirements for licensure, such a national organization is a necessity in helping the pharmacist who wishes to change locations.

The very basis for the legislation and regulation which it is the task of the state board of pharmacy to administer and to develop is the protection of the patient whom the pharmacist is to serve. Toward this end it is the obligation of the state board of pharmacy to ensure that the pharmacist is qualified to practice at the highest possible level and, further, to see that he does structure his practice in this way. It is for this reason that the state boards administer licensure examinations to graduating students of pharmacy school; inspect the premises, equipment, and qualifications of those practicing pharmacy; and more recently have moved toward requiring continued education of pharmacists beyond the time of their graduation from pharmacy schools (4).

Some critics have claimed that state boards of pharmacy on occasion are more interested in serving the needs and wishes of practicing pharmacists in the state than they are the public. One treatment on this subject, for example, has accused state boards of pharmacy of restraint of trade in the retail drug business (5). Pfeffer hypothesized that one of the functions of the state board licensing functional activities was to raise the income of health practitioners. Pharmacy was a part of his study; however, he found little evidence that the licensing activity per se had a major effect on the income of pharmacists (6).

One of the reasons for criticism of state boards has been their administration of control over pharmacy licenses. However, the court in North Dakota upheld the right of that state board to restrict pharmacy ownership to pharmacists.

Since the passage of the first state pharmacy law in Rhode Island in 1870, state boards of pharmacy have become involved in increasingly complex regulatory matters. In 1979, on the occasion of the seventy-fifth year of the NABP, an historical review published in the Proceedings demonstrated just how complex these matters had become (7). Some of the issues facing the NABP over the years had been:

1. *Mandatory continuing education*—The concept of mandating continuing education as a step toward continued competence appears to have taken hold in the early 1960s, and by 1972 the NABP adopted a resolution favoring mandatory continuing education. This resolution followed by 5 years the first state requirement (Kansas), and by 1985, 34 states had such requirements.
2. *National pharmacy examination*—The idea of a national pharmacy examination has been one which seems logical, which would be likely to ease the process of transferring licenses from state to state, but which has been fraught with problems. In addition to the sheer complexity of constructing such an examination, there has been resistance from states' rights perspectives. In spite of the problems, a "Blue Ribbon" examination was developed and used widely by 1968. This has been followed by the development of the NABPLEX (*N*ational *A*ssociation of *B*oards of *P*harmacy *L*icensure *E*xamination), which was administered in 1979 in 48 states (all except Louisiana and Oklahoma). A *Candidate's Guide* to the NABPLEX is available from NABP headquarters.
3. *Consumerism*—During the 1960s many institutions came under increased scrutiny from organized consumer groups. Pharmacy boards were not excepted, and in 1962 California became the first state to require the appointment of a lay person to the state board of pharmacy. By 1978 some 14 states required consumer representation on state boards.

The state board remains the central force in the regulation of the practice of pharmacy. In this capacity it is important to practitioners and students alike. In a course in pharmacy law, it is general practice for the details of practice regulation to be conveyed to the pharmacy student late in the professional program. Because of the increasing involvement of the student in the practice setting early in his education, however, brief attention is given here to recommendations and activities of the state boards of pharmacy as they relate to the student or intern.

Because many students are concerned about their role in the pharmacy, a good rule of thumb is "that the student may not function except under supervision and all of his acts are the legal responsibility" of the supervising pharmacy (F. T. Mahaffey, Executive Director of NABP, personal communication).

The NABP has suggested guidelines for attention to consideration of legal matters in structured internship programs with formal preceptors. Knowledge of these principles should be acquired by the student even if no such formal system exists. Specific recommendations of the NABP follow.

The intern is responsible for knowing and observing the legal restrictions that are applicable to him. The laws and board regulations vary from state to state. He must understand clearly his legal rights and the limitations of practice imposed upon him. The intern should know the extent to which he is legally liable during his internship. He should inquire about the liability insurance carried by the pharmacy and his coverage under the policy.

The intern is responsible for applying for his certificate of registration as an intern in those states where this is required. He is also responsible for keeping a formal record of his progress if this is required by the board. He is responsible for requesting whatever certification of internship is required. Instructions on all of these matters can be obtained from the secretary of the appropriate board of pharmacy.

The intern must understand that he is preparing for a profession whose primary purpose is to give service to the public. He should remember that professional acts and suggestions are done with the best interests of the patient in mind. All personal contacts with the public should be carried out with proper respect for the individual as a person as well as a patient. . . .

Federal restrictions on the sale of exempt narcotic preparations should be reviewed with the intern. State regulations on exempt narcotics may be more stringent and they should be clearly spelled out. Because the pharmacist is now responsible for authorizing the sale of these items for proper medical use, the intern should observe the procedure followed by his preceptor. . . .

The regulation of professional practice is the responsibility of each state rather than the federal government, although there are a number of significant facts which the intern should know recognizing that no two states laws are identical. Not only should the intern be responsible for a working knowledge of state and federal law but he should review all supplementary statutes that relate to the establishment of a business and particularly the distribution of drugs, devices, and cosmetics.

The poison or hazardous substance laws vary from state to state. State law differs somewhat from federal law. The intern has the responsibility to know those poisonous substances for which he must register each sale and determine its use (e.g., muriatic acid). The intern should also know and observe any special restrictions on the sale of poisons that apply to him as an intern. In addition to observing recording requirements and limitations on sale, he should have an opportunity to see the preceptor exert professional conscience where the purchasers or users will have linguistic or sensory handicaps that make the written cautionary labeling limited in value.

The intern should be briefed on public poison control and assistance units in the area and antidotal information generally (8).

In addition, the student will be interested in the examination administered by the state board of pharmacy before his licensure.

The NABPLEX examination is administered several times a year, but at the *same* times in each state. It is carefully prepared by practitioners, educators, and other experts. Its administration is carefully monitored. Each section of the NABPLEX is related to and purports to test the ability to meet the criteria of competency statements in the areas of Practice of Pharmacy, Pharmacology, Pharmacy, Mathematics, and Chemistry. An example of such a competency statement, from the area of Practice of Pharmacy, is:

Given a patient medication profile, and taking into consideration the patient's disease state, sensitivities, or related problems, the candidate shall be able to monitor the patient's therapy and recognize the possibility of an interaction or adverse reaction between:

— drugs already recorded
— newly prescribed drugs
— a newly prescribed drug or a requested OTC product and drugs already being consumed: the patient's disease state, sensitivities, or related problems.

In the preparation of the Blue Ribbon examination, the precursor to NABPLEX, the examining committees identified six thought processes which they believed to be involved in the performance of pharmaceutical functions. Each of these was to have been included in the testing process. They were as follows:

1. Knowledge: ability to define essential terms and recall important facts, materials, phenomena, processes, or abstractions;
2. Comprehension: demonstration of a thorough understanding of major concepts and relationships and the ability to translate these into other communication;

```
  HAROLD RHEMSTRAND, M.D.                              DOCTORS CLINIC
                                                       Galen, Iowa


  FOR:   Mrs. Regina Conrad                    DATE:   April 19, 1981
         603 Tintagel Drive

  AGE:   Adult



                 Rx       Valium 5 mg.

                          Disp. #20

                 Sig:     Take one tablet before each meal three times daily.



                                        Reg. No. 6743
```

Figure 9.1   A typical prescription.

3. Application: the ability to apply appropriate knowledge, understanding, and skill to situations which stimulate the basic health functions of the pharmacist;
4. Analysis: the ability to analyze information given so that the major elements, relationships, and principles are made clear;
5. Synthesis: the ability to relate various facets of education and experience in order to explain differences between drugs or drug products, to propose ways at evaluating an assumption, and to arrive at reasonable deductions;
6. Evaluation: the ability to make judgments, form valid opinions, and arrive at sound professional opinions (9).

It should be pointed out that the prescription order itself is normally regulated by the state. Figure 9.1 shows an example of a typical prescription, with all of the important parts identified. Such a prescription is a legal document with many ramifications, among which are legal permission to dispense the drug, an obligation to dispense exactly what is prescribed, and certain legal liabilities which are mentioned later in this chapter.

Finally, mention should be made of the fact that the states do exercise some control over the drugs themselves, even though the major drug regulation comes from federal authority.

Criminal and Civil Controls

It should be obvious that any pharmacist who fails to abide by the laws and regulations governing his practice and the distribution of drugs is subject to criminal prosecution. Historically, the bulk of such actions has been the result of violations of regulations controlling narcotics and other dangerous drugs and of state board of pharmacy practice regulations.

Any student or pharmacist would be foolish to overlook, in addition, the liability of the pharmacist to civil damage suits arising from charges of malpractice. The financial sequelae as well as the professional repercussions of such actions can be considerable, and most pharmacists carry malpractice insurance. Even more important, of course, is the potential for human suffering.

Garson Kanin in his moving novel *A Thousand Summers* (10) provides one of the few pharmacist "heroes." His account of a dispensing error provides a good description of the nature of the pharmacist's legal and moral responsibilities. In the novel the hero learns that he has made an error in compounding the prescription, resulting in the death of a child. In the suit which follows, the pharmacist himself states his position in painfully personal terms.

> I wish to state that I have never been involved in a court proceeding and I have been greatly gratified to observe our form of justice in action. I believe that my trial was fair, the judge considerate, the jury attentive—mostly—and the witnesses truthful. The prosecutor seemed to me to be seeking no more and no less than the truth of the matter, and my own counsel, Mr. Coburn Saltonstall, represented me in the most exemplary possible manner. So much for that. I maintain that I made a terrible blunder, an unforgivable mistake and that, for this, I should indeed be punished. My regret and remorse and sense of guilt are, I fear, beyond my power to express. To the parents of the infant whose death I inadvertently, but surely, caused, I offer my abject apology. No term in prison can restore life to that hapless infant, yet I mean to serve it, as a reminder, I trust, to others of my calling, of how often we hold life and death in our hands, and with what unrelenting care and caution we must perform our responsible duties. . . . No amount of money, no material gain can make up to the parents the forever absence of their child, yet it is my intention, as a penance, to turn over to them a basic part of my estate. . . . The suspension of my license is, in many ways, the most painful part of this ghastly misfortune—yet I must accept it as just. I shall dispose of my establishment here and shall never again practice pharmacy anywhere. . . . My good

counsel has recommended an appeal of this verdict. With all due respect to him—and to you, Your Honor—I do not wish such a maneuver to take place. I wish now only to pay my debt. Thank you (10).

Professional negligence, generally known as malpractice, is the breach of the standard of care due to a patient. It may be grounds for civil court action if the negligent act (whether of omission or commission) causes harm or injury to the patient.

Most pharmacists carry malpractice insurance, which is insurance against the costs of litigation and awards. The cost of premiums, presumably reflecting increasing claims and amounts of awards, has been rising rapidly, particularly for physicians.

All of the states, responding to a perceived "malpractice insurance crisis," have in the past few years enacted various laws relating to medical malpractice litigation. These have included changes in statutes of limitation (time within which suits must be brought), ceilings on total awards, and provisions for pretrial screening of cases by special panels or for binding arbitration. Suits against pharmacists have been comparatively few, but this situation certainly could change.

Ethics and Self-Regulation

One of the often cited earmarks of a profession is a code of ethics. Implicit in the existence of such a code is the general belief that "a profession involves a sense of service and responsibility to the community, and the conduct required of a professional man is above that required of other men" (11).

Generally speaking, it is expected that the professions will be accorded special status in society. A part of that status is the special trust given the professional by his client. Adherence to a code of professional ethics and possession of a specialized body of knowledge provide the basis for this trust. Both are necessary; neither is sufficient.

Professional Interests

One of the tasks of the ethical code—probably the major one—is to reconcile professional interests with those of society. There are a number of elements involved in professional interest. *Extrinsic* interest may be devoted to socioeconomic status, reputation, prestige, and success, which accrue to the profession as a whole. Also included may be the *technical* interests that are a part of the craft and art of the profession. Included here are concerns about the training of new recruits, maintenance and improvement of standards of efficiency, and the seeking of new and better methods and processes. Sometimes these internal interests are in conflict.

When a certain level of professional development is achieved that results in a satisfying level of *extrinsic* progress, members of a profession may find it difficult to pursue further the *technical* interest that, while a part of the professional ideal, may provide discomfort in the short term.

The Interests of Society

Any profession monopolizing some socially important body of knowledge is likely to be considered potentially dangerous. It might use its monopoly to enrich itself or enlarge its power rather than to serve in the best interests of its clients. The symbol of the profession, however, portrays a group whose members have altruistic motivations and whose professional activities are governed by a code of ethics that heavily emphasizes devotion to service and the good of the client and condemns misuse of professional skills for selfish purposes.

From society's viewpoint, a strong and enforced code of ethics is the springboard from which the status "profession" arises. Profession is a symbol that people in society use in thinking about occupations, a standard to which they compare occupations in deciding their moral worth. It represents consensus in the society about what certain kinds of work groups *ought* to be like.

With professional status comes autonomy, which Freidson has called the single most important criterion of professional status (12). Autonomy cannot and should not be granted unless the client can count on the professional whose service he retains to have his best interests at heart. He cannot count on this without the existence of a code of ethics which is both adhered to and enforced.

Teaching Ethics to the Pharmacy Student

Students in professional education must become competent in their professions. There is a limit on the usefulness of this competence, however, unless the student is able to place his skills within the context of society. Every professional practitioner needs social understanding to do his work well. It is necessary even in the introductory phases of his practice to provide a framework within which to accumulate and interpret his experience. He needs it to relate his practice to the larger social issues facing his profession and society.

It is both obligation and enlightened self-interest for the profession to ensure that its entering members understand and subscribe to its ethical code. As McGlothlin notes:

. . . a student in a profession who is unable or unwilling to value the ethical principles of this profession should be prevented from entering—ever. Universally, the professions expect ethical behavior from their members. Universally, then, the professional school must do what it can to assure ethical behavior among its graduates (13).

The message is clear. As noted above, professional competence *and* ethical behavior are necessary for practice. While it is possible for the incipient pharmacist to have a well-defined sense of *personal* ethics, it is highly unlikely that he will come to pharmacy school with an appreciation for the nuances of *professional* ethics. It is the duty of all those involved in pharmacy education to be sure that the pharmacist trainee knows the standards of professional conduct and understands that deviation from those standards cannot and will not be tolerated.

Surely, instruction in professional ethics is a responsibility of the faculty of the schools of pharmacy. Just as surely, however, it is a responsibility of many practicing members of the profession. At no time since all training was done by the guilds have so many practitioners been involved formally in pharmacy education. Nearly every school of pharmacy in the country now has a cadre of practitioners who serve as preceptors in a clinical program. Many have faculty titles.

Not to be overlooked is the substantial, and perhaps most important, role played by pharmacists who give the neophyte his first position and thus are responsible for much of the early socialization to the profession. "As the twig is bent . . ."—so goes the axiom—and the new pharmacist, bent toward nonethical behavior by the example of his first employer, may grow "crooked."

As noted previously, practicing pharmacists have a great opportunity and obligation to assist in instruction in professional ethics. There are at least three ways in which this can be done. The first and most obvious is by setting a good example. The implications of this statement require no elaboration.

Pharmacists who are involved as preceptors have a special opportunity, not only to set a good example, but to articulate the reasons for their action to the student. When good ethical practice is the norm, it may require special effort to identify incidents that provide an opportunity to explain the decisions made. The effort is worthwhile.

Finally, pharmacists individually and through their professional organizations must demonstrate their willingness to enforce the code of ethical conduct by sanctions against those who fail to abide by it. This is perhaps the most difficult task of all, but the most important. To do less, to be content only with high personal standards of ethics, is to risk the loss of professional status given by society.

McGlothlin points out that professions would be lost without their ethical codes.

> The professions must live up to the codes as fully as it is humanly possible or face the probability that Society will so alter their freedom that they cannot effectively practice. The monopoly which a profession enjoys is based on its guarantee of ethical behavior. With these guarantees, the professions are awarded a status which few other groups in a democracy can boast (13).

There is a whole series of situations into which a professional person may be drawn and which have no real counterpart in basic human moral codes. It is not always clear from intuition what is best for the patient, for the profession, and for society. These are the reasons professions—and particularly the healing professions—have throughout history tended to adopt and adapt ethical codes.

History shows that responsibility for the development of codes of ethics has fallen usually to the professional association. Just as personal codes of ethics are developed and refined through years of personal experience in both simple and complex situations, so codes of professional ethics have been honed through many years of practice and by application in a multitude of professional situations. It is also true that a professional code of ethics, through a professional association, has greater public visibility, thus affording society the opportunity for comment and suggestion. The code of ethics in these circumstances is most likely to be consistent with the prevailing social view of "right" and "wrong."

In pharmacy the only national professional association which has developed a code of ethics is the APhA. Because it is unique and because the APhA is the only professional association offering full membership to all practicing pharmacists, it is the APhA Code which is most likely to be judged by society. The code is reproduced here.

APhA Code of Ethics

Preamble. These principles of professional conduct are established to guide pharmacists in relationships with patients, fellow practitioners, other health professionals, and the public.

A Pharmacist should hold the health and safety of patients to be of first consideration and should render to each patient the full measure of professional ability as an essential health practitioner.

A Pharmacist should never knowingly condone the dispensing, promoting, or distributing of drugs or medical devices, or assist therein, that are not of good quality, that do not meet standards required by law, or that lack therapeutic value for the patient.

A Pharmacist should always strive to perfect and enlarge professional knowledge. A pharmacist should utilize and make available this knowledge as may be required in accordance with the best professional judgment.

A Pharmacist has the duty to observe the law, to uphold the dignity and honor of the profession, and to accept its ethical principles. A pharmacist should not engage in any activity that will bring discredit to the profession and should expose, without fear or favor, illegal or unethical conduct in the profession.

A Pharmacist should seek at all times only fair and reasonable remuneration for professional services. A pharmacist should never agree to, or participate in, transactions with practitioners of other health professions or any other person under which fees are divided or that may cause financial or other exploitation in connection with the rendering of professional services.

A Pharmacist should respect the confidential and personal nature of professional records; except where the best interest of the patient requires or the law demands, a pharmacist should not disclose such information to anyone without proper patient authorization.

A Pharmacist should not agree to practice under terms or conditions that interfere with or impair the proper exercise of professional judgment and skill, that cause a deterioration of the quality of professional services, or that require consent to unethical conduct.

A Pharmacist should strive to provide information to patients regarding professional services truthfully, accurately, and fully and should avoid misleading patients regarding the nature, cost, or value of these professional services.

A Pharmacist should associate with organizations having for their objective the betterment of the profession of pharmacy and should contribute time and funds to carry on the work of these organizations.

An Historical Perspective

In Sonnedecker's marvelous *History of Pharmacy* a vivid picture is painted of the early struggles of the APhA to balance its desire to develop a "truly national and all-embracing" organization against the knowledge that many pharmacists to whom membership was to be offered were simply not qualified to practice (14). The Code of Ethics was one of the stumbling blocks in this early organizational effort.

APhA membership was limited inter alia to pharmacists who were willing to subscribe to its Code of Ethics, and this presented practical difficulties. The Code of Ethics required that the member "discountenance quackery." Yet, Edward Parrish, then operating a private School of Practical Pharmacy, noted that this was new to many "druggists." "It is mainly by the sale of quack medicine that many druggists subsist, who yet desire a reform in their business, and would be glad to cooperate in the laudable objectives of the Association." The ethical code should be rather the goal than the condition of membership.

Shortly after the APhA was formed, subscription to the Code of Ethics as a requirement for membership was dropped, but the standards of conduct were then incorporated into the "objectives" of the Association as set forth in the constitution. With revision and expansion in 1870, seven objects set the ethical tone for the ideal of pharmacy practice for the century ahead. They bear repeating here.

> To improve and regulate the drug market by preventing the importation of inferior, adulterated, or deteriorated drugs, and by detecting and exposing home adulteration.
>
> To establish the relations between druggists, pharmaceutists, physicians, and the people at large, upon just principles, which shall promote the public welfare and tend to mutual strength and advantage.
>
> To improve the science and the art of pharmacy by diffusing scientific knowledge among apothecaries and druggists, fostering pharmaceutical literature, developing talent, stimulating discovery and invention, and encouraging home production and manufacture in the several departments of the drug business.
>
> To regulate the system of apprenticeship and employment so as to prevent as far as practicable, the evils flowing from deficient training in the responsible duties of preparing, dispensing, and selling medicines.
>
> To suppress empiricism (i.e. quackery) and to restrict the dispensing and sale of medicines to regularly educated druggists and apothecaries.
>
> To uphold standards of authority in the education, theory, and practice of pharmacy.
>
> To create and maintain a standard of professional honesty equal to the amount of our professional knowledge, with a view to the highest good and greatest protection to the public.

The Code of Ethics was revived as a membership requirement in 1922 and revised in 1952 and 1969. One amendment was added in 1975. The present code touches on three major areas. The first two pertain to the profession itself:

> The pharmacist's personal duty to maintain and utilize the best professional knowledge and skills; and to practice only in situations which allow him to do so.
>
> The need to practice in such a way as to bring credit to the profession of pharmacy; and to participate in professional organizations.

The third and most important area covered by the code describes duties to the patient. Included are directions to:

1. Put the health and safety of the patient first
2. Use only drugs of high quality and therapeutic efficacy
3. Seek fair and reasonable remuneration
4. Respect the confidentiality of the patient
5. Provide appropriate and never misleading information to the patient

As the present code is read, one notes the degree of similarity between the present code and the APhA's first effort over a century ago. This is perhaps as it should be because the basics of ethical pharmacy practice, as they relate to the needs of society, have not changed.

This is not to say that there has been no change. The 1952 version, for example, noted that the pharmacist "makes no attempt to prescribe for or to treat disease." This prohibition is no longer a part of the code. In another section of the 1952 version it is stated that: "The pharmacist refuses to prescribe or diagnose." This, too, has been deleted.

Another more recent change (1975) is the deletion of the prohibition against advertising. The 1969 statement read: "A pharmacist should not solicit professional practice by methods inconsistent with his opportunity to advance his professional reputation through service to patients and to Society." The current version reads: "A pharmacist should strive to provide information to patients regarding professional services truthfully, accurately, and fully and should avoid misleading patients regarding the nature, cost, or value of these professional services."

This most recent change exemplifies well the role of society in the development of professional ethical codes. The courts, presumably reflecting the views of society, have held that prohibition of advertising is illegal. The pharmacy profession has reacted to this message.

Ethics and the Law

The APhA Code of Ethics, like most other professional codes, is quite general. Such codes are living documents whose real value to the practitioner comes through their interpretation. As often happens, the ethical standards have often been involved, indirectly, with the legal environment. The mandatory continuing education statutes and regulations in many states, for example, certainly are directly related to the provision in the current code that: "A pharmacist should always strive to perfect and enlarge his professional knowledge."

There are at least two ways of looking at the developments just described. One viewpoint holds that legal action consistent with a provision of a professional code is society's way of endorsing it. Thus, "The profession has done such a good job of delineating standard of practice, that we will mandate it for all."

A second, somewhat more gloomy, outlook is that legal action of this kind is evidence of the failure of the profession to enforce its code of ethics. Thus, "If the profession cannot keep its house in order, Society will take over."

In fact, enforcement is the issue on which legal-ethical decisions turn. The 1952 version of the APhA Code included this: "The pharmacist will expose any corrupt or dishonest conduct of any member of his profession which comes to his certain knowledge, through those credited processes provided by the civil laws or the rules and regulations of pharmaceutical organizations, and he will *aid in driving the unworthy out of the calling*." (emphasis added.)

Enforcement is only possible with adequate sanctions. If expulsion from a professional association has little practical significance (which many would argue is the case in pharmacy today), legal sanctions are the only recourse. Unfortunately for society, there tends to be a substantial gap between unethical and illegal conduct. The model arrangement is that which exists in Great Britain where licensure is contingent upon membership in the Pharmaceutical Society. A member who is expelled from the Society for unethical conduct simultaneously loses his license to practice.

The code of ethics of the APhA is interpreted and enforced by the Judicial Board of the Association. Members of this board are elected by the membership. Disciplinary proceedings by the Judicial Board are instituted on the basis of formal complaints alleging that a member of the APhA has violated provisions of the Association Code of Ethics. The bylaws of the Association provide an individual charged with a violation with an opportunity for a hearing before the board. The penalty for violations so judged by the Judicial Board can be expulsion from the Association.

Relation of Legal and Ethical Control

The interface between the professional and ethical control of pharmacy and the legal control is one which is not clearly defined. The APhA Code of Ethics takes note of this problem when it states that "the pharmacist has the duty to observe the laws of the states and nation." It is seldom true, however, that the laws or regulations will lend legal status to any specific ethical code, although many state pharmacy laws refer in a general way to "ethical" practice. Two examples may be cited of situations in which ethical practice and legal practice may not be identical.

The first deals with the matter of "substitution." At its national convention in 1970, the House of Delegates of the APhA approved a resolution calling for repeal of the various state laws prohibiting substitution (substitution in its usual definition means the unauthorized dispensing of a brand of drug other than that which is ordered or prescribed). Thus, we see the Association defining as ethical (since it is moving for repeal of the laws) the practice which was at that time in those states illegal.

The second example deals with legal tests of the APhA Code of Ethics. Among such tests was a ruling in 1980 in federal court that actions of the Iowa Board of Pharmacy (consistent with the APhA Code) to restrict mail-order pharmacies were a violation of antitrust regulations. The mail-order house plaintiff, Federal Prescription Service, was awarded damages in excess of $100,000.

It is a mark of the professionalization process that the increasing control of professional activity as well as extension of professional functions precedes the formal recognition of either by the law. This may be expected to be the case in pharmacy. Indeed, it seems safe to state that the self-regulatory practices of a profession should be more stringent than the laws that regulate it.

Pharmacists in the future may be expected to face a variety of circumstances in which legal guidelines either are inadequate or seemingly inappropriate but in which the ethical thing to do will be clear. Consider, for example, the problem of substitution. It is possible at the time this is being written for a pharmacist to be perfectly within the law by following to the letter the directions of the prescribing physician. It is possible at the same time that the best interests of the patient are not being served. Which, for example, is more important: adherence to the direction, sometimes ill considered, of the physician who prescribes the most expensive brand name product, or the suggestion that a less expensive but equally efficacious product may be used? Some pharmacists would say that the latter course should be chosen regardless of the law. It is in fact characteristic of the law that it will change to meet the changes in the system but that these legal changes will follow by some period of time changes in actual practices.

Another example: in most states pharmacists are not required by law to maintain extensive family record systems such as are necessary for adequate monitoring of potential drug interactions and adverse reactions. Ethically, however, it seems a necessity that the pharmacist include in this his total professional activity. It now seems possible that the courts may begin to interpret this ethical responsibility as a legal responsibility in malpractice cases. Legal and ethical controls of pharmacy or any profession are irrevocably related. They are not, however, identical, and pharmacy will be judged by its ability in the area of self-regulation.

A final example is the case of continuing education. Even though some state board of pharmacy regulations now provide for compulsory continuing education, leaders of the profession have made efforts to go beyond these legal requirements. Among the recommendations of a Task Force on Continuing Competence jointly sponsored by the APhA and the American Association of Colleges of Pharmacy were these:

> Recommendation 1: Responsibility for assuring continuing competence should be borne primarily by the profession and its individual members but also shared by colleges of pharmacy, state agencies and employers.
> Recommendation 2: Standards for continuing competence should be established by the profession and its recognized specialty groups in conjunction with representatives of related professions and the public (15).

There is always the danger of viewing the law as the lowest common denominator in evaluating the performance of the pharmacist. Written law generally evolves through the years as a reaction to events rather than as some omnipotent a priori code. In many cases there is no relevant law. Where no law exists, the basic question can only return: is it right?

Responsibility for Medical Care

A word or two also should be said about the larger responsibilites pharmacists must bear because they labor in the field of health care. Such a discussion would seem to belong in this chapter inasmuch as the determination of how health care is to be organized and provided will determine in large part the amount of external control exercised over pharmacy practice.

Probably the best contemporary description of the problems and the alternatives has been provided by Donabedian, who summarized the distinctive characteristics of medical care as follows:

> Briefly, medical care is a service, both necessary and unpredictable, which must compete with other necessities for which the need is more constantly pressing, or with non-necessities the satisfaction of which is more pleasurable. It must be purchased by a relative ignorant consumer in a market in which the free operation of consumer choice and the price mechanism are hampered by a variety of restrictive devices. It is, moreover, a service whose receipt or nonreceipt by individuals affects society as a whole (16).

These distinctive characteristics complicate attempts to approach a truly efficient and effective system of health care because of the existence of two fairly distinct viewpoints concerning the relevance and content of four social values to the provision of health services. These values are:

1. Personal responsibility
2. Social concern
3. Freedom
4. Equality

Although Donabedian applies his exposition to the issue of "the acceptability of greater government responsibility for the provision of health services to a particularly vulnerable population group," the issues are as basic as the values.

What we are in fact talking about is the responsibility of the pharmacist, in his larger role in a position of public trust, not just to deliver technically adequate pharmaceutical services but to assist to the best of his ability in the delivery of optimal health services for all. We are suggesting that each pharmacist must personally address the question of the public good in his reaction to all issues facing him as a health professional. We offer for consideration the viewpoint that the pharmacist cannot allow himself to be satisfied with merely following the dictates of current laws and formal codes of ethics. Rather, he has an obligation as a professional to seek out needed changes in both toward a goal of optimal health for all.

Pharmacist/ethicist Robert Veatch has observed that pharmacists today face a challenge from patients and health professionals "who insist the time has come when patients have grown up, when they have rights that must be protected even at the expense of some risks to their health" (17).

We think it is fair to say that the health professions have not taken much initiative in forming solutions to the problems of developing an equitable health policy. Pharmacists especially have been reluctant to get involved. The primary impetus for drug product selection has been the consumer. Pharmacists have made little or no contribution in developing solutions to the "drug lag" problems of our nation. Even the legal challenge to the maximum allowable cost (MAC) regulations was brought not by the pharmacy community but the American Medical Association and the Pharmaceutical Manufacturers Association (PMA). The legal action that pharmacists have undertaken has been distinctly self-interested, as when an FDA regulation denied community pharmacist access to methadone (18) or when a loose interpretation of the Robinson-Patman Act placed community pharmacists at a competitive disadvantage (19).

Some years ago Schneller suggested a host of areas for pharmacist participation in asserting the duty of scientists to contribute to the formations of public policy (20). These include the development of sensible criteria for drug approval, problems in the possible overuse of certain medicines, and the importance of bioavailability data in determining drug interchangeability. The importance of pharmaceutical expertise is emphasized by his question: "Should a branch of the government or a volunteer organization like the USP determine the tests and standards which are to be used to govern the quality of pharmaceutical products?"

Summary

While the control of the practice of pharmacy may be nicely divided into external (or legal) and internal (or ethical) parts, the actual division is not so precise. There is an extensive mechanism for the legal control of the practice of pharmacy and the drugs with which it is associated at all levels of government. There is further a developed and, to a certain extent, tested code of ethics available against which to judge pharmacy practice within the profession. Both ethics and the law are interrelated, however, and pharmacy faces an immediate and long-range future of resolution of the problems of living up to the expectations of both.

The future certainly will see changes in the nature and degree of control of pharmacy practice as well as the origin of that control. The NABP is taking stronger steps to lead the profession in promoting and requiring total pharmacy services. In 1979, for example, the first steps were taken in the direction of a recommendation for requiring pharmacists to consult with patients at the time prescription medication is dispensed (21).

Ultimately, of course, all professional controls emanate from social needs. In Chapter 10 we take a closer look at some of the organizations in pharmacy. Some of these are involved directly in formulating policies of professional control and, as we shall see, many other important activities.

REFERENCES

1. Freidson E: *Profession of Medicine*. New York, Dodd, Mead & Co., 1970.
2. Denzin NR, Mettlin CJ: Incomplete professionalization: The case of pharmacy. *Soc Forces* 46:357–382, 1968.
3. Anon.: How FDA regulations have affected family physicians. *Med Times* 101:32, 1973.
4. Lawrence GD: Voluntary or compulsory continuing education? *J Am Pharm Assoc* NS9-510, 1969.
5. Fletcher FM: *Marketing Restraints in the Retail Drug Industry*. Philadelphia, University of Pennsylvania Press, 1967.
6. Pfeffer J: Some evidence on occupational licensing and occupational incomes. *Soc Forces* 53:102–111, 1974.
7. Anon.: Epilogue and prologue. *Proceedings, NABP*. Chicago, National Association of Boards of Pharmacy 1979, pp 1–41.
8. National Association of Boards of Pharmacy: *Introduction to the Practice of Pharmacy—A Guide for Preceptors and Interns*. Chicago, 1971. Reprinted with permission.
9. Anon.: *NABPLEX, A Candidate's Guide, 1979*. Chicago, NABP, 1979.
10. Kanin G: *A Thousand Summers*. Garden City, NY, Doubleday & Company, Inc., 1973.
11. Jeffrey CR: The legal profession. In Davis EF (ed): *Society and the Law*. New York, Free Press of Glencoe, Inc.
12. Freidson E: *Profession of Medicine*. New York, Dodd, Mead and Co., 1960.
13. McGlothlin WJ: *The Professional Schools*. New York, Center for Applied Research in Education, Inc., 1964, pp 26–27.
14. Sonnedecker G: *Kremers and Urdang's History of Pharmacy*, ed 4. Philadelphia, J. B. Lippincott Company, 1976, p 200–202.
15. Anon.: Task Force proposes standards commission. *APhA Newsletter* 13:1, December 14, 1974.
16. Donabedian A: Social responsibility for personal health services: An examination of basic values. *Inquiry* 8:3–19, 1971.
17. Veatch RM: 'The Pharmacist and the patient's rights movement. *U.S. Pharmacist* 4:93–94, 1979.
18. APhA v. Weinberger 317 F. Supp. 824 (U.S.D.C.C., 1974).
19. Portland Retail Druggist Assoc. v. Abbott Labs 96 S. Ct. 1305 (1976).
20. Schneller GH: Do public assistance patients deserve access to all prescription drugs? *Am Pharm* NS19:471, 1979.
21. Anon.: NABP moves toward backing of mandatory consultation. *Am Drug* 175:51, 1979.

CHAPTER *10*

Pharmacy Organizations and Periodicals

Pharmacy seems to be the most organized unorganized field in the country. An array exists of national, state, and local organizations that are concerned with one aspect or another of pharmacy or drugs. The large number of groups is an indication of the great diversity of pharmacy. There are organizations of hospital pharmacists, independent community pharmacists, consultant pharmacists, black pharmacists, clinical pharmacists, and pharmacy students. There are organizations of chain stores, drug manufacturers, and wholesalers. Pharmaceutical scientists, educators, and colleges of pharmacy have organizations. And the APhA seeks to be the "foundation organization" of all (1). It is not difficult to understand why close cooperation among pharmacy groups may be difficult with such wide-ranging interests.

One of pharmacy's nagging problems has been a frequent inability to avoid excessive internal divisiveness over important profession-wide issues. Organizations within pharmacy often are at odds with one another as well as outside groups. Because many pharmacists are members of a variety of pharmacy groups, it is not unusual for a pharmacist to support, with membership and money, organizations holding opposite points of view on several matters. Recently, however, there are indications that the major national practitioner groups are cooperating to a greater extent than in the past. For example, in 1985 seven associations representing a spectrum of pharmacy interests joined to defeat proposed cuts in drug product cost reimbursement in the Medicaid program (2).

This chapter will discuss a number of specific pharmacy organizations, as well as the major periodicals of the profession. First, however, the functions of the professional association in general are considered.

237

Functions of the Professional Association[1]

Merton defines a professional association as "an organization of practitioners who judge one another as professionally competent and who have banded together to perform social functions which they cannot perform in their separate capacity as individuals" (3, p 58). Thus, the association's reason for being is to perform *social* functions; these functions usually are outlined in a lofty statement of objectives toward which the group will strive. What is actually done, however, may differ significantly from these published objectives since the association must perform multiple functions not always consistent with each other or with specific objectives.

For example, some functions of the professional association may come into conflict with the best interests of the public, at least in the short run. The association usually is committed to strive for the economic welfare of its members; this may result in higher charges for services to the clients served. Efforts to raise the educational standards of practitioners may result in extended training periods and sometimes in shortages of personnel, which again serve to increase charges made to clients. Both the members and the leaders of associations must be aware of conflicts such as these so that they may be handled equitably.

To make it easier to discuss the many kinds of things professional associations do, it is useful to classify functions by those units that benefit from them. These beneficiaries include: (a) the individual member, (b) the profession as a whole, (c) the association itself, and (d) society at large. In the discussion of specific functions that follows, it should be remembered that not only professional associations perform functions such as these; scientific, industrial, and trade groups also carry out many analogous activities. Consideration in this section is limited to professional organizations, while realizing that many other types of groups exist to serve the interests of various segments of pharmacy.

Functions for Individual Members

Perhaps the most obvious activities of associations are those carried on for the direct benefit of their members: the most pervasive of these activities serve to provide social and moral support for the members in their roles as professionals. Thus, individual practitioners gain strength from the knowledge that they need not deal with professional problems

---

[1]This section of loosely based upon an article of the same name, reproduced with permission from the *American Journal of Nursing*: Merton RK: The functions of the professional association. *Am J Nurs* January: 50–54, 1958.

and issues alone. This is especially important for many practicing pharmacists, who often work in settings with little opportunity for contact and communication with other members of the profession. In fact, much of the contact that does exist in the community is competitive rather than cooperative. Membership in a professional association helps to ease the feeling of aloneness which may be present in the independent practitioner.

Concern on the part of the association for the social and economic welfare of its members is especially important to employee pharmacists. This concern is expressed most often through efforts to establish desired salary levels and standards for working conditions and professional autonomy. The development of employer-employee guidelines by the APhA and several state associations is an example of this approach. Several organizations, including the American Society of Hospital Pharmacists (ASHP), the American Association of Colleges of Pharmacy (AACP), and, most recently, APhA's Academy of Pharmaceutical Sciences, conduct salary surveys of their members; these surveys provide useful information for both employers and employees.

Another important set of functions revolves around improving and maintaining the knowledge, skills, and level of practice of practitioners. Often this is attempted through planning and sponsoring continuing education activities such as institutes and seminars and through the preparation and distribution of publications. The association strives to motivate individual member to take advantage of these services in order to meet established standards of practice.

During this discussion we have examined activities and services provided only to association members. It is clear, however, that nonmembers also benefit from the results of these activities. The importance of this point has been stressed by Merton:

> . . . Members of the profession who are not members of the association typically receive an unearned increment of social, moral, and economic gain from the work of their professional colleagues in the association. In the not inappropriate idiom, those who remain outside the organization are the "free-loaders": they do not pay their way, either in dues or in kind. True, the free-loaders in a profession often do not see themselves as such. They do not realize that they are nonpaying and nonparticipating beneficiaries of the sustained work done by those who make up the associations representing their profession. Yet they are in much the same condition as citizens who would avoid paying taxes and taking part in public service while benefiting from the taxes and activities of the rest who contribute to the commonwealth. It is a task confronting every professional association to convert the free-loader into

the member, preferably an actively participating member, not only that he may do his share of the work which the organized profession needs to have done but also in order that his voice may be heard when the organization formulates its policies (3, p 52).

Functions for the Profession

The association is involved in a number of functions that serve to promote the best interests of the profession as a whole. Many of these functions benefit nonmembers as well as members; separation is not always possible. Of foremost concern is the establishment and promotion of standards in the profession. Thus, common activities include recruitment of qualified students into the field, active interest in educational programs, concern with the regulation of practice, and stimulation of relevant research activities. A progressive professional association always will be pressing for higher standards of excellence in all that the profession endeavors; it is in a sense "committed to dissatisfaction" with the current scene. This constant push for upgraded standards often produces conflicts among members since these members represent a wide range of education, abilities, and philosophies. Unless the association can handle such conflicts wisely, dissension and even the formation of competitive groups may result. This has occurred from time to time in pharmacy when one organization failed to successfully accommodate diverse points of view among its members.[2]

Profession-wide functions include the promotion of research in the field, thus encouraging the accumulation of new knowledge for the benefit of practitioner and client alike. Here the association takes on some of the functions of a scientific society; in fact, the APhA has a separate arm, the Academy of Pharmaceutical Sciences, to deal with such activities. To be useful the fruits of research must be disseminated, hence the involvement of the association in the publication of scientific and professional journals and related materials.

If well done and communicated adequately to the lay public, these activities provide the basis for increasing the standing of the profession in the eyes of society. Public relations activities must, however, be rooted in real accomplishments to have significant long-term effects.

---

[2]For example, the APhA Section on Commercial Interests split off to become the National Association of Retail Druggists in 1898. More recently, the ASHP ended its affiliation with APhA to become a separate organization, and, at this writing, Academy of Pharmaceutical Sciences members are proposing to begin a new scientific association independent of the APhA.

Functions for the Association

Certain activities carried out by associations are designed to forward their own private interests, which are often but not always consistent with those of the profession and of society. For example, membership recruitment, which is vital to the continued existence of the association, may not be in the best interest of the profession if the tactics used include attacks on other groups. In a field such as pharmacy, in which several associations are in existence, certain activities may serve to strengthen a particular organization while weakening others and causing divisiveness in the profession. Such a result could be bad not only for the field as a whole but also for the public, which frequently looks to professional groups for guidance in many matters requiring expertise. Major disagreements among similar organizations can be confusing unnecessarily when cooperation with outside organizations is required.

Functions for Society

> The functions of the professional association for individual practitioners and for the profession are, in the main, conspicuous ones, readily identifiable by those who would look and see. But one of the association's principal functions for the society of which it is a part is far from evident; it has often gone wholly unnoticed. This is its function, as one of the great intermediate associations, to help prevent the atomization of society into a sandheap of individuals, each intent on pursuing his own private interests. Such an atomized condition is a step toward totalitarianism, which consolidates power over these socially disconnected individuals into a single center.... In a word, the professional association helps furnish the social bonds through which society coheres (3, p 53).

Thus, the professional association performs an important social function by helping to relate disconnected practitioners to each other and to other important groups such as other professions, educational institutions, government bodies, and consumer groups. Without such formal associations, communication would be much more difficult, if not virtually impossible.

The overall effectiveness of a professional association depends upon many things: the quality of its leadership, its financial base, and so forth. But most important is its membership. A successful organization must have within its ranks a high proportion of those eligible, or its objective of fulfilling its multiple functions will not be met easily, if at all.

Professional Pharmacy Associations

American Pharmaceutical Association

Practicing pharmacists in the United States first organized into local associations called colleges. As might be expected, the first of these local groups began in an eastern city with the founding of the Philadelphia College of Pharmacy in 1821. Over the next 30 years similar colleges were formed in Boston, New York City, Baltimore, and Cincinnati. Among other things these groups were concerned with regulating pharmaceutical affairs in their communities. There was little *legal* regulation of practice until the 1870s.

Because Philadelphia, New York, and Boston were major entry points for drugs imported into this country, it was natural that their pharmacists were concerned about the problem of adulteration of imported drugs that arose in the late 1840s. To cope with this problem, a meeting of delegates from the three colleges was held in New York in 1851. In addition to dealing with the specific problem of adulteration, the delegates unanimously passed a resolution which would lead directly to the founding of the national organization of pharmacists:

> ... that a convention be called, consisting of three Delegates each from incorporated and unincorporated Pharmaceutical Societies, to meet at Philadelphia, on the First Wednesday in October 1852, when all the important questions bearing on the Profession may be considered, and measures adopted for the organization of a National Association, to meet every year (4, p 199).

Thus, in the fall of 1852 in Philadelphia, less than two dozen pharmacists from around the country met to create the APhA. Since that time, the Association has had an increasing voice in the affairs of American and international pharmacy, with its most rapid growth occurring since World War II. By the time of the Pharmaceutical Survey in 1947, the APhA had 11,000 members; in 1985 membership totaled more than 40,000 active members and more than 11,000 student members. Since 1934 the Association has been housed in the American Institute of Pharmacy in the heart of Washington, D.C.

Objectives. The wisdom and foresight of the small group of APhA founders can be seen by a close examination of the original objectives of the Association as written and adopted into the constitution in 1856. Although the language and details have been modified and modernized several times to keep up with changing times, the underlying soundness of the original statement still is evident:

> Article I. This association shall be called the American Pharmaceutical Association. Its aim shall be to unite the educated and

reputable pharmaceutists and druggists of the United States in the following objects:

1st. To improve and regulate the drug market, by preventing the importation of inferior, adulterated and deteriorated drugs, and by detecting and exposing home adulteration.

2nd. To establish the relations between druggists, pharmaceutists, physicians and the people at large, upon just principles, which shall promote the public welfare and tend to mutual strength and advantage.

3rd. To improve the science and the art of pharmacy by diffusing scientific knowledge among apothecaries and druggists, fostering pharmaceutical literature, developing talent, stimulating discovery and invention, and encouraging home production and manufacture in the several departments of the drug business.

4th. To regulate the system of apprenticeship and employment so as to prevent as far as practicable, the evils flowing from deficient training in the responsible duties of preparing, dispensing and selling medicines.

5th. To suppress empiricism. i.e. quackery, and as much as possible to restrict the dispensing and sale of medicines to regularly educated druggists and apothecaries.

In 1870 the following additional objectives were added:

6th. To uphold standards of authority in the education, theory and practice of pharmacy.

7th. To create and maintain a standard of professional honesty equal to the amount of our professional knowledge, with a view to the highest good and greatest protection to the public (4, pp 201–202).

As the first national pharmacy organization in America, the APhA was concerned, as the objectives state, with a wide range of interests: drug regulation, pharmaceutical education, regulation of practice, business affairs, and so forth. Over the years subgroups have been organized within the APhA to deal with specialized interests, and from time to time these subgroups have split off to become either autonomous or affiliated separate organizations. Thus, the APhA has fostered such diverse groups as the American College of Apothecaries (ACA), the National Association of Boards of Pharmacy (NABP), the National Association of Retail Druggists (NARD), and the AACP.

Membership and Activities.   Active membership in the APhA is open to any pharmacist in the United States. Currently, only pharmacists may be active members and thus vote and hold office, but a proposal is under consideration to extend active membership to non-pharmacists involved in pharmacy through positions in industry, government, education, the press, and associations. The APhA has a strong student organization, with a provision for smoothly moving into active membership at graduation.

In 1984, following a change in executive leadership, an intensive period of strategic planning ensued, and substantial changes in the organization's structure have been proposed. No textbook can deal adequately with rapidly changing events, so readers are referred to *American Pharmacy* for up-to-date accounts of changes.

The monthly publication *American Pharmacy* is the official journal of the Association; in it can be found the record of annual and special meetings and news of the organization and its members. A weekly newsletter to members covers current events. A scientific journal, the *Journal of Pharmaceutical Sciences*, is a monthly publication of the APhA's Academy of Pharmaceutical Sciences.

The Association also publishes books and monographs, including the well-respected *Handbook of Nonprescription Drugs*, now in its eighth edition.

In recent years the APhA (and most other pharmacy associations) has stepped up its activities in the government affairs and political arenas. A national political action committee (PAC) was formed in 1985, and a Government Affairs Office was created. Both were created, at least in part, as a response to the growing influence of public and private third-party programs on pharmacy.

Recent actions of the House of Delegates have called for a greater influence on the part of the APhA in educational affairs, particularly the provision of clinical components in pharmaceutical curricula, improvement of internship programs, and increased emphasis on the recruitment of minority students into pharmacy programs. These actions continue the Association's longstanding concern for pharmaceutical education, expressed earlier in its encouragement of the founding of the AACP and currently through its membership on the American Council on Pharmaceutical Education. Recently, this activity resulted in the completion of the Standards of Practice for the Profession of Pharmacy, which are described elsewhere in this text.

American Society of Hospital Pharmacists

The ASHP represents pharmacists in hospitals and other organized health care settings. Founded in 1942, the Society makes its headquarters in Bethesda, Maryland; by 1985 its membership totaled over 21,000.

ASHP active membership is open to pharmacists who currently are practicing pharmacy in a hospital or related institution. Student memberships also are available, as is participation in one of eleven Special

Interest Groups (SIGs), which represent members of the Society who have a common interest in a particular area (such as psychopharmacy) of institutional pharmacy practice.

A dynamic and rapidly growing organization, ASHP has an active publication program, including its official journal, *The American Journal of Hospital Pharmacy*, and a new monthly journal, *Clinical Pharmacy*. The widely used *American Hospital Formulary Service* contains detailed, unbiased information on virtually every drug entity available in the United States. *International Pharmaceutical Abstracts* is a semimonthly abstracting service of the world's pharmaceutical literature. ASHP has extensive educational programs designed to help members improve pharmaceutical services. The Society also is a national accrediting organization for pharmacy residency and pharmacy technician training programs.

Objectives. In 1984 ASHP revised its charter and adopted the following goals:

1. To advance public health by promoting the professional interests of pharmacists practicing in hospitals and other organized health-care settings through
   a. Fostering pharmaceutical services aimed at drug-use control and rational drug therapy.
   b. Developing professional standards for pharmaceutical services.
   c. Fostering an adequate supply of well-trained, competent pharmacists and associated personnel.
   d. Developing and conducting programs for maintaining and improving the competence of pharmacists and associated personnel.
   e. Disseminating information about pharmaceutical services and rational drug use.
   f. Improving communication among pharmacists, other members of the health-care industry, and the public.
   g. Promoting research in the health and pharmaceutical sciences and in pharmaceutical services.
   h. Promoting the economic welfare of pharmacists and associated personnel.
2. To foster rational drug use in society such as through advocating appropriate public policies toward that end (5).

National Association of Retail Druggists

Throughout the years, pharmacy, unlike most other health occupations, has been practiced primarily in retail settings. The pharmacist therefore has been involved with the sale of nonhealth merchandise as well as drug products and has confronted not only the problems of the health professions but also those of the retail merchant and store owner. Just as he turned to associations to help him cope with professional problems, he turned to those same associations for help with commercial problems. Thus, in 1887 the Section of Commercial Interests was formed as a part of the APhA to assist the pharmacist in his business dealings. This section survived for only 12 years.

> It soon became evident that, while the Section on Commercial Interests, with the moral weight of the American Pharmaceutical Association at its command, could effectively *assist* the endeavor to protect the business interests of pharmacy owner, it was entirely beyond the ability of the Section to watch the situation adequately and to *initiate* and pursue consistently and effectively the actions and the counteractions required (4, p 188).

Therefore, a new and separate organization, the NARD, was formed in St. Louis in 1898. Through the years it has been a powerful force in defense of the independent pharmacy. In recent years it has become the principal advocate of entrepreneurial activity in pharmacy. Active membership is restricted to the owners of independent pharmacies, while employee pharmacists may become associate members. Student membership also is available. The Association has developed a substantial continuing education program in pharmacy management, home health care, and computer applications.

From its headquarters in Virginia, the Association publishes the *NARD Journal* and is active in government affairs and politics. In 1985 it had well over 20,000 members.

National Pharmaceutical Association (NPA)

The NPA is a professional association for black pharmacists. It was formed as an outgrowth of two meetings held in Washington, D.C., in 1947 and 1948, and the organization adopted its present name in 1949. It publishes the *Journal of the National Pharmaceutical Association* and is fostering an active student organization.

American Society of Consultant Pharmacists (ASCP)

The ASCP is the only national organization devoted solely to matters pertaining to long-term-care pharmacy. The Society was founded in 1969 as an educational and information vehicle for the consulting function of pharmacy services to long-term-care facilities. Specific goals of ASCP include promotion and improvement of consulting pharmacist services to health care institutions, hospitals, home health agencies, industry, and other institutions. Other goals involve representing the interest of consultant pharmacists before legislative and administrative branches of government, and sponsorship and encouragement of educational facilities and courses for advancement of the profession. The Society has over 1500 members.

Consultant pharmacists provide numerous services to long-term-care facilities, including a monthly drug regimen review of each patient's chart, in-service education presentation to facility staff, nursing station inspections, checking for proper storage and use of medications, and serving on committees such as the Pharmaceutical Services Committee, Infection Control Committee, and Drug Utilization Review Committee. This role provides an opportunity for the consultant to utilize clinical skills and have direct patient contact and interaction with the nursing home's professional health care team, including the physical therapist, laboratory technician, physician, nursing staff, and the nutritionist. Many consultant pharmacists also are involved in the dispensing of medications and all aspects of pharmacy involved in delivering this service.

American College of Apothecaries

This organization of about 1200 members was founded in 1939. Membership is limited to those pharmacists who can meet and maintain a specified set of standards; these include practicing in a pharmacy that is primarily a prescription shop, agreement not to carry certain types of non-health-related merchandise or to engage in certain types of sales promotion, and earning a specified number of points annually, based upon participation in professional associations and meetings. Hospital pharmacists, faculty members of schools of pharmacy, and certain others are eligible to become associate members, but the organization is made up primarily of owners of prescription pharmacies and their pharmacist employees.

The ACA has developed an extensive continuing education service and offers speakers and programs for presentation nationwide. It publishes the *Voice of the Pharmacist*, a commentary on contemporary pharmacy. The college has a permanent staff with headquarters in Memphis, Tennessee.

State and Local Pharmacy Associations

Pharmacy associations exist in each of the 50 states and function in a fashion analogous to that of the major national groups, except, of course, for geographic limitations. Because there is only one such organization per state, it must meet both the professional and business needs of its members. Thus, stresses apparent between national organizations often occur within a single state association. Sometimes separate subsections or affiliated groups are formed within state associations to permit more latitude in dealing with business or commercial matters.

Historically, most state associations were predominantly business oriented. Founders, early supporters, and a majority of members were often the owners of independent pharmacies. In some cases, only owners were permitted the right to vote or hold office, perhaps in recognition of the fact that their financial support was vital to the success of many association activities. As state groups have evolved, more and more are extending the full rights of membership to all pharmacists residing in the state, without regard to ownership status.

State associations generally have been very influential in the construction of state legislation regarding pharmacy practice. In the professional sphere legislators often look to pharmacists for guidance on matters of professional or technical nature, and in the business realm pharmacy owners often band together with other independent retail merchants to press for favorable commercial legislation and regulation. In many states the pharmaceutical association nominates a slate of candidates from which the governor selects appointees for the state board of pharmacy. Because of the involvement of state associations in this process, boards of pharmacy in most states have been and continue to be dominated by independent pharmacy owners.

State associations usually have at least one full-time staff member, and some of the larger associations have several. Most of the groups publish a monthly journal of statewide pharmacy news and occasional professional articles, and all hold annual conventions. The executive secretaries of the associations are members of the National Conference of State Pharmaceutical Association Secretaries, which meets periodically to discuss problems of mutual interest.

State Hospital Pharmacy Associations

Most of the states have an active hospital pharmacy association that often works closely with the ASHP. These organizations provide a focus for the concerns of hospital pharmacists and usually sponsor regular business and continuing education meetings.

Local Pharmaceutical Associations

Local pharmaceutical associations of varying degrees of activity are widespread throughout the country. They provide an opportunity for local pharmacists to get together both professionally and socially. Legislative involvements usually are limited to pressing for or reacting to local ordinances related to drugs, for example, additional controls on certain drugs such as exempt narcotics that may have become a community problem. The local association often helps to mediate disputes between individual pharmacists and state or county welfare departments or with insurance companies; it also promotes good relations between pharmacy and other health professions in the area.

In many states local associations are becoming affiliated with the state group for more effective representation and communication statewide. The total impact of organized pharmacy in general depends a great deal on such strong grassroots organization linked successively to state associations and to the national body. Some progress is being made, although slowly, in this direction.

Associations of Companies

The associations discussed so far in this chapter have had individuals as their members. Many organizations, however, are made up of corporations, companies, colleges, boards, or other groups. This section examines organizations of firms engaged in retail pharmacy, wholesaling, and drug manufacturing.

National Association of Chain Drug Stores (NACDS)

Formed in 1933, the NACDS shares similar interests and objectives with the NARD, but it is made up of executives of large drug chains and pharmacy operations in department stores, discount houses, and food supermarkets, rather than owners of independent pharmacies. Thus, while similar in many ways, the two associations are also active competitors. The NACDS can be thought of as representing profit-oriented corporate pharmacy practice. With the rapid growth in prescription sales and the financial strength of chain operations, this organization undoubtedly will grow in size and power in the coming years. It currently has nearly 200 corporate members and occupies headquarters in Arlington, Virginia.

The NACDS objectives include:

1. Identify common opportunities and trends incident to merchandise distribution and chain drugstore operations and to initiate appropriate programs and services that best serve member needs and interests.
2. Encourage membership and participation of drug chains of every size and geographic area of the United States.

3. Promote and preserve the general welfare of the chain drug industry and of the consumers it serves.
4. Monitor the activities of legislative, regulatory, pharmacy, and special interest groups and initiate appropriate action when it best serves the general welfare.

National Wholesale Druggists Association (NWDA)

Founded in 1876, the NWDA includes as members full-service drug wholesalers, that is, those that stock and distribute a complete line of pharmacy merchandise and offer complete distribution services. The Association, which has long been active in the development of improved methods of drug distribution, works closely with the customers of drug wholesalers, primarily independent pharmacies, on management, computer, and business problems.

Pharmaceutical Manufacturers Association (PMA)

The manufacturers that produce over 95% of the prescription drugs sold in this country belong to the PMA, which was formed by the merger of two older manufacturer groups in 1958. Because of the close regulation of drug research, development, production, and distribution by federal and state agencies, a major function of the Association is to keep its members up to date on regulatory activities and to lobby on their behalf. Thus, the PMA is headquartered in Washington, D.C., and maintains a large, well-financed staff. The Association develops and distributes statistics on the industry and provides a focus for communication among member firms and between the manufacturers and society.

National Pharmaceutical Council (NPC)

The NPC consists of 23 drug firms "dedicated to the enhancement of the quality and integrity of pharmaceutical services in the manufacturing, distributing, and dispensing of prescription medications and other pharmaceutical products." Originally formed to deal inter alia with the substitution issue, the NPC has broadened its activities considerably in recent years.

National Association of Pharmaceutical Manufacturers (NAPM)

The NAPM, reflecting a major change in the drug industry, represents the manufacturers and distributors of generic drug products.

Proprietary Association

Firms that manufacture nonprescription drug products make up the Proprietary Association, which was organized in 1881. Over 90% of the sales of OTC products are accounted for by member firms. The organization continues to play an important role in the OTC review, begun in the 1970s, and helped to coordinate the industry's conversion to tamper-resistant packaging in the aftermath of the 1982 Tylenol tampering.

Organizations Related to Pharmaceutical Education

American Association of Colleges of Pharmacy

The AACP was formed in 1925 from an earlier organization of pharmacy schools, called the American Conference of Pharmaceutical Faculties. Its annual meeting serves as a forum for discussion of mutual problems and interests among the member schools and their faculties. The Association is governed by a board of directors that meets several times during the year, while day-to-day activities are handled through an executive office in Bethesda, Maryland.

In 1974 the AACP was reorganized from an organization of schools to an organization with a membership base consisting of individual deans and faculty members. Both are represented in the House of Delegates, which sets policy for the Association. In addition to the annual meeting, the AACP also publishes a quarterly journal entitled the *American Journal of Pharmaceutical Education*.

American Council on Pharmaceutical Education

The Council is an independent, nonprofit corporation formed in 1932 through the efforts of three primary sponsoring organizations: the NABP, the APhA, and the AACP. These associations were concerned with the need to establish standards for pharmaceutical education, and the Council is charged with the responsibility of establishing such standards and seeing that they are met by schools applying for such accreditation. Schools apply for accreditation on a voluntary basis, but most state boards now require their applicants to be graduates of an accredited school.

As stated in the Council's Accreditation Manual, the purposes of accreditation are to:

> A. Advance the standards of pharmaceutical education in the United States and associated commonwealths;
> B. Formulate the educational, scientific, and professional principles and standards for undergraduate professional programs which a college or school of pharmacy is expected to meet and maintain for accreditation of its programs, and to revise these principles and standards when deemed necessary or advisable;
> C. Evaluate the undergraduate professional programs of any

college or school of pharmacy that requests accreditation of its programs;

D. Publish a list of accredited undergraduate professional degree programs of colleges and schools of pharmacy for the use of state boards of pharmacy or appropriate state licensing agencies in pharmacy, and other interested agencies and for the interested public, and to revise such list annually or as frequently as deemed desirable;

E. Satisfy itself that the colleges and schools whose undergraduate professional programs have been accredited maintain the proper standards through evaluation in a manner similar to that for original accreditation for any or all colleges or schools of pharmacy at regular intervals or at such times as may be deemed advisable. The accreditation by the ACPE of the undergraduate professional programs of any college or school of pharmacy failing to maintain the standards as formulated shall be withdrawn or the program shall be placed on probation;

F. Assist the advancement and improvement of pharmaceutical education and prerequisites and procedures for licensure and to provide a basis for inter-institutional relationships.

Each school of pharmacy is re-evaluated every 6 years by an accreditation team from the Council. Representatives from the state board and/or a general educational accrediting agency may also be present during the visit. The accreditation team prepares a report, and its recommendation for action by the Council as a whole, and copies of the approved report are sent not only to the dean of the school involved but also to the president of the institution and the state board of pharmacy.

The Council is composed of 10 members appointed for 6-year terms by four organizations: three members by the NABP, the APhA, and the AACP, and one member from the American Council on Education. It also accredits continuing education programs.

American Foundation for Pharmaceutical Education (AFPE)

The AFPE was organized in 1942 by a group of pharmacy leaders from the profession, industry, and education to provide a national focus for efforts to obtain and wisely use private contributions in support of pharmaceutical education. Because of the relatively small size of most pharmacy schools, in the years previous to the formation of the Foundation it had been extremely difficult to obtain contributions for education on a national scale. Through the efforts of the Foundation and its chief contributors, pharmaceutical manufacturers and wholesalers, pharmaceutical education has benefited greatly. Since 1942 the AFPE has spent over $8 million in support of programs related to pharmaceutical education, and annual grants have been well over $400,000, although there have been reductions recently.

Over half of current AFPE expenditures are in support of graduate fellowships and undergraduate scholarships; thus, pharmacy students are the most frequent direct beneficiaries of the Foundation's efforts. A part of the annual budget goes to the AACP for support of its journal and other programs. The American Council on Pharmaceutical Education also receives support from the AFPE.

Other Education-Related Organizations

There are, of course, many organizations with a deep concern for the state of American pharmaceutical education. Most national and state pharmacy groups have standing committees devoted to education, and these committees serve an important function as a focus for the concerns of the parent association. But there are other important organizations in pharmacy that deserve to be mentioned here not so much for their substantive concern with education but because their membership (at least their active membership) is composed largely of students. A few of these national organizations are mentioned below.

Rho Chi Society. Pharmacy's scholastic honor society was founded to provide recognition for academic excellence and to stimulate scholarship and professionalism in pharmacy. The society's members are selected from among professional students in their last year and a half of study, from graduate students and from faculty.

Professional Fraternities. Several national professional fraternities foster professional ideals and public service in schools of pharmacy and also play an important social function. These include Alpha Zeta Omega, Kappa Psi, Omega Psi Chi, Phi Delta Chi, Rho Pi Phi, Kappa Epsilon, and Lambda Kappa Sigma.

Student Professional Organizations. Many national and state pharmaceutical organizations offer students an opportunity to join these associations at a reduced membership rate. The most important aspect of these student memberships is usually the opportunity for communication with future members of the profession through the parent association's publications. In some cases, however, students are offered positions on important committees and are given speaking and voting seats in the parent organization's governing body.

Other Specialized National Associations

Scientific and Scholarly Organizations

Pharmaceutical scientists and scholars belong to a variety of associations serving primarily intellectual needs. Mention has already been made of the Academy of Pharmaceutical Sciences of the APhA, which is made up of sections concerned with specific pharmaceutical disciplines. The American Institute of the History of Pharmacy, founded in 1941, is composed of both professional historians and pharmacists interested in their heritage. It is housed in the School of Pharmacy at the University of Wisconsin. The American Society of Pharmacology is another scientific organization composed of scholars and researchers. The American Society for Pharmacy Law was formed to further legal knowledge in pharmacy.

Many pharmaceutical scientists also are members of scientific associations in the basic fields related to their areas. For example, the American Chemical Society has a Division of Medicinal Chemistry; pharmacologists may join the American Society for Pharmacology and Experimental Therapeutics; and any pharmaceutical scientist may join the Pharmaceutical Sciences Section of the American Association for the Advancement of Science, an interdisciplinary organization that, among other things, publishes the weekly journal *Science*. Individuals from pharmacy may belong to many other smaller scientific or scholarly societies.

Regulatory Associations

The boards of pharmacy in the individual states are responsible for the administration of the state pharmacy laws governing licensure and the practice of pharmacy. Although the autonomy of individual states with regard to pharmacy regulation was and still is recognized, the boards desired a means through which they could communicate and discuss recommended policies and standards to be considered among the states. Thus, the NABP was founded in 1904 to provide such a forum. Much progress has been made through the efforts of the Association to achieve reasonably consistent standards relative to qualifications for licensure, practice regulations, and so forth. Since internship generally is under the supervision of boards of pharmacy, the NABP has been active in programs to upgrade this aspect of the pharmacist's training.

A major contribution to national standards for pharmacy licensure has been the development by the Association of a standard examination for licensure (NABPLEX). Finally, the NABP coordinates and expedites the transfer of licensure by pharmacists from one state to another (reciprocity).

Pharmacy Periodicals

In pharmacy as in any profession, a constant flow of relevant, up-to-date information is necessary to keep the practitioner from becoming intellectually obsolete. In these days of scientific and professional progress, pharmacists must devote considerable effort to maintaining and improving their knowledge through a personal program of continuing education. A vital component of such a continuing education program is a planned method for keeping up with the professional and scientific literature.

This portion of the chapter considers one segment of that literature—pharmacy periodicals. In addition to a general discussion of periodicals, a selection of general interest journals and newsletters will be considered. Specialty journals and other kinds of pharmacy literature such as reference books, abstracting services, indexes, and texts are beyond the scope of this chapter and are left for study in conjunction with specific disciplines and subject areas.

Reading periodicals is a highly efficient and personally rewarding way of gaining information. Compared with attending lectures, for example, reading is much faster and may be done much more selectively. The reader himself chooses what to read and when to read it, rather than delegating the responsibility for information selection to a lecturer. Access to information in printed form permits convenient storage, retrieval, and restudy when required. Readers also can progress at their own pace.

On the other hand, readers must assume more personal responsibility for their own education. They have no third party to peruse a mass of material and organize it into a cohesive unit. This job must be done by the reader himself, and that takes work. It requires a knowledge of what information sources are available, judgment concerning the relevance and quality of written material, and programing of the time available for careful reading.

The only sure thing in the process is the fact that no one can read everything. There are literally thousands of periodicals dealing with some aspect of pharmacy and thousands more that could be relevant in some respect. Making rational decisions about which periodicals to read requires an introduction to a meaningful cross-section of what is available. Every pharmacist should develop a personal list of periodicals to be scanned or studied thoroughly on a regular basis. Only in this way can the professional's knowledge base be updated continuously.

Periodicals Covering News and Current Events

Required reading on anyone's list should be a selection of periodicals designed to provide an overview of pharmacy, health-related news, and current events affecting the profession. Because being a well-informed citizen is a prerequisite to being a well-informed professional, regular reading of major daily newspapers and news magazines is a must. In addition to providing general news and information, many major newspapers employ specialized journalists who concentrate full time on health care issues. Their reports and columns often offer vital analyses of issues affecting pharmacy from a viewpoint outside the profession. These viewpoints are essential in developing a personal position on important issues.

Two periodicals are devoted primarily to reporting news of direct interest to practicing pharmacists. These are *American Druggist*, a monthly magazine, and *Drug Topics*, a bimonthly. These publications report pharmacy-related events and include news stories and columns devoted to both professional pharmacy and business topics. Both sacrifice depth for breadth of coverage, although a few articles in each issue deal with a given topic in more detail. Both frequently conduct opinion polls and collect data relevant to pharmacy operations, providing the basis for occasional special reports. Both publish annual drug price books—the *American Druggist Blue Book* and the *Drug Topics Red Book*—as well as continuing education series.

A source of current in-depth information on specific subfields of pharmacy is provided by a growing number of newsletters. Such newsletters carry no advertising, are expensive, and specialize in providing up-to-date coverage of a variety of topics. The most prominent in this category is a rainbow of newsletters published by the same company. Each appeals to a different segment of pharmacy and is printed on a different color paper. Included are *Weekly Pharmacy Reports* (the Green Sheet), aimed at practicing pharmacists and covering community and hospital pharmacy practice; *Food, Drug, Cosmetic Reports* (the Pink Sheet), for drug company executives and government administrators and covering the industry and FDA activities; and *Drug Research Reports* (the Blue Sheet), for scientists and covering biomedical research and NIH activities. Other newsletters include the *Washington Drug and Device Letter*, the *Washington Report on Medicine & Health*, and *Dickinson's FDA*.

Because of their weekly publication schedule and aggressive reporting, these newsletters represent the most up-to-date printed source in the pharmacy field. They feature in-depth analyses of issues which may run for several pages. If a subject is of outstanding importance, a special supplement may be produced. A frequent objective is to give the reader not only the facts but the context of the situation. Thus, an insider's view and opinion is frequently encountered, obviously as filtered through the reporter's eyes. As freedom-of-information legislation opens more news sources in the federal government, weekly newsletters become an even better source of fast information by having the advantage of on-the-spot reporters at important news events.

In addition to these independently published newsletters, just about every national pharmacy association has a newsletter reporting on current association activities. These newsletters, which report and analyze general news from the viewpoint of their constituency, also serve as a public relation vehicle for the association. After a major policy decision by government or industry, it is interesting to read a variety of newsletters published by different associations to watch the scramble to take credit on behalf of the association if the action was favorable or to be the first to deplore it if the action was negative. Needless to say, when information on a controversial issue is sought, reliance should not be placed solely on association newsletters. They do, however, represent an excellent source of recent information on association activities and provide current statements of their policies.

Many state pharmaceutical associations also publish newsletters, if not on a regular basis, at least during meetings of their state legislature. During this period, lobbying activities are reported and membership support on pending legislation is solicited.

Association Journals

Each national pharmacy association publishes a monthly journal as its "official magazine." This publication serves as the formal record of association activities and is one of the major means of communication from the organization to its members and other interested persons. Because of the official nature of the journal, certain information appears on a routine basis: the names and addresses of the officers and major staff members, a record of the functions of the association such as annual meetings, elections, policy statements, testimony before Congressional committees, comments on government regulations, and addresses and articles by officials.

In addition, editorials regularly appear, arguing the viewpoint of the association. Most of these journals include news items, particularly reporting the activities of state and local affiliates or noteworthy accomplishments of members. Because the interval of publication is monthly and the lead time required is lengthy, most truly newsworthy items have already appeared in a variety of other publications geared to more rapid reporting. Thus, the purpose of the news columns in association journals usually is more to provide a historical record and to satisfy public relations motives than it is to serve an information function adequately. Nonetheless, readers like to scan such columns to search for their own names and those of their friends, and thus the columns serve a very real purpose for the journal and its editorial staff.

An important category of published material in most association journals is that of authored or signed articles reporting scientific or professional topics. These articles serve as a major source of new and relevant information on what is going on in the field; they may include reports of innovative practice ideas, advances in drug therapy, or reviews of a pharmaceutical science discipline such as clinical pharmacology or biopharmaceutics. There are several ways in which such articles may come to be published. They may be solicited specifically by the editor or contributed directly by the author. Many papers originate as presentations at annual meetings or as speeches before pharmacy groups. After submission, papers are reviewed by the editorial staff and in some cases referred to outside editorial reviewers for criticism. The latter system, using referees, usually is employed by scientific journals and, to some extent, by professional journals as well. The more complex the review system, the longer it takes to make a decision on a paper and the greater the time lag before publication. Of course, the purpose of outside review is to ensure the quality of published articles.

The important thing to realize, however, is that most signed articles appearing in any scientific or professional journal may have been written months or even years prior to actual publication. Thus, if for some reason it is important to obtain very recent information, other avenues must be explored.

Professional associations often publish journals other than their official periodical. For example, the APhA publishes the *Journal of Pharmaceutical Sciences*, a scientific journal dealing primarily with pharmaceutics, industrial pharmacy, and quality control, and the ASHP publishes *Clinical Pharmacy*, a journal reporting studies of advances in clinical practice. The ASHP also publishes *International Pharmaceutical Abstracts* (IPA), which provides abstracts of pharmacy or drug-related articles originally appearing in over 1000 worldwide publications.

In addition to pharmacy groups, many other professional organizations publish official journals that can be of great use to practicing pharmacists. Examples include *JAMA*—the *Journal of the American Medical Association*—and the *American Journal of Public Health*, published by the American Public Health Association. Both frequently include articles of interest to pharmacists, either specifically pertaining to drugs and pharmacy or more generally related to health and medical issues. *Hospitals*, a publication of the American Hospital Association, has a regular feature on pharmacy and therefore should be useful to pharmacists practicing in this setting. Many other journals in the hospital field regularly include pharmacy articles.

Privately Published Pharmacy or Drug Periodicals

Obviously, not all pharmacy journals are published by professional associations. Just as obviously, it is not possible to describe here each of this growing number. As pharmacy has grown in its importance in the drug selection process, the profession has seen a concomitant growth in its professional literature. A sample of this growing list, with selected comments, follows.

> *Apothecary.* Published by the Massachusetts College of Pharmacy.
> *Drug Store News.* One edition of a series of magazines aimed at chain store managers and employees.
> *Drug Intelligence and Clinical Pharmacy.* Addressed to the growing specialty of clinical pharmacy, this journal is professional and scientific in nature.
> *Hospital Formulary Management.* Deals with matters of drug utilization and institutional practice.
> *Lippincott's Hospital Pharmacy*
> *Medical Marketing and Media.* Deals with aspects of drug promotion and marketing from an industry perspective.
> *Pharmacy Times.* Originally titled *American Professional Pharmacist*, the journal is intended primarily for community pharmacists.
> *U.S. Pharmacist.* A clinically oriented journal that features continuing education series for credit.

A number of pharmaceutical manufacturers publish private periodicals for distribution to pharmacists, physicians, and others on special mailing lists. These are often extremely well edited and contain useful, readable information in well-illustrated formats. They serve primarily as a public relations mechanism for the publisher. There has been a proliferation of these publications in recent years, with each containing one or two articles on a currently important topic. Each issue contains a prominent advertisement for one of the sponsor's products. While the companies claim to give writers total editorial independence, charges of interference have sometimes been made. These publications are not included in standard indexing sources such as *Index Medicus* or *Current Contents*.

Summary

This chapter covered the organizations and periodicals of pharmacy. The topic of professional associations was put into perspective initially by a discussion of their functions drawn from the writings of sociologist Robert Merton. He points out that, in addition to the obvious functions that serve association members and the profession, the professional association also serves a vital function for society by providing a means for independent practitioners to communicate more efficiently and effectively with other groups in society. Such communication is vital to the cohesiveness and proper functioning of society.

The major organizations in pharmacy were described and discussed briefly. These included professional associations, organizations to companies, educational organizations, and others.

The literature of pharmacy not specifically scientific in focus was classified into three categories: news publications, official organization journals, and privately published periodicals. These classifications should help in developing a personal reading list to follow on a routine basis. Regular reading cannot be overstressed as the key to keeping current with practice in this time of rapid change.

Not covered in this discussion were the many scientific journals one must read to keep abreast of the technical aspects of practice. Their exclusion in no way reflects upon their importance but is due to the limited coverage possible in a book of this nature.

REFERENCES

1. Schlegel JF: New ideas for pharmacy's "foundation organization." *Am Pharm* NS24:538–544, 1984.
2. Joint action stops HCFA plans. *Am Pharm* NS25:781, 1985.
3. Merton RK: The functions of the professional association. *Am J Nurs* 58, 1958.
4. Cited in Sonnedecker G: *Kremers and Urdang's History of Pharmacy*. Philadelphia, J. B. Lippincott Company, 1976.
5. Governing documents of the American Society of Hospital Pharmacists. *Am J Hosp Pharm* 41:2424, 1984.

CHAPTER 11

Toward Optimal Pharmacy Services

The goal of any profession is to see that optimal professional services are provided to those who need them. The problems and questions that arise in this connection do not concern the goal itself but involve instead varying definitions of optimal services and differences of opinion over how to provide them. In this concluding chapter a definition of good pharmacy services is offered, based upon the American Public Health Association's prescription for good medical care. Evidence of pharmacy's performance is presented and discussed in conjunction with each criterion.

The major issues and questions facing pharmacy then are summarized. All have been covered previously, and the purpose in this chapter is to highlight those issues the authors believe are most important to pharmacy and health care. This analysis necessarily reflects our biases, and readers are encouraged to pursue the issues and consult other sources of opinion.

Consideration in this chapter is limited to the professional practice of pharmacy, while omitting detailed consideration of pharmacists in industry, academia, government, and other areas. The latter topics are excluded not for lack of importance or because they have a less interesting or more predictable future, but because this book's prime concern is with the practice of pharmacy.

Good Medical Care and Pharmaceutical Services

"The fundamental goal of the medical care complex is to make good medical care available to the population" (1). It follows that the fundamental goal of pharmacy is to make good drugs and pharmaceutical services available to all who need them; but what are the elements of "good drugs and pharmaceutical services," and how does pharmacy measure up to reasonable standards?

Beverlee Myers, writing for the American Public Health Association, has described the elements of good medical care as: (a) accessibility, (b) quality, (c) continuity, and (d) efficiency. These elements or objectives are equally applicable to pharmacy, and they serve as a starting point for our discussion.

Included in that discussion will be reference to the Policy Statement of Principles for Pharmaceutical Sciences adopted by the American Public Health Association (2).

Accessibility of Drugs and Pharmaceutical Services

One is tempted to say that drugs and related services obviously are accessible in this country; in some cities there is a pharmacy on almost every street corner. (Some would argue that drugs are *too* accessible, given the rampant drug abuse problem.) But accessibility in a medical care sense means more than just physical availability; it also refers to the provision of comprehensive drug-related services and to the absence of artificial barriers to the receipt of care.

Availability of Drugs and Pharmaceutical Services.   The physical distribution of drug products from producers to pharmacists in this country is excellent. Not only are the nation's pharmacies serviced by a network of full-line drug wholesalers, but pharmaceutical manufacturers have prided themselves on their ability to supply rare or seldom-used drugs on short notice wherever needed. Community pharmacies are ubiquitous; they blanket the nation. Over 5000 hospital pharmacies serve ambulatory as well as institutionalized patients. Several mail-order pharmacies serve hundreds of thousands of clients on maintenance therapy or with transportation problems (3).

The recent increase in pharmacy school enrollments and the relative youth of most practitioners are factors that seem to assure that the profession can keep up with the projected growth in prescription demand. Thus, pharmacists should be quantitatively able to continue to dispense however many prescriptions are written. Unfortunately, pharmacists often have failed to make good use of time *not* spent in dispensing prescriptions. Thus, much unmet need for pharmaceutical services of other kinds results from less than optimal use of resources rather than from personnel shortages. Other problems related to the availability of pharmaceutical services include the geographic maldistribution of practicing pharmacists and great variation in the productivity of individual practitioners.

The profession and its organizations long have had an active interest in the manpower situation and have undertaken a number of studies and continuing surveys, often with government support, to assess the availability of an adequate supply of pharmacists to meet the population's needs.

Comprehensiveness of Services. Good medical care requires accessibility to a complete range of professional pharmaceutical services. Whereas dispensing services are offered universally by pharmacists, these services are not always comprehensive, and often nondispensing services are not readily available at all, even upon request. For example, few community pharmacists actively engage in general health education activities, poison control functions, or the provision of drug information to physicians.

The dispensing function itself involves much more than just passing out drugs. Yet complete services are not always available in all pharmacies. An obvious example is personal consultation with the pharmacist at the point of dispensing. This function often is essential to the proper use of the medication, that is, the patient must know how to take the prescription properly to gain its benefits.

The profession has long supported and encouraged consultation with patients. Continuing education efforts are widespread. One state board has required that pharmacists discuss dispensed medication with the recipient, but enforcement is virtually impossible.

Absence of Barriers to Service.   Optimal pharmaceutical services imply that no unnecessary barriers to such services should exist. Possible barriers include geographic factors, sociocultural differences, and financial limitations.

The geographic barrier to accessibility of pharmaceutical services may arise from the maldistribution of pharmacy outlets. This has been discussed previously. Probably the most severe access problem exists in urban ghettos and in poverty stricken rural areas such as Appalachia. In the case of the ghetto, physical distance to a pharmacy may be small but the effort necessary to reach it high, because of a lack of private or public transportation. Pharmacists have reduced this problem substantially through the use of delivery service, but some personal services still are hampered. On the other hand, in poor areas one is much more likely to find pharmacies than to find medical practitioners.

Sociocultural barriers often arise from differences in social class and in ethnicity between pharmacists and their patrons. These differences may foster suspicion and difficulty in communication, although the problems here appear much less prevalent and significant than in other areas of medical care.

For patients with acute illnesses, the financial barrier to the receipt of drugs and pharmaceutical services is not great and is in a way indirect. Because prescriptions must stem from a physician contact, this contact would be the most directly affected by a financial barrier. On the other hand, physician services often are covered by insurance plans, whereas outpatient drugs usually are not.

Patients on chronic drug therapy are those most likely to feel a financial squeeze. One group in particular, the elderly, spends three times as much annually for drugs as do those under 65. Medicare now takes care of in-hospital drug needs for this group, but outpatient coverage is not yet provided although it has been proposed on numerous occasions.

All in all, access to needed drugs and related services in this country seems high.

The American Public Health Association Policy Statement, mentioned previously, lists the following as appropriate patient expectations relative to accessibility. Services should be provided which:

— Are appropriately directed toward the health needs of the individual whether preventive, curative, or restorative in nature

— Provide the patient, before using a drug, the right of informed consent based on information including the name of the drug, intended purposes and benefits, and consequences or risks

— Provide for a choice of source of services or a choice of medical care system in which they are provided

— Provide, in advance, information about both the range and cost of professional services that are available from the setting

— Are available when and where needed, including emergency drug services

Quality of Drugs and Pharmaceutical Services

Quality is an elusive element of medical care that defies precise definition or measurement. Although one can never be completely satisfied with the current level of practice, quality as the term is used here means implementing the most up-to-date knowledge available to the profession. This presupposes that drug products themselves are of high quality and that the drug choice decisions of physicians are rational. Although tangential to the main issue of the quality of pharmaceutical services, this subject warrants some attention since the pharmacist may well be in a position to influence decisions related to drug quality and quality of drug choice.

Drug Quality.   Drug quality has long been the concern of not only drug manufacturers, health professionals, and patients but also of the FDA, the federal agency responsible for regulating the activities of the pharmaceutical industry. Federal law requires that a new drug meet specified standards of purity, safety, and efficacy before it may be marketed in the United States. In addition, studies of the efficacy of hundreds of drugs marketed before the 1962 amendments went into effect (see Ch. 9) have now been completed, and many regulatory activities have been carried out. Some reviewed drug products were withdrawn from the market for ineffectiveness, while others were relabeled to reflect more limited usefulness. A similar review of OTC medications by the FDA is now in progress.

The issue of the clinical equivalence of chemically identical drugs manufactured by different companies has been discussed. The problem of selecting with discrimination is a difficult one because in many cases adequate information is either unknown or not available to the prescriber or the pharmacist. The issue will become more prominent as more manufacturers become involved in the production of identical drugs after the expiration of patents on previously sole-source drugs. The patents on many of the leading drugs are scheduled to expire within the next few years.

On the other hand, some commentators argue that many prescriptions that may seem irrational may serve nonpharmacological ends that are quite rational. For example, the physician may provide for continuing contact with a patient by prescribing a small quantity of an innocuous drug with instructions to return for a renewal at a set time. Prescriptions sometimes serve an important psychological function to both patient and physician by legitimizing their relationship: the patient is in effect reassured that his decision to seek care was correct, and the physician himself believes that through prescribing he has accomplished something for the patient. Support for the latter argument is found in the large number of prescriptions written for symptomatic relief or at nontherapeutic dosage levels. At the same time, the number and severity of drug-related adverse reactions is large enough to question many drug choice decisions, regardless of rationale.

A frequently heard criticism is that a physician is unduly influenced by advertising and promotion in his choice of drug therapy. Observation has shown time and again the changes in prescribing that take place when drug company detail men make a pass through a community. Undoubtedly, the physician is subject to the same appeals that influence all of us. This criticism raises the major issue of the adequacy and usefulness of information about drugs. Much of the physician's information, particularly about new drugs, is received from the manufacturer, and while this source is educational, it is often one sided. In addition, physicians are not well trained in the retrieval and evaluation of drug information. Most are inclined to try a product out to see how it works on their own patients, despite the obvious deficiencies in such a procedure.

It is in this problem area that pharmacists have accomplished a great deal, especially in hospitals. Most institutions have active pharmacy and therapeutic committees which review drugs proposed for use in the institution and make recommendations to the medical staff. These committees sometimes are involved in drug utilization review procedures designed to raise and maintain the quality of drug use in the hospital. Another major contribution often made by pharmacists is the establishment and implementation of a system of drug information. Such a system may consist of a simple library of reference materials or a complex, computer-linked regional network. When properly used, the drug information center can be a major factor in improving the use of drugs not only in the institution in which it is located but also in the entire community or region.

All in all, the quality of drug products marketed in this country is high, despite occasional well-publicized incidents and recalls. Generally speaking, it is the *use* of drugs that seems to offer more hazards than the quality of the products per se.

Quality of Drug Choice by Prescribers. Prescribers, be they physicians, osteopaths, dentists, or others, are the gatekeepers for the legitimate supply of legend drugs to society. They decide whether or not a drug will be used by patients; they choose the specific drug product in most instances and decide how it should be used. The quality of these decisions is not only of life or death importance to patients, it is crucial to the fortunes of pharmaceutical manufacturers, dispensers, and programs providing and paying for drugs.

As is the case for questions of quality in all areas of medical care, sufficient knowledge does not exist to provide a thorough assessment of the quality of drug choice by prescribers. There is no lack of opinion, of course, and some of it may be quite well informed. Some authorities argue that physicians grossly overprescribe, with many prescriptions constituting unnecessary or inappropriate treatment.

A major international study has classified "abuse of prescription medicines by the prescriber" into four categories: (a) underprescribing, (b) overprescribing, (c) multiple prescribing, and (d) incorrect prescribing (4).

It lists as causative factors the conditions of medical practice, overtreatment, patient expectations, patient pressures, and commercial pressures. One of the corrective measures proposed was the use of the pharmacist as a special advisor to the physician.

Quality of Pharmaceutical Services. Pharmacists (and other health professionals) often use their years of education and experience as an indicator of the quality of their work. This argument frequently is produced as a defense against encroachment by less well-trained personnel. The fact is that little objective evidence exists that relates education to performance in practice; we do not even have a very clear idea of the general level of quality of pharmaceutical services being rendered. When specific studies of quality are performed, the results often are disheartening.

Over the past few years numerous studies of the quality of pharmacy services have been conducted (see, for example, reference 5). Several of these studies have required the pharmacist in the field to be challenged to perform a variety of functions such as compounding prescriptions, providing drug information to physicians, answering client questions about nonprescription drugs, and so forth. Other investigators have examined the contents and labeling of dispensed drugs, and still others have interviewed patients concerning pharmacists' advice to them. Many of these studies have been reviewed by the authors:

> The literature . . . is notable because it reports data; not speculation or hopes, but information based on pharmacy as it is practiced today. Despite the paucity of the data, results are remarkably consistent: except for dispensing fundamentals, activities offered by the pharmacist are utilized infrequently and often tendered with low quality. In addition, and more disturbing, pharmacist performance in dispensing is frequently poor. Even when liberal criteria are employed, demonstrated performance is often unacceptable. It should be pointed out, however, that such findings are not unique to pharmacy; evaluative studies of medicine, for example, report similar findings (6).

It is hypothesized that a major difficulty in keeping performance high at all times has to do with the commercial atmosphere in which community pharmacy is practiced. It is very easy to forget that the person with a prescription order is a patient or represents a patient, when it is so convenient and easy to consider him or her a customer for a specialized item of merchandise. It is in the attempt to overcome the "product orientation" that has characterized much of pharmacy for so long that schools of pharmacy vigorously have embraced the clinical pharmacy approach. The chief hallmark of clinical pharmacy is attitudinal: a patient-centered approach to all elements of practice. To the extent that this attitude is adopted in practice, quality can be expected to improve, provided that the basic knowledge is there.

The motivation and the means for quality improvement in an occupation such as pharmacy must come from within the profession. External efforts, including legal requirements, probably have little effect on quality although they do set minimal standards for admission to practice and offer some guidelines for its structure by, for example, specifying minimal equipment and reference book requirements for a community pharmacy. The ASHP has established minimal requirements for pharmaceutical services in hospitals, and the ACA enforces certain quality-related requirements for initial and continuing membership.

The APhA and the AACP have established a joint Pharmacy Standards Commission charged with establishing competencies for the practice of pharmacy and devising ways of helping individual practitioners develop and maintain these competencies. One approach would be through voluntary self-assessment and continuing education. Another, already adopted by several states, is a mandatory system of continuing education. A third possibility, not yet being tried in pharmacy, would be mandatory re-examination for licensure renewal.

The APHA Policy Statement lists the following quality-related items as necessary to comprehensive pharmaceutical services:

— Are provided by competent and skilled practitioners from adequately equipped, staffed, and maintained settings.
— Provide services in a courteous, concerned, and culturally sensitive manner.
— Are organized to provide comprehensive and complete personal or family drug information for the purpose of providing appropriate drug services to patients.
— Provide information on drugs received, including name and strength, explicit directions for use, including the amount per dose, dosage interval, and for how long, any particular potential for bodily harm and damage to physical and mental health, and, if applicable, the expiration date, storage requirements, and manufacturer or distributor of the drug.
— Additionally, patients should be informed of possible long-range effects of drugs used continuously, such as oral contraceptives, and should be instructed on detecting adverse effects and on the appropriate actions to take when these occur.

In summary, although there is no public outcry over deficiencies in pharmaceutical practice from a quality point of view, limited studies and careful observation of practice indicate that there could be much improvement in the quality of pharmaceutical services provided patients. In this respect pharmacy is very similar to the other health professions: given the lack of an organized overall system of practice, incentives and/or penalties associated with quality performance are difficult to devise and implement. Quality is largely determined by the will of the practitioner.

Continuity of Care

Good medical care must not only be accessible and of high quality but also must have continuity. That is, for optimal care the patient should be treated as a whole person, not as a cluster of organs, a peculiar sort of disease, or a customer seeking an expensive drug. Care provided by different practitioners, often in separate locations, should be coordinated by a central person, usually the primary physician. Only in this way can the individual components of medical care most effectively contribute to the successful outcome of treatment.

Toward this end, then, drugs and pharmaceutical services should be thoroughly integrated into the care of the patient for optimal results. The drug-related services provided must be appropriate to the overall needs of the patient, and they should include monitoring of the drug therapy prescribed, either by the pharmacist or by another competent person. This type of continuity often is found in hospitals, where inpatients can be monitored relatively easily. Drug administration and observation are the direct responsibilities of the hospital staff, and accountability can be built into the system. In some hospitals the pharmacy department is responsible for *all* aspects of drug use, including administration and monitoring patients. Provided that proper communication is established and maintained with the medical and nursing staffs, this system seems to provide almost complete continuity of pharmaceutical services.

Such systems are not widespread, however, and even in this advanced system continuity may be threatened when the patient is released from the hospital and becomes responsible for his own medication. The same situation exists, of course, in virtually all outpatient prescription transactions, posing a problem of great magnitude for the community pharmacist. He can play a significant role by establishing a sound pharmacist-physician-patient relationship, but this is extremely difficult to accomplish in our fragmented medical care system and with our mobile population. Patients tend to patronize several outlets for their drug needs, and modern pharmacies are becoming bigger and busier, making extended patient contact difficult. A good system of patient records is necessary for proper monitoring of drug therapy, but we have already noted their limited use and numerous deficiencies. In the typical community pharmacy communication between physicians and pharmacists may be strictly limited to the written prescription or a hurried telephone call. When this is the case, the pharmacist may find himself, in effect, walled off from the rest of the medical care system; his role as viewed by the patient may simply be that of the purveyor of a restricted commodity, prescription drugs.

Improvement in this situation is probable, however. There is no question that monitoring a patient's drug therapy can be extremely useful, even if limited merely to drug procurements and prescription renewals. Physicians often have little or no evidence or knowledge of their patients' compliance with drug therapy instructions and often find such information vital. Factors which hold promise for improving the pharmacist's contribution in this area include the trend to clinical pharmacy, which emphasizes the patient orientation that is so necessary to assuming new responsibilities in medical care, and the development of better record-keeping systems using modern computer technology which will permit pooling of patient data among pharmacies and physicians. The pharmacist's contribution in monitoring drug therapy could be most significant in the general improvement of medical care.

Continuity requirements addressed by the APHA Policy Statement are:

— Services are provided by either one drug service provider or coordinated through a group of drug service providers;
— Inform and advise about the patient's appropriate use of drugs and other related health products and supplies;
— Provide educational services to groups of citizens about timely drug-related community health problems and issues such as drug abuse, family planning, and venereal disease;
— Refer persons to physicians and other health care providers when appropriate.

Efficiency of Providing Drugs and Pharmaceutical Services

The final element making up good medical care is efficiency, both in the organization and financing of necessary products and services. Despite the essential nature of medical care, other essentials such as food, housing, clothing, and defense compete for limited resources. Therefore, unbridled costs and inefficient organization cannot be tolerated, even in medical care, and attention must be given constantly to optimal organization and financing of services. The APHA Policy refers to services which "are organized and provided in a cost-effective manner."

Organization of Pharmaceutical Services. Although the system for distributing drugs from manufacturer to pharmacist was described earlier as very good, the inefficiencies of pharmacy outlets themselves were pointed out. Some critics have characterized the situation as a twentieth century manufacturing system attached to an eighteenth century distribution system. The root of the problem is the large number of comparatively small community and hospital pharmacy outlets which supply outpatient prescriptions. The vast majority of these outlets are independent of one another. What was viewed earlier in this chapter as a virtue when using convenient availability as a criterion is a drawback from the viewpoint of efficiency and economy. The thousands of independent practitioners are the pharmaceutical equivalent of the solo practice of medicine, which has been long criticized for its inefficiency.

Single-unit pharmacy outlets are characterized by high costs of operation, including high drug costs due to low-volume purchasing. The physical separation from physicians, other health professionals, and other pharmacists leads not only to care that is discontinuous but also to inefficient practice. Lacking integration with other health care units, community pharmacies are dependent almost entirely upon the abilities of the individual pharmacist for efficiency, with economy limited by the scale of practice.

One function that has been improved significantly, however, is the drug distribution function. The entrance of chain pharmacies into the drug market brought greater buying power, specialized management, and large financial resources to retail drug distribution. The result has been an ability to dispense prescriptions at a lower price than most independent pharmacies, providing a definite advantage to patients. Many independent pharmacies have begun to counter the chains by forming voluntary buying groups or otherwise cooperating in certain aspects of business. Drug wholesalers, themselves threatened by the growth of chains (which often bypass the wholesaler to deal directly with manufacturers), are offering increased services to independent pharmacies to help them operate more efficiently and thus compete more successfully in the prescription drug market. Thus, many product-related services are becoming more efficient.

The impact of the computer cannot be overlooked. Dozens of systems now are available to pharmacies which can take much of the drudgery out of buying and selling merchandise. Inventory control, pricing, accounts receivable, and the generation of a host of business reports can all be accomplished by entering information at the point of sale into what was once a cash register. Computer processing not only increases the efficiency of many functions but also provides the pharmacist with better control by providing more accurate and more complete reports than previously possible. In addition, more time should be made available for professional functions.

Computers are also being used to process prescription data, both for financial reasons and to monitor drug therapy. Although some experimentation is being done in the area of computerizing patient prescription records, on-line systems permitting prospective review of patient drug use are not yet generally available.

Unfortunately, economies initiated in order to lower prescription prices may also conflict with other goals of good medical care. Care must be taken not to neglect or eliminate necessary pharmaceutical services when cost cutting is undertaken.

Summary

The degree to which the profession is able to meet its goal of providing good pharmaceutical care is a function of four interrelated elements: accessibility, quality, continuity, and efficiency. Pharmacy is far from perfect in discharging each of these elements, but then so is every health profession. The degree to which pharmacy is willing to recognize its deficiencies and seek positively to improve them is one measure of its viability. The contributions of enthusiastic recent graduates, combined with the realism and experience of current practitioners, promise progress in the coming years toward the elusive goal of good pharmaceutical care.

The Next Ten Years

No book of this sort can fail to consider some of the major issues that now and will continue to affect pharmacy over the next 10 years. The important issues are directly related to the crucial question of how to provide good pharmaceutical care in the complex American medical care system. Thus, the most relevant issues involve the identification of barriers to the provision of better services and the determination of ways to surmount or circumvent them. Four key issues relate to *knowledge, economics, regulation,* and *attitudes.*

Knowledge

At first glance, knowledge hardly seems to have the glamour or the controversy necessary to be labeled as a major issue for pharmacy in the coming decade. A closer look, however, reveals an almost explosive expansion of underlying knowledge in the drug field. For a scientifically based profession such as pharmacy, this presents the question of what pharmacists need to know in order to do best what they have to do. All professions derive much of their strength, autonomy, and distinctiveness from the unique body of knowledge they control. In the case of pharmacy, the knowledge base has been changing rapidly over the last few years, at least as perceived by the academic community. A major shift in emphasis has occurred in the direction of clinical pharmacy. More experience-based education is now required and the length of curriculum has been increased at many schools.

Paradoxically, the lengthening curriculum and the shift to clinical pharmacy has caused some observers to worry that the underlying pharmaceutical sciences may be neglected, thus weakening the overall intellectual base of the profession. In part because of the lessened flexibility in a clinically oriented curriculum, fewer recent pharmacy graduates are seeking advanced training in the pharmaceutical sciences. Thus, schools of pharmacy face the prospect of recruiting future faculty members from among persons with nonpharmacy backgrounds. Pharmacy input into research and administration in the pharmaceutical industry could also be diminished by this factor.

Of most direct relevance to patients is not what pharmacists know but what they can do. An important trend in many colleges of pharmacy over the last few years has been the translation of educational objectives from knowledge-based statements to competency-based behavioral objectives. This approach is helpful in concentrating the attention of both the educator and the student on the prime reason for obtaining a professional education: providing services to the patient.

Another aspect of the knowledge issue is that of mandatory continuing education. Many states now require the accumulation of a specified number of continuing education credits before license renewals are issued. Whether mandatory continuing education actually increases the knowledge of practitioners or influences practice is frequently debated. At its best, such a requirement can stimulate pharmacists to assess their personal needs for continuing education and provide the impetus to plan a formal effort to improve knowledge. At the least, mandatory continuing education forces practitioners to go through the motions of attending seminars, completing correspondence courses, or reading journals. In the process it is hoped that some improvement will occur.

In the context of day-to-day practice, perhaps the most significant immediate knowledge deficit is that of more complete patient-related information. Pharmacists typically do not have access to diagnostic information, and in many cases a previous drug history is not available. This problem is directly related to the element of continuity of care and reflects the relative isolation of the pharmacist from the rest of the therapeutic team. Great strides have been taken in developing standardized patient record systems for pharmacies, and the advent of inexpensive micro- and minicomputer systems has permitted more efficient record keeping, but the lack of a complete data base is destined to be a problem the pharmacist will face for some years to come. Given this situation, it is important that pharmacists be able to make the best professional decisions they can even, in the absence of complete information, and not use it as an excuse to avoid responsibility for making necessary decisions.

A major knowledge-related issue for many current practitioners is the question of what will happen to the thousands of B.S. graduates if the Pharm.D. degree becomes the established first professional degree. Will B.S. graduates be labeled as inferior, destined to be discarded? The APhA has taken the stand that a professional doctoral degree is the preferred first degree and that schools of pharmacy should institute programs in the near future to make it possible for practicing pharmacists holding the baccalaureate degree to obtain a professional doctorate through part-time adult education programs. As yet, schools of pharmacy have not moved very far in this direction, with most of them taking the position that education equivalent to a professional doctorate would require so much time to obtain the necessary clinical experience that part-time programs would be difficult if not impossible to establish. However, a concerted effort is being made to develop an external degree program to make it possible for pharmacists to earn a Pharm.D. degree without returning to school full time.

In practice, it would seem that knowledge deficits are not the major barrier to pharmacists seeking to perform optimally in their profession. Knowledge gaps can be identified and ways found to eliminate them. From a practical standpoint, it has been pointed out that "Pharmacists in general will rise to a competency level sufficient to protect their incomes if not for the altruistic purpose of meeting societal expectations" (7). Thus, although the knowledge issue is one which will consume a great deal of attention in the 1980s, it is likely that increasing the pharmacists' knowledge base will not solve the profession's problems. As the young county agricultural agent was told by the old farmer: "I don't need more new information—I'm not farming half as well as I can now!"

Economics of Practice

Few would disagree that economics, inflation, and cost containment will be major concerns of the health professions in the next 10 years. Personal health care expenditures already account for over 10% of the gross national product. Prices and insurance premiums continue to rise, yet still the public demands more and better medical care. Pharmacy cannot escape these pressures even though drugs and related services account for less than 10% of the medical care dollar.

Although the cost of drug products has increased to a lesser extent than any other component of medical care, the "high cost of drugs" is of constant concern to the public, the press, and consumer groups. In a sense, pharmacists suffer from their own success in making drugs widely available. Because only a small proportion of outpatient prescriptions are paid for by insurance and other third-party programs, consumers pay directly and, thus, know immediately the price of their prescriptions. In addition, a drug is a product, and a small one at that, and it is often difficult for the consumer to understand the professional services included in preparing and dispensing it. The public nature of the community practice of pharmacy, coupled with the economic structure of the retail distribution system in the country, often leads to competitive situations where the economics of practice tends to force prices down. Although this may be good for the consumer in the short run, it provides little economic incentive for the development of high quality professional services. Some pharmacists believe it is easier to compete by stressing product and price rather than professional services.

One aspect of the economic situation is the degree to which drugs and pharmacy services are or should be covered by government and private third-party programs. In the outpatient sector, as mentioned, only about 20–25% of prescriptions are covered by third-party programs. For those prescriptions covered, the pharmacist must cope with the often bewildering regulations of a plethora of public and private programs. Because most of these programs developed their drug benefit long after physician services and hospitals costs were covered, they were designed specifically to avoid some of the abuses which have occurred and continue to occur in these other types of benefits. For example, few drug programs reimburse on the basis of usual and customary charges of permit pharmacists to automatically pass along cost increases. Until the recent past, such provisions in physician and hospital insurance programs were necessary to gain the participation and cooperation of providers. Thus, even if third-party coverage of outpatient drugs were expanded drastically, pharmacy's economic problems would be far from solved.

The segment of outpatient prescribing paid for by the private sector is still greatly influenced by rising government and personal health care expenditures. For example, the Medicare program (which does not have an outpatient drug benefit) has been doubling in cost every 2 years recently. The taxpaying consumer has little direct control over Medicare costs or those services paid for through insurance policies and thus tends to pay more attention to those health care costs that can be directly controlled. This naturally includes the drug component.

In the hospital situation, drugs and pharmacy services are paid for primarily by third-party programs which cover hospital costs without a separate accounting for drugs. The recent switch to prospective payment under the Medicare program has provided pharmacy a rare opportunity to demonstrate how the application of clinical pharmacy services can reduce overall hospital length of stay and total health care costs. It is clear that many institutional pharmacy departments are rising to this challenge.

Returning to the outpatient situation, pharmacy is greatly influenced by the retail nature of the drug distribution system. The influence of corporate chains in the industry has increased enormously in the past few years and is predicted to rise even further. The provision of expanded professional services within the context of large profit-making corporations has been debated for years, not only in pharmacy but also in medicine. If community practice is to be dominated increasingly by the chains, which appears likely, pharmacists must act vigorously to retain control of the professional services aspects of these ventures. Pharmacy is not alone in having to face such problems. As the supply of physicians grows, some have predicted the growth of more highly organized group practices in medicine to implement the same sorts of economies of scale and control of market practiced by chain drug stores. In the hospital field, hospital management corporations operating for profit now control more hospitals than ever before either through management contracts or outright ownership. This large growth has taken place without much public discussion or debate over the propriety of such profit-making control over the health services industry. In the past, for example, proprietary hospitals had notoriously lower quality records than community and public hospitals.

Only feeble efforts have been made thus far to change methods of reimbursement for community pharmacists in order to encourage the development of greater professional services. For the most part, incentives in public and private third-party programs have been designed to control the cost of the physical drug product and not to improve pharmaceutical services.

Time is money, and therefore the use of time in pharmacy practice is an important economic issue. Many pharmacists, particularly in community settings, complain that they cannot increase or improve their professional services because they do not have time. Pharmacy transactions carry a fairly low dollar value, so many must be performed in a given time period in order to produce sufficient income to support pharmacists. Thus, practitioners are under constant pressure to dispense more prescriptions. Because the prescription load is not evenly distributed across the day, the situation is complicated even further.

Some see the development of technical personnel to support pharmacists as being the key to solving the problem, whereas others fear that if dispensing functions are delegated to technicians, pharmacists will not use the time freed up to expand professional services. The impact of computer technology in improving the pharmacist's efficiency also will be important to resolving this problem.

Regulation

The over-regulation of American enterprise is a common complaint of the 1980s. Almost every activity of our daily lives is influenced by laws, rules, guidelines, and regulations imposed upon us by ever-vigilant agencies of local, state, and federal governments. Business, education, transportation, and the health professions all are significantly affected by regulations even in our supposedly free society. The pendulum of regulation is now beginning to swing the other way, with more and more groups calling for deregulation and a drastic cut in those interventions seen as being unnecessarily restrictive.

Pharmacy and the other components of the health care industry are caught in the web of legal requirements and government regulations. In fact, if anything, regulation is still increasing with the deregulation movement not yet affecting pharmacy. It is not surprising that pharmacists are concerned with the breadth and specificity of regulations which directly affect them and reduce their professional autonomy. For example, depending upon the state, on a typical day practicing pharmacists may be required by law to:

> *1)* dispense certain drugs only on prescription, *2)* store their Schedule II drugs in a certain way, *3)* include specified information on drug labels, *4)* apply a rubber stamp of a letter "C" of specified size in a specified color on specified prescriptions, *5)* earn a specified number of continuing education credits annually, *6)* keep patient records with specified information, *7)* provide specified oral information to patients when dispensing prescriptions, *8)* charge the Medicaid program no more than 2.05 cents per ml for ampicillin oral suspension (250 mg/5 ml strength) plus a reasonable dispensing fee to be determined unilaterally by the state, and *9)* *etcetera* (8, p 356).

It is clear that efforts are needed to bring some sense to the chaos of regulations to ensure that quality services are provided to patients while not overly interfering with the professional discretion of the pharmacist.

If a profession is self-regulating and autonomous, how did pharmacy get into this situation? Part of the problem is related to the central role of the drug product in the profession's activities. Many of the laws and regulations affecting pharmacy stem from an attempt to regulate the proper distribution and use of the drug product. Laws regulating the labeling, storage, and packaging of drug products were stimulated by a desire to control drugs rather than to interfere with the practice of pharmacy. Most of these laws and regulations, as well as most state pharmacy practice acts, were passed with the support of and, in many cases, at the initiation of pharmacists themselves.

State practice acts have developed incrementally over time in order to encourage good pharmacy practice or to deal with specific problems as they arise. As a result, these acts often are fragmented and unsystematic and sometimes retain antiquated approaches to regulating a profession that has changed dramatically over the years. The basic solution to this problem is a well-planned effort to totally revise pharmacy practice acts in order to account for modern practice. This has been accomplished in some states. The more usual approach is to add new regulations that deal with specific situations rather than attempt to revise an entire act.

There has been a great deal of activity in recent years in mandating additional professional services through changes in state law. For example, some states require pharmacists to keep and use patient medication records, whereas others require pharmacists to consult with patients on every new prescription. Mention has already been made of the more than 20 states that require mandatory continuing education. Still others require auxiliary drug labeling and drug product selection. Recent revisions in three states provide a limited prescribing function for pharmacists.

Advocates of the legislative approach to improving pharmacy services point to the desirability of making a public statement of what is required of pharmacists in the hope that consumers will be mobilized to demand such services. They also argue that regulation may be the only way to stimulate certain pharmacists to undertake necessary services. Critics of the legislative approach argue that such regulations are ineffective from a practical standpoint, that is, requiring patient records will not ensure that pharmacists will keep or use them properly. They suggest that by establishing such regulations, the sponsors may decide they have solved the problem and thereafter forget it.

In any event, whether the strategy is to pass new legislation that would mandate higher quality professional services or to completely revise and update the pharmacy practice act, it requires serious effort by the profession to achieve the desired result. The responsibility for working meaningfully with legislators and regulators must be assumed by pharmacy in the years to come if the profession is to avoid being stifled by unnecessary red tape, paper work, and arbitrary regulations.

Attitudes

The last and most important issue to be discussed is that of the attitudes of pharmacists themselves toward their work and the people with whom they deal. In any profession an individual practitioner has an immense degree of latitude in how to practice. The attitudes of individual pharmacists toward utilizing this latitude determine both the scope and complexity of the individual's contribution to practice. The sum of the contributions of all practitioners determines the character and reputation of the profession. Thus, how pharmacists view their relationships with other health practitioners, the patient, their profession, and themselves shapes pharmacy not just in this decade but at all times.

In the vast majority of individual patient transactions, practicing pharmacists can act as autonomous professionals. Despite all that has been said about the constraints of legal regulation, the pressures of economics and time, and the gaps in the knowledge base, pharmacists *can* transcend these barriers and, in an individual case, render complete, appropriate, and high quality pharmaceutical services to the patient. No one can stop them from doing it if they want to. In the individual practice setting, no one is looking over their shoulders to determine whether or not laws and regulations are being met. No one can see over the prescription counter to notice that a dirty tablet counter was used or an expired drug dispensed. No one will note if pharmacists are abrupt with confused patients or provide garbled or wrong information. No one will know if the answer to a drug information question is guessed rather than looked up. In individual patient interactions, pharmacists can do just about anything and probably get away with it. By the same token, pharmacists can go beyond the regulations, the economic constraints, and the need for new knowledge and perform in an outstanding manner if they are motivated. In large part, the performance of individual pharmacists in individual situations will be determined more by the pharmacist's personal attitudes toward what is being done than by external constraints. External constraints can be and are dealt with if the proper motivation and attitudes are present.

Performance would suggest that pharmacists have had difficulty with their attitudes toward their profession. Part of this can be attributed to working in the shadow of the physician. To a great extent the activities of pharmacists are influenced by the desires of physicians who initiate drug therapy. Pharmacists are human, and like all of us, have been socialized from childhood to the concept that the doctor knows best. Even though medicine has encountered much criticism in recent years, the criticism usually is aimed at medicine as a profession rather than to individual physicians. Most people have high regard for their own doctor. Given this kind of socialization, it is difficult for pharmacists to deal on an equal level with physicians on the turf of medicine. For example; "Despite the voluminous literature about inappropriate prescribing by physicians, many pharmacists find it difficult to accept that the physicians with whom they deal individually could be prone to prescribing errors. Since the pharmacist often believes the physician always has complete information about the patient, it is very easy to be convinced that the physician has a defensible rationale for prescribing almost anything" (8, p 359).

Another attitudinal problem for pharmacists is to define a professional role and stick to it. For example, because reviewing all prescriptions for appropriateness is a prime function, a somewhat skeptical, vigilant attitude must be developed to avoid missing problems which may occur infrequently. Certainly many more prescriptions are appropriate than are inappropriate, and it is easy to be lulled into security and miss significant problems. When a problem is detected, the impending discussion often is viewed with alarm by pharmacists. After all, pharmacists want to be accepted on the health care team with physicians, and they do not like the idea of being perceived as constantly questioning or criticizing the physicians' prescribing.

The pharmacist's attitude toward the patient is an essential component of practice. It is all too easy in the commercial environment of many community pharmacies to forget that the person receiving the prescription is often a person at his or her most vulnerable, either personally sick or with a sick family member.

Finally, we come full circle back to the central issue for pharmacy, and that is the attitude of the pharmacist toward himself. Unless the pharmacist can develop and maintain a strong self-image as an important contributor to the health care system, it will be difficult for pharmacy to fully maximize contributions to the health of patients. As is so often the case, the resolution of the attitudinal issue in pharmacy is largely controllable by pharmacists themselves. If it can be resolved successfully, it will be much easier to deal with the other major issues facing pharmacy in the 1980s.

The Challenge to Pharmacy: Optimal Services

It has been the purpose of this book not only to discuss pharmacy and drugs but also to examine society and its need for drugs and the services of pharmacy. Only with a clear understanding of the interrelations among pharmacy, the medical care system, and society as a whole can pharmacists move with confidence into the next 10 years.

Drugs have never in history played as important a role in society as they do now. Few other substances can affect society so profoundly. It is the role of pharmacy, as the health profession devoted to the application of knowledge of drugs, to serve as the link between drugs and society. Never has there been so great a need for a corps of well-educated, well-motivated pharmacists to aid in the proper use of drugs and to deter their misuse. This, then, is the challenge to the pharmacists of the 1980s: the control of the use of drugs by society.

REFERENCES

1. Myers BA: *A Guide to Medical Care Administration; Volume 1: Concepts and Principles*. New York, American Public Health Association, 1965, pp 23–24.
2. Anon.: Policy statements adopted by the governing council of the American Public Health Association, October 18, 1978, statement of principles for pharmaceutical services . *Am J Public Health* 69:300–301, 1979.
3. Wertheimer AI, and Knoben JE: The mail-order prescription drug industry. *Health Serv Rep* 88:852–856, 1973.
4. Working Party 1975 Council of Europe, European Public Health Community: Abuse of medicinés. II: Prescription medicines. *Drug Intell Clin Pharm* 10:94–110, 1976
5. Jang R, Knapp DA, Knapp DE: An evaluation of the quality of drug related services in neighborhood pharmacies. *Drugs in Health Care* 2:21–38, 1975.
6. Knapp DA, Smith MC: *Evaluating Pharmacists and Their Activities: A Review of Methods and Findings*. Washington, D.C., ASHP Research and Education Foundation, 1973.
7. Baumgartner RP, Jr.: Overcoming the barriers to pharmacist intervention in problems associated with the use of drugs—institutional pharmacy. *Am J Pharm Ed* 43:362, 1979.
8. Knapp DA: Barriers faced by pharmacists when attempting to maximize their contribution to society. *Am J Pharm Ed* 43, 1979.

Index

283